Women in the Military

Other books in the Current Controversies series:

The AIDS Crisis
Drug Trafficking
Energy Alternatives
Iraq
Police Brutality

Women in the Military

David L. Bender, *Publisher*
Bruno Leone, *Executive Editor*
Bonnie Szumski, *Managing Editor*

Carol Wekesser, *Book Editor*
Matthew Polesetsky, *Book Editor*

Current
Controversies

Library of Congress Cataloging-in-Publication Data

Women in the military / Carol Wekesser & Matthew Polesetsky, book editors.
    p. cm. — (Current controversies)
   Includes bibliographical references and index.
   ISBN 0-89908-579-2 (lib) — ISBN 0-89908-585-7 (pap)
   1. United States—Armed Forces—Women. 2. Women in combat—United States. 3. Women soldiers. 4. Women in combat. I. Wekesser, Carol, 1963-   . II. Polesetsky, Matthew, 1968-   . III. Series.
UB418.W65W67   1991
355.4'082—dc20   91-25056

Printed on
recycled paper

Contents

Because the United States has an all-volunteer military, the armed forces are recruiting increasing numbers of women. This practice should be stopped because women weaken America's military by causing morale and other problems.

Chapter 2: Should Women Serve in Combat?

Yes: Women Should Serve in Combat

No: Women Should Not Serve in Combat

Chapter 3: Does Discrimination Harm Women in the Military?

Yes: Women in the Military Are Harmed by Discrimination

sending the message that discrimination against women is acceptable.

No: Women in the Military Are Not Harmed by Discrimination

Chapter 4: How Have Other Nations Integrated Women into the Military?

Foreword

By definition, controversies are "discussions of questions in which opposing opinions clash" (*Webster's Twentieth Century Dictionary Unabridged*). Few would deny that controversies are a pervasive part of the human condition and exist on virtually every level of human enterprise. Controversies transpire between individuals and among groups, within nations and between nations. Controversies supply the grist necessary for progress by providing challenges and challengers to the status quo. They also create atmospheres where strife and warfare can flourish. A world without controversies would be a peaceful world; but it also would be, by and large, static and prosaic.

The Series' Purpose

The purpose of the Current Controversies series is to explore many of the social, political, and economic controversies dominating the national and international scenes today. Titles selected for inclusion in the series are highly focused and specific. For example, from the larger category of criminal justice, Current Controversies deals with specific topics such as police brutality, gun control, white collar crime, and others. The debates in Current Controversies also are presented in a useful, timeless fashion. Articles and book excerpts included in each title are selected if they contribute valuable, long-range ideas to the overall debate. And wherever possible, current information is enhanced with historical documents and other relevant materials.

Thus, while individual titles are current in focus, every effort is made to ensure that they will not become quickly outdated. Books in the Current Controversies series will remain important resources for librarians, teachers, and students for many years.

In addition to keeping the titles focused and specific, great care is taken in the editorial format of each book in the series. Book introductions and chapter prefaces are offered to provide background material for readers. Chapters are organized around several key questions that are answered with diverse opinions representing all points on the political spectrum. Materials in each chapter include opinions in which authors clearly disagree as well as alternative opinions in which authors may agree on a broader issue but disagree on the possible solutions. In this way, the content of each volume in Current Controversies mirrors the mosaic of opinions encountered in society. Readers will quickly realize that there are many viable answers to these complex issues. By questioning each author's conclusions, students and casual readers can begin to develop the critical thinking skills so important to evaluating opinionated material.

Current Controversies is also ideal for controlled research. Each anthology in the series is composed of primary sources taken from a wide gamut of informational categories including periodicals, newspapers, books, United States and foreign government documents, and the publications of private and public organizations.

Readers will find factual support for reports, debates, and research papers covering all areas of important issues. In addition, an annotated table of contents, an index, a book and periodical bibliography, and a list of organizations to contact are included in each book to expedite further research.

Perhaps more than ever before in history, people are confronted with diverse and contradictory information. During the Persian Gulf War, for example, the public was not only treated to minute-to-minute coverage of the war, it was also inundated with critiques of the coverage and countless analyses of the factors motivating U.S. involvement. Being able to sort through the plethora of opinions accompanying today's major issues, and to draw one's own conclusions, can be a complicated and frustrating struggle. It is the editors' hope that Current Controversies will help readers with this struggle.

Introduction

History is replete with stories of women in battle. The ancient Greeks, for example, told of Amazons so dedicated to warfare that each cut off one breast to improve her ability to shoot and throw spears. The British recount tales of Queen Boudicca, famous for leading a revolt against the Romans in A.D. 61 and sacking London, Colchester, and Verulamium after the death of her husband the king. And Americans can point to colonist Margaret Corbin who, during the British attack on Fort Washington in the Revolutionary War, operated a cannon until she was seriously wounded.

For the most part, however, the history of women in battle is a combination of myth and exaggeration, mixed in with a few true accounts of unique women. Indeed, throughout history most societies have banned women from military service. Those women who did fight were often forced by circumstances into positions of military leadership, as was Boudicca, or were conscripted only when men were in short supply, as was the case in the Soviet Union during World War II. In the absence of these extreme circumstances, most societies have restricted women from serving in the military to the same extent that they have restricted women from other male-dominated occupations.

These restrictions are largely based upon each society's perceptions of the appropriate roles for men and women. In ancient Greece and Rome and in the Jewish and Christian faiths, women were perceived as nurturers and care givers in the home, while men were viewed as protectors of the home. In general, all of these cultures held women to be subordinate to men. In accordance with Aristotle's assertion that women should be passive and obedient, Greek women were legally considered to be minors, had few rights, were not educated, and were encouraged to remain at home, caring for their children. Neither Greek nor Roman women could vote or hold public office, and both the early Jewish and Christian faiths prevented women from teaching or preaching. None of these cultures even considered the possibility of women serving as professional soldiers.

The subordination of women continued into the Middle Ages, when women had no legal rights and were not educated. During the Renaissance, however, women began to be allowed access to education, and more and more women were involved in managing business and property. Women such as Elizabeth I of England, Catherine the Great of Russia, and Isabella of Spain became powerful, influential leaders. Progress in women's rights was still slow, though, and the traditional view of women as dependent and domestic continued to be upheld by most philosophers of the age.

When European colonists came to the United States, they brought this Western philosophy concerning the roles of men and women with them. Women in most states were denied the right to vote and own property, and, with few exceptions, participated only as nurses in the Revolutionary War. Americans believed the appropriate role for women was domestic, and this is reflected in author Fanny Kemble's journal entry in the late 1830s: "Maids must be wives and mothers to fulfill the entire and holiest end of woman's being."

Gradually, laws began to change in support of women's rights. Reforms in child custody, divorce, and property rights came about in the mid-1800s. Another sign of progress was the 1848 Seneca Falls convention on the rights of women, which sparked the women's suffrage movement. Despite the actions of this new movement, women's activities were still largely confined to caring for husband, children, and home. In 1869, Sarah Ann Sewell, author of *Woman and the Times We Live In*, wrote: "It is a man's place to rule, and a woman's to yield. He must be held up as the head of the house, and it is her duty to bend so unmurmuringly to his wishes, that the rest of the household will follow her example, and treat him with the due respect his sex demands."

"The status of women in our society is fraught with contradictions and confusion."

The women's movement in the United States strove to change such attitudes, and succeeded in gaining women the right to vote in 1919. However, society continued to strictly define the appropriate roles for men and women. With the exception of poor women (who have always worked), women in general continued to be discouraged from working outside the home. This social pressure and discrimination against women continued during World War I. Although many women worked for the armed forces during the war, they were denied military rank and benefits and were prevented from remaining in the military once the war ended.

Women's roles changed abruptly in both the domestic and military arenas with the onset of World War II. While American involvement in World War I had lasted just over a year, the four-year-long World War II proved to be a severe drain on the nation's resources. As more and more men were drafted into the military, the country desperately needed women to fill men's positions in factories and other workplaces. The nation's need opened up opportunities for women, who were no longer restricted to domestic duties. As author Marjorie Rosen observed: "On December 7, 1941, the Japanese bombed Pearl Harbor. Johnny got his gun. America mobilized. And social roles shifted with a speed that would have sent Wonder Woman into paroxysms of power pride." Women were recruited for noncombat military service, and by the end of the war were granted military rank and benefits.

Post-War Discrimination

While the expansion of women's opportunities during World War II brought about much change in the perception of women's abilities, after the war the nation quickly went back to its narrow definition of male and female roles. As men returned from the war seeking jobs, women were forced out of the work force and back into the home. While most women relinquished their jobs to returning veterans, others refused. Many of these women were discriminated against. This discrimination was also evident in the military, where women were organized into their own institutions, such as the Women's Army Corps, rather than being integrated with men. During the post-war era, society seemed uncertain as to the appropriate role for women. "The status of women in our society is fraught with contradictions and confusion," author Mirra Komarovsky stated in 1953. This confusion especially applied to occupations that seemed to require the "male" characteristics of strength and aggressiveness. In the 1950s and 1960s, women were still prohibited from serving alongside men as firefighters, police officers, and construction workers.

These occupations finally opened up during

the 1970s, when social and economic changes and the growing women's movement combined to increase opportunities for women. Roles became much less defined as women became 45 percent of the work force and men increased their involvement in child care and household duties. The military reflected this social change when it abolished the all-female service organizations and integrated men and women in the mid-1970s. While at first the positions open to women were limited, they gradually expanded so that by 1990, women comprised 11 percent of the U.S. armed forces and were allowed to serve in nearly all noncombat positions. In 1991, Congress passed a bill allowing Air Force servicewomen to fly in combat missions.

Expanding women's roles in society has not entirely erased the controversy concerning women in the military, however. While many Americans have accepted women as soldiers and even as combat pilots, there still exists much debate about whether women should serve in combat positions. A 1991 poll revealed the nation's split: 52 percent of those surveyed said women should be assigned to ground-combat troops, while 44 percent said they should not. For many Americans, the battlefield remains a unique workplace, where soldiers are required not only to be physically strong and emotionally aggressive, but also brutal and capable of killing. Many Americans are still unprepared to acknowledge these qualities in women. As social anthropologist Sharon Macdonald explains, "Where war is defined as a male activity, and where highly-valued masculine characteristics are often associated with war, a female warrior must be seen as inherently unsettling to the social order." Perhaps more than any other issue, the question of women in combat exposes the nation's continued confusion about the appropriate roles for men and women.

Examining the Issues

Women in the Military attempts to address the controversy concerning women in the military from a variety of perspectives. The opinions of scholars, defense experts, politicians, and male and female soldiers are presented in four chapters that debate the issues of women in the military, women in combat, servicewomen and discrimination, and the experiences of servicewomen of other nations. Examining these issues can lead to a greater understanding of how Americans perceive women and how these perceptions influence the nation's opinions concerning women in the military.

Chapter 1:

Should Women Serve in the Military?

Preface

Although American women have long served as nurses and in other supportive roles during wartime, they were not officially enrolled in the armed forces until World War I. While most of the thirteen thousand women who served in World War I were clerks and secretaries, some were assigned to translation, recruitment, and other tasks that had traditionally been done by men. These women were not given military rank or benefits, and they were prohibited from remaining in the military once the war ended.

With the outbreak of World War II, however, the military once again encouraged the recruitment of women by establishing the Women's Army Auxiliary Corps (WAAC), the Navy Women's Reserve, and the Marine Corps Women's Reserve. Women in these organizations were given military rank and benefits. More than 350,000 women served in World War II. As in World War I, these women served in clerical and support positions.

Women's status in the military remained unchanged until the late 1960s, when the armed forces began opening up more positions for women. The first women generals in U.S. history were appointed in 1970, and by 1976 the military academies at West Point, Annapolis, and Colorado Springs were opened to women. By the end of the 1970s, all of the women's military organizations were discontinued, and women and men were integrated within the regular military. Today, women comprise about 11 percent of America's armed forces. They are allowed to serve in nearly all noncombat positions.

Although women have been part of the regular armed forces for more than a decade, several issues remain divisive. Disagreement focuses on several points: how having women in the military affects the nation, women themselves, and their families.

Critics lambast the performance of female soldiers and question the wisdom of having them serve with men. James Webb, former secretary of the navy, argues that women who serve in the military are harming themselves as well as America's defense. "It is easy to say these women are pioneers who are breaking barriers, moving along the fabled cutting edge of social change," Webb states, "but there is a cost, and they, along with society and the men, are paying the price." Webb and others maintain that women are harmed when they force themselves to play the role of soldier and thereby strip themselves of their femininity. Webb's primary concern is that the nation's defense is compromised when women, who are physically weaker than men, are allowed to serve in physically demanding military positions. In addition, Webb and other critics point out that the frequent travel required by the armed forces often causes military mothers to be separated from their children. These separations, critics contend, harm children and threaten the stability of families.

Supporters of women in the military argue that military service benefits women, strengthens the nation's defense, and strengthens the family. Jeanne M. Holm, retired major general in the U.S. Air Force, believes that "the greatly expanded employment of military women in our services has strengthened our national defense." Whereas women's skills were once overlooked by the military, such skills are now valued as integral to the nation's security. Holm and others assert that women benefit from the career and educational opportunities provided by the military. In addition, supporters maintain that military women can be positive role models for their children by showing that women are strong, confident, and capable soldiers.

The debate concerning the role of women in the military is unique in that it concerns both the issue of equality for women and the issue of national defense. The authors in the following chapter discuss how having women in America's armed forces affects women and the nation.

Should Women Serve in the Military?

Yes: Women Should Serve in the Military

Military Service Benefits Women
Mothers Should Be Allowed to Serve in the Military
Women Served Effectively in the Persian Gulf War

Military Service Benefits Women

Fern Marja Eckman

About the Author: *Fern Marja Eckman is a free-lance writer.*

At Fort Dix, a United States Army training base in New Jersey, the sunny day crackles with gunshots. Drill Sergeant Upright, a tall, dashing figure in woodland camouflage, combat boots and swashbuckling headgear known here as the Smokey the Bear hat, strides over to two young recruits waiting to take their M16 rifle qualifying test.

The sergeant crisply assigns them their testing stations. Each replies, "Yes, Drill Sergeant." Grasping the first trainee's rifle, Upright snaps, "Let go of that," then swiftly demonstrates the correct hold, returns it and adds, "Good luck." The two respond, "Thank you, Drill Sergeant."

As they walk toward the shooting range, Upright comments with a smile, "They're getting nervous," then shouts at the departing pair, "Let's go, you two, before they cancel you out!" Both abruptly quicken their pace.

Nothing unusual in that scene, but it is worth noting that all three soldiers are women.

Today more and more women are choosing to join the military. As of April 1989 they number 222,000, or 10.4 percent of our total active force. About 32,600 are officers, a dramatic development since the early 1950s, when there were so few that they were virtually invisible.

Although the majority still gravitate toward the administrative and medical fields, females have made bold inroads into what was only recently regarded as exclusively male territory. Women fly missions, serve as officers aboard

Fern Marja Eckman, "Women in the Armed Forces," *McCall's*, April 1989. Reprinted with permission.

ships, repair planes and assorted motor vehicles, operate in intelligence units and even—though rarely—command brigades.

Their new and varied occupations also take women into areas where they are inevitably exposed to greater danger during hostilities. As a result, they are more likely to be killed, once another exclusively male prerogative.

"We can no longer go to war without women," General Colin Powell, Chairman of the Joint Chiefs of Staff, sums up bluntly.

Women flew on tankers that refueled bombers in midair during the Libyan operation in 1986. Two hundred fifty-eight women sailed on the *Arcadia* to the Persian Gulf. One hundred seventy women participated in the invasion of Grenada as military police, signal operators and munitions specialists. In the event of war, women will launch nuclear missiles, risking enemy retaliation.

The armed forces are not for every woman any more than they are for every man. It's a demanding life physically, with heavy responsibilities that cannot be shirked. Why, then, do so many young women join the services? For the same reasons men do: to learn new job skills, to benefit from Uncle Sam's college funding program or to shape a military career, all three enhanced by a sense of fulfilling a patriotic duty.

> ## "Females have made bold inroads into what was only recently regarded as exclusively male territory."

"There are two distinct groups predisposed to join the services," says Lieutenant Colonel Greg Rixon, a Pentagon spokesman. "They are the job-oriented and the college-oriented. We've really gone after the college-oriented, and we've been extraordinarily successful."

Under the new G.I. Bill adopted in 1981, members of the armed forces who enlist for two or more years and contribute $100 a month for

12 months are eligible to receive $10,800 for education from the Veterans Administration. In addition, the Army—only the Army—offers a juicy financial plum to high school graduates who score in the upper 50 percent on intelligence tests and enlist in critical military specialties. By the end of their hitch, qualified soldiers can accumulate from the G.I. Bill plus the Army College Fund a tidy $25,200.

"College financing is the chief lure for Army women."

"If you go to college nine months a year for four years," Rixon points out, that's seven hundred dollars a month. Not bad!" Which is why, he says, college financing is the chief lure for Army women. In 1987, 64,833 women on active duty were enrolled in the G.I. college program.

Private First Class Joanevia Coleman, 20, five feet tall, wide-eyed and dimpled, ranked third academically in her graduating class at John L. LeFlore High School in Mobile, Alabama. Deprived of a sizable scholarship after her first year at Livingston University because she refused to major in education, Coleman volunteered for the Army. "I don't want to teach," she says. "I want to be a forensic pathologist. When I finish my two years, I'll be back in college."

Coleman shares barracks with seven other trainees. Six days a week, they rise at four A.M. and clean their barracks, which means making up the bunks with almost mathematical precision, sweeping the floor and buffing it electrically. At five A.M. they march to the dining hall, and at 5:45 A.M. they proceed to the training area for the most rigorous event of the day. Until 11:10, when they have a half-hour break for lunch, the women are put through the rugged exercises dubbed "drill and ceremony." Under their sergeant's all-seeing eyes, the platoon learns how to march, stand at attention, perform the manual of arms.

At 12:15, already bone weary, the trainees march to their afternoon classes, which may include four hours of first aid and another hour of physical training. Dinner is at five P.M.

At eight P.M., the unit heads back to the barracks for a blessed hour of personal time. They can write letters (most are away from home for the first time and homesick), read, take showers or just rest. No TV, though, until Sunday.

Lights go out at nine P.M., and even the night owls appreciate early bedtime. "The girls hurt all over because of the exercises we give them," Gabriele Upright says. "And after the second week, we march them from two to four miles in formation, carrying twenty-pound rucksacks and their rifles."

Sunday is, comparatively, an easy day. The women can sleep until five. After chow, they burnish their barracks. Then those who want to—and most do—go to church (Jewish trainees attend synagogue on Saturday). From noon to 4:30 P.M., they are free to watch TV in the dayroom, play ball in the gym, purchase items at the PX, eat at the snack bar, read, chat, relax. By the sixth week they have the privilege of attending on-post movies. They may not leave base until training is completed. After the recruits graduate, they move on to schools around the country for the specialties they selected upon joining.

The Military Option

So many women are satisfied with their initial hitch that an astonishing 54.5 percent reenlist, topping the 48.2 percent figure for their male counterparts. As time goes on, however, those figures are more or less reversed, possibly due to the demands of marriage and children on females. Still, 81 percent of women who have completed their second hitch join again, compared to 86.6 percent for males.

What makes the military attractive to so many women? To a nonmilitary visitor, the superficial benefits were striking. The strenuous regimen had produced glowing complexions, clear eyes, enviable posture and flat tummies—in short, the kind of fitness the most expensive spas would be hard-pressed to equal.

More important, of the ten women we interviewed, every one voiced unreserved enthusiasm for her military experience. Black or white, young or mature, ranging in age from 19 to 51, none harbored regrets about joining, even though several matter-of-factly mentioned the disadvantages of service life, and the two with children confessed that at times it's "a real hassle."

The Upper Ranks

Judging from their own comments, the women who reach the upper ranks share a willingness to make the most of the services' good features and the best of the not so good. Talk to them and they impress you as superior in intelligence and looks, admirably fit and well organized, bandbox neat—and ambitious. It's clear that they can be counted on to put their obligations to the service *first*, ahead of their private lives, even if that creates problems in the family. Domestic disruptions are accepted as necessary sacrifices.

"I think everybody goes through periods of wondering, 'Do I want to commit myself to more time?'" reflects Navy Commander Marsha J. Evans, 41, currently a student at the National War College in Washington, D.C. Auburn-haired, willowy, just a half-inch under six feet, with considerable charm, Evans is married to a retired Navy lieutenant commander. "I use the 'cup is half-full' rule," she says.

"I love the Air Force. I'd like to make general!"

"On the days I say, 'Gee, I want to get up and go to work,' then my job is a good job. I've had periods when it's been less than wonderful—my husband and I were stationed apart for a year. But we knew that by marrying in the service there was at least a chance of that. I'm very lucky. I've had a happy life."

Brigadier General Myrna Hennrich Williamson, 52, the senior female officer in the Army and a divorcee, is now on the Pentagon's Army staff after five years of command assignments. All snap and polish in her beautifully tailored uniform, with an elegance of carriage and a gentle, precise voice that conveys complete authority, she says: "I joined the Army twenty-nine years ago because I wanted to travel, meet people and have a variety of challenging jobs. And that is exactly the reason I am still in the Army."

Upright, 29, fresh-looking and wholesomely attractive without a smidgen of makeup ("Trainees can't wear cosmetics in uniform, so we try to set an example"), simply says, "I'm an active person—I enjoy the road marches, rifle shooting, throwing hand grenades."

For her, as for many of her sisters-in-arms, financial security is a bonus. "I get about fourteen hundred dollars a month, free medical care, thirty days of vacation," Upright says. She trains male and female troops but prefers the latter, "because I like to see women better themselves. Men say, 'Oh, I can do that.' Women aren't sure. I tell them, 'Look at me. I was you. And I did it.'"

Upright says there is one serious drawback to Army life, one cited by women in other branches of the military: "If you want to stay in one place and buy a home, you can't do it because you have to be ready to move. At first that's fun. But after nine years you want to think about putting down roots."

On balance, Upright plans to stay in 11 more years. "I want to do my twenty years, see how high I can get and then retire, go to college and major in physical therapy or psychology," she says. Her reward after 20 years of active duty would be a lifetime pension of half her retirement pay (about $20,083 or three-quarters of her retirement pay after 30 years.)

Career Choices

Candidates for officer commissions must meet stiff requirements. A baccalaureate is essential. A graduate degree, while not a must, can spell the difference between acceptance and rejection and later can provide a boost toward promotion.

That extra lift up has not escaped Major Alicia (Cissy) Lashbrook, 39. A green-eyed, blond dynamo, she is a helicopter pilot and a full-time public affairs officer in the Arkansas National Guard at Camp Robinson, North Little Rock. She doubles there one weekend a month, two weeks a year, as public affairs officer for the State Area Command of the Army National Guard. If that were not enough, Lashbrook flies a Huey, a utility helicopter that can transport troops on 24 flight-training missions a year. Her triple job load earns her about $50,000 a year.

"Sexism in its multiple guises is just as prevalent in the armed forces as it is in the civilian world."

Married to a pilot who has a schedule almost as crowded as her own, Lashbrook has three stepsons. Robert, 16, and Michael, 15, live with the Lashbrooks; Jeremy, 13, is a frequent visitor. "I never thought I'd enjoy being a parent," Lashbrook says. "Now I wouldn't take anything for the boys."

Eager for promotion, Lashbrook says: "I'm convinced you have to have a master's degree to go ahead, so I'm looking at getting one, probably in business administration." And how many hours at home will that leave her? "Enough," Lashbrook says briskly, "to sit down with the boys and help with homework."

A tough dilemma confronted Air Force Major Paula W. Haley, then stationed in Washington, D.C. She was handpicked for the elite Air Command and Staff College in Montgomery, Alabama, an honor that was hardly an unmitigated blessing.

Friendly, breezy, with wheat-colored hair and a ripe Texas drawl, she is in her early 40s, the wife of a retired lieutenant colonel and the mother of Kristen, 12, and David, nine. "I had to decide whether I wanted to come way down here to Alabama for *ten* months," Haley says, making that period sound like forever. "Or did I want to get out? But I love the Air Force. I'd like to make general! So here I am."

"My kids were very unhappy, my husband was very unhappy. I brought the kids with me. And I left Bob behind for almost a *year*—because he has a job he really likes with a communications firm. But this was a career decision I had to make. I could not turn it down."

Sergeant Beatrice Stallworth, 30, one of Upright's cohorts at Fort Dix, is a single mother. Her daughter, Tara, is 13. The sergeant, lithe and good-looking with a quirky sense of humor, is from Woodside, Long Island. Stationed in Germany for four and a half years, she has traveled all over Europe and "loves every minute" of her 11 years in the Army.

The sergeant rates her job as "interesting," but she is much more emotionally involved than that tepid adjective suggests. Informed that her platoon had come in first in the company in the rifle tests, Stallworth flung down her gloves, leaped into the air and shouted, "All *right!*"

How do men react to taking orders from women? "I personally do not go around taking surveys of that," Williamson says tartly. "If they mind, they don't show it," says Lieutenant Sandra Woodbury, 33. "They mind but they can't show it," says Stallworth.

New Skills and Opportunities

For the many thousands of women who join the military for comparatively short stretches, the main objective is acquiring valuable new skills in any of the assorted specialties available to them, such as computers, electronics, languages, meteorology and communications—skills that are marketable in the civilian world.

"Women have an opportunity in the Air Force for leadership experience and management skills that they would have a much more difficult time obtaining in civilian life," says Richard E. Carver, former assistant secretary of the Air Force for Manpower and Reserve Affairs. "And a woman officer who is given the responsibility for supervising people and perhaps handling millions of dollars in assets may be only twenty-two years old. Should she decide to walk out of the Air Force and look for a job, she has advantages over *any* civilian of her age—*period.*" Other officials said much the same for the Army, Navy and Marine Corps.

The Male Perspective

From the male perspective, how well do women perform in the armed forces? "We need the best people we can find," Carver says, "and it so happens many of them are women."

"If you want equality," says a pretty 26-year-old West Point graduate and ordnance captain from Massachussetts whose husband is also a captain, "then join the Army."

Well, equality up to a point. Yes, the pay is absolutely equal for both sexes. Yes, female opportunities have expanded and are still expanding. But a Congressional law enacted in 1948 bars women from direct combat and, by extension, from all jobs viewed as hazardously close to combat, where the risk of capture is high. The Pentagon acknowledges that combat experience is not only a push toward promotion but, in the top ranks, a prerequisite.

"As long as there is combat exclusion, there will be career limitations for women," says David J. Armor, Ph.D., a sociologist and the Principal Deputy Assistant Secretary of Defense for Force Management and Personnel. "If you want to change that, you've got to change Congress, you've got to change the people in this country, many of whom believe women should *not* be war fighters."

The truth is that sexism in its multiple guises is just as prevalent in the armed forces as it is in the civilian world. Promotion for women can be grudging or stalled. Female officers are sometimes assigned to duties below their rank. Verbal offenses rankle. Grievances filed by women are frequently pigeonholed.

It must be emphasized here that each of the senior female officers who were consulted spoke in glowing terms of the tremendous strides made by military women in recent years. Only eight years ago Cissy Lashbrook, then Captain Alicia Coleman, was the first woman in the Arkansas National Guard to go to flight school, where she became the first female class leader. At a reception for class leaders, the commanding general shook Lashbrook's hand and said, "Good evening, Mrs. Coleman. Captain Coleman could not be with us this evening?" Cissy drew herself up and said, "Sir, I am Captain Coleman." Today, Lashbrook says, "it would never occur to that general that there was *not* a female class leader."

"Have we been victims of sexism and sexual harassment? Of course we have!"

"Women in the military have two choices," sums up Commander Evans, who is refreshingly spontaneous and candid, unlike so many high-ranking officers, male and female. "You can mope about inequality and get out at the end of your obligation. Or you can look for personal growth, professional development and an opportunity to contribute in all the ways you can.

"Have we been victims of sexism and sexual harassment? Of course we have! Every woman who's been in business or industry has encountered that. You can complain about how bad things are, or you can try in a constructive way to change people's behavior where you *can.* Where you can't," Evans continues with vehemence and fervor, "you've got to go on, charge ahead and do the best job you can."

Mothers Should Be Allowed to Serve in the Military

Dorothy and Carl J. Schneider

About the Authors: *Dorothy and Carl J. Schneider both spent two years teaching college courses at military bases for the University of Maryland's Far Eastern Division. During this time the Schneiders interviewed more than three hundred military servicewomen for their book,* Sound Off! American Military Women Speak Out. *The following viewpoint, excerpted from their book, includes quotes from some of the women interviewed.*

For long years after World War II, a woman could not remain in the service if she married, became pregnant, or accepted responsibility for a minor child, even as a stepmother. In the 1970s servicewomen fought for and won the right to have families and to receive the same military benefits for them as servicemen for their families. Pregnant soldier is no longer an oxymoron, but a fact of military life: the pregnant servicewoman may choose to stay or to leave, provided that she has not incurred a service obligation by accepting an enlistment bonus or specialized training or education and that she is not considered essential. . . .

[Some] servicewomen believe that, like their spouses and male colleagues, they are entitled to both the human relationships that families provide and a military career. Hormones, social pressures, *and* the example of the many military mothers triumph over doubts and fears. As a financial management officer put it, a bit wistfully,

"I don't think it would be a problem doing both, being in the military and being a mother. It would be what my husband was doing [combining career and parenthood]." "For me there wasn't even an option when I found I was pregnant," an airman first class in the security police told us. "I was going to stay in, no matter what. I guess it was the way I was brought up. Don't depend on anybody to do for you. You've got two arms and two legs and you can go out there and do for yourself. I've always believed that. And I'll get my daughter to believe that too!"

Naturally servicewomen face the same problems as other American working women with families—the same strains and stresses of managing a household and raising children with no full-time homemaker, the frets and fatigues of doing two jobs at once, and the frustrations of the conflicting demands of two careers. . . .

But if the service, a jealous god, taketh away, it also giveth. If the servicewoman and her family have to face special difficulties, they also reap benefits. Impelled by concern for its personnel, a desire for improved retention, and a number of court cases, the military helps its families cope.

> ## "Pregnant soldier is no longer an oxymoron, but a fact of military life."

While their situation falls far short of the ideal, American military women fare better than most of their civilian sisters in maternity leaves, guaranteed jobs after childbirth, and child-care facilities. The servicewoman may wish she had more time to recuperate and to bond with her new baby, but she can count on four weeks off *and* a job to which to return, without loss of rank, seniority, or pay. Her doctor can lengthen her disability leave. And if her job and her boss permit, she may save up leave time beforehand so that she can extend her time at home after her baby is born. . . .

Servicemen's complaints about the special treatment of women's getting leave after the birth of a baby ring loud; indeed some servicewomen believe that the length of this leave, formerly six weeks, was shortened because of male complaints. Women point out that even allowing for pregnancy and leave after the birth of a baby, servicewomen lose less time from work than servicemen. "My neighbor, bless his heart, he's a real good guy, but he's always complaining about his pregnant WAVES [acronym for Naval women], and I just say, 'Well, George, I see a lot of cases that come in on discipline [for misconduct] and they're mostly on men.'" "The men have to understand," says an Air Force tech sergeant. "They go to the hospital to have their appendix out, and they get four weeks' convalescent leave. I have a young guy that cut his hand severely; he had three weeks, and it was just his hand. I don't agree with them when they start complaining."

Healthy and Pregnant

And an Air Force lieutenant remarked in irritation, "I would put some of my women up against five good guys. They're always there. Don't have the least problem: AWOL [absent without leave], sickness. So they get pregnant; they're usually right back after their four weeks. I've known guys to play football; they banged up their knees and were in the hospital for six months."

The lieutenant's point was ironically proved years ago, as Captain Patricia Gormley (USN) recalls: "When I was at the Justice School at Newport, I had my first child. They were just in the process really of changing the rules: instead of being automatically discharged, you could stay on active duty with the approval of your department. Of course you had to use your own leave, and they didn't have maternity uniforms. I didn't teach a normal schedule, because they were afraid that I would have the baby in the middle of one of the courses, so I had a lot of the short schedules. Plus we had a lot of the men out sick or injured that summer. One in-

structor got hurt playing football, and another broke his leg some other way. I was reasonably healthy, so I would show up at the other schools in normal clothes, very pregnant, and say, 'I'm Commander Gormley, and I'm here to teach the course in nonjudicial punishment for your surface warfare officers.' They would just look at me. 'Who is this large creature who comes in claiming to be a Naval officer and is so clearly pregnant? Somebody's playing a joke on us.' Yet they were too polite to indicate that, and they'd show me into the classroom, and I'd start teaching. I ended up teaching more hours than the other folks—which was fine. I was in very good health and did not have to leave until the baby was born, and the men seemed to be having all these disability problems.". . .

As a matter of fact, I was pregnant, wearing orthodontic braces, and was selected Sailor of the Year. I was kind of embarrassed, standing in front of the admiral, getting my plaque. I felt a little silly, but I still was proud of myself. I've even got pictures in my daughter's album of Mommy making Sailor of the Year while pregnant with her.

My daughter has two [parachute] jumps. When I was pregnant I jumped twice. Yeah, she got two jumps on her daddy. No, the Army didn't know I was pregnant. Not by far. I told them after that and they about had a conniption.

"American military women fare better than most of their civilian sisters in maternity leaves, guaranteed jobs after childbirth, and child-care facilities."

Most military women work almost to the day they deliver. Often the military alters assignments to make the situation a little safer for the prospective mother, but many women take pride in having performed their regular tasks throughout their nine months. Some women protest not being allowed to do their regular jobs. "Right now I'm grounded," a helicopter pilot said. "I think that's an area that very little research has been done in, is pregnant aviators and their ability to fly. I feel I am capable of flying. At times, you know, when I'm feeling well. I think someone's put a stamp down and said that pregnancy does not correspond with flying. I just don't think there's been enough research."

Work and Pregnancy

A twenty-one-year-old insisted that the Army regimen improved her experience of pregnancy. "The two children that I had before I came in the service were both premature babies. I guess I just was bored and I didn't get out and do any exercise. Now I'm in really good physical shape, and I've carried the baby, no problems. I feel fantastic. I still did PT [physical training], up until they told me 'You're not doin' PT no more.' 'Cause it makes me feel relaxed. You run to be a road-guard [a servicemember who runs ahead of her unit to stop traffic while troops march through an intersection, and then runs to catch up with the unit], and if I've fallen out to do that, the sergeant says, 'No, thanks. What's the matter with you? You know you can't run.' I say, 'My goodness, I'm pregnant, not handicapped.'"

Women are going to continue to have babies! That's not going to stop, whether they're in the military or not! And they should be afforded the personal help that the Air Force provides in all other factors.

She just had a baby. Her husband went to sea for six months, about a month ago. She works eight to eight during the day, or eight to eight at night, so it costs her about $400 to $500 a month for a baby-sitter.

Child-care facilities are far from free, they never seem to have enough spaces for all the children who need them, and they are never open long enough (even though some stay open twelve hours a day and take babies as young as three weeks). With servicepeople subject to call at any of the twenty-four hours, child-care centers need to be open twice around the clock—but seldom are. . . .

Assignment abroad may complicate or ease the situation, depending on the local traditions and economy. In the Far East reliable mamasans (maids) are relatively easy to find; in Germany their equivalents are scarce and expensive.

Military parents must arrange beforehand for the emergency care of their children for periods of up to a year. "They came out with this thing where you had to make out a power of attorney for this person [the caregiver] and you have to sign this paper every year saying that this person here will take care of your child while you're gone. It's a bummer."

Bummer or not, it's hard to see how the military could function without such assurance. . . . The babies' grandmothers, aunts, even grandfathers and uncles figure largely in these arrangements, especially when they're for protracted absences—a year on a remote or three months at sea. A black intelligence analyst on her way to Okinawa planned for her son to stay "with my parents for a year. He's the first grandson and they're spoiling him to death." "I have an uncle that doesn't work, so every time I go out to sea, he comes down and watches my little boy for me." The divorcée may rely on her child's father. Thus with a keenly ambitious Air Force tech sergeant: "It works out real well. My children are nine and eleven. When I go overseas, they stay with their daddy. Of course, me and their father have a real good understanding. He's a civilian. I've been overseas several times for a year at a time, and there's no problems. It's great. I can do what I want and he can do what he wants.". . .

"I would put some of my women up against five good guys."

Families can also turn to the relatively new Family Support Centers. On many military bases these exist only as uncoordinated bits and pieces: a volunteer group here, the chaplain's office there, and an inadequate child-care center. The most advanced centers are state-of-the-art, staffed by professional counselors, who assist military families in every imaginable way, from certifying baby-sitters sane and nonsadistic and locating housing to marital counseling and parenting education. They provide an umbrella for the official and volunteer organizations that help families in times of stress. A single parent with four children who received no cash from the Army for a year, because she was repaying Army loans, survived by grace of a moonlighting civilian job and help from Army Community Service. "Well, when I got here I didn't have any furniture. ACS gave me three cribs. They gave me clothes. They gave me diapers. I'm stubborn but I didn't mind taking help from them, because I support them, and in turn when the kids grew out of clothes and grew out of their cribs, I gave 'em back. They gave me three brand-new high chairs. I didn't turn 'em down—they cost too much!" . . .

The unwed mother, our interviewees say, may meet with anything from disapproval to friendliness and helpfulness. . . .

Whatever the difficulties they encounter, some sole parents win out. Take a Marine on the verge of retirement: "My children are nine and eleven, a girl and a boy. In the military, everyone I've worked with has been most cooperative. I have never had a problem with someone objecting if I take the children to the doctor and those kinds of things. It could be that I've never taken advantage of it. Some people did. But I like to work, and I'm not much of a baby-sitter! I don't think I was ever meant to be a mother! But I've not had any bad problems with the kids. Sometimes when they get into trouble I think maybe it wasn't such a great idea. Other times I think

I've done a pretty good job of blending being a mother and being a Marine.

"I don't even know if my kids know that I'm in the military. It's a job I go off to every morning and come home from every night, just like any other person's job, except that I do wear a uniform. They don't have any concept of my rank. Of course when I got promoted to master sergeant, I made a big deal out of it, told them what this meant to us, more money and all.

"The wide world of the military makes room for all sorts of families, and many kinds of women."

"Several months ago we went through the Quantico basic school's obstacle course in the morning and through their combat course in the afternoon. Wow! I would probably have *loved* that sort of thing had I been nineteen or twenty years old, but at age forty climbing up the side of a mountain on a rope? Laying on a little rope that's no bigger than that and going across this big culvert? Crawling through mud, going under water? That night I said to the kids, 'I've got to tell you guys what I did today.' And I drew them some diagrams of me crawling on this rope, pulling myself across this big ditch, and said, 'Now I want you to be proud of your mom!'"

The wide world of the military makes room for all sorts of families, and many kinds of women.

Women Served Effectively in the Persian Gulf War

Carol Barkalow

About the Author: *Carol Barkalow is a special assistant to Army Chief of Staff General Carl Vuono. A 1980 graduate from the U.S. Military Academy at West Point, New York, Barkalow is the author of* In the Men's House, *a book about her West Point experiences.*

I went to Saudi Arabia on temporary duty after the air war started. I volunteered and was picked up by the 24th Infantry Division (Mechanized) on the day it started its eight-day move to its positions before the start of the ground war. I was lucky in that I didn't have to weather all the months in the desert that preceded the war. The 24th ID had been in the desert longer than any other unit.

The first thing that struck me about the soldiers of the 24th ID was the high morale. After living through conditions so austere that only someone who was there could accurately describe them, everyone was still highly motivated, trained and ready to perform their wartime missions. This operation has proven soldiers, male and female, can adapt to tough conditions. Soldiers, officers and enlisted, worked together daily to accomplish the mission. Not everything went as planned . . . it never does. But the adaptability of the soldiers in the 24th ID is a testament to the proficiency and professionalism of those who serve. The soldiers of the Victory Division wear their pride on their sleeve, as they should.

Because I didn't get to Saudi Arabia until after the air war began, I had witnessed the focus and attention of much of the news media during the months of Operation Desert Shield. Without fail, every few days there was a story about women deploying to the Persian Gulf region. The stories ranged from grandmothers leaving grandchildren, to new mothers leaving their infants, to members of Congress demanding investigations because women had to endure the horrible living conditions and sleep in the same tents with men.

What didn't get much attention, though, was the thousands of women and men just doing their jobs, jobs they had been trained to do. It just wasn't news to find that men and women adapted to the conditions and that everyone missed loved ones at home. Many of the mothers I spoke to, who were never interviewed, said they understood their commitment, and yes, they missed their children, but they knew they had a job to do, and yes, they would do it again. These news accounts also ignored the pain and difficulty caused by fathers leaving home. Parents having to leave children is a human cost of defending our country, and that's the way it should be viewed.

> ## "Women were accepted as an integral part of Operations Desert Shield and Desert Storm."

Men and women in the desert, for the most part, were treated the same. Living conditions varied depending on the unit and its location. In one of the forward brigades of the 24th ID, the intelligence officer was a woman. She slept in the same tent with the male officers on the staff. During the redeployment phase, at the port of Dammam, I shared a tent with five men and one other woman. We had only one tent, so the officers and enlisted soldiers lived together. In some coed tents, a blanket was put up as a partition to give both sexes a little more privacy. There are only problems when someone who hasn't lived

Carol Barkalow, "Women Really Are an Integral Part of the Military," *Army Times*, May 27, 1991. Reprinted by permission.

in such an environment raises a fuss because they think it is a problem. For the record: It's not a problem. Women don't want to be treated differently.

I also witnessed the Direct Combat Probability Coding Policy fail to work. Men and women worked in all areas of the battlefield, and commanders made prudent decisions, even though they may not have been in line with the policy, to assign the best-qualified soldiers to the job, regardless of gender. That's what our combat leaders should be called upon to do.

"More than 33,000 women served in Desert Shield and Desert Storm."

While I was in the desert, I witnessed the same type of relationships forming between men and women as has traditionally been described as occurring among men: mutual respect and caring borne out of enduring the same dangers and the same hardships. Because of that, women were accepted as an integral part of Operations Desert Shield and Desert Storm.

I consider myself lucky to have been part of the Victory Division during Desert Storm. Professionally, as a transportation officer, this was the golden opportunity of my career. The 24th ID had the toughest mission of moving the most soldiers and equipment the farthest distance: an incredible transportation challenge. Personally, I've met some of the finest people, officers and enlisted, I have ever served with. I truly believe that today's Army has the finest soldiers ever.

Now, I think, the hardest part begins. The next five years will bring a lot of change for the military as a whole. We will all feel the effects of the downsizing. Many soldiers are concerned about their futures. It's the future that we have to plan for now.

For years, military women just put their heads down and went to work, hoping their performance would be enough to sway the "non-believ-ers." In many cases it was enough, and to those women we owe a debt of gratitude. But in some critical cases, it has not been enough. Women never really have been able to plan for their futures because the "rules" kept changing. Sometimes, the changes increased opportunities for women, and in some cases, opportunities were taken away.

In 1983, I switched my branch from air defense artillery, or ADA, to the Transportation Corps because I felt in ADA I would hit the "glass ceiling." By policy, I am prohibited from being assigned to the low-level air defense weapons systems, Chaparral and Vulcan. That limited my opportunity to command at the battalion and brigade level. Soon, though, the Army will have the first female combat arms colonel in air defense. That's progress.

It took a major deployment and conflict for a nation to realize that women really are an integral part of the military, and not just assigned to traditional jobs. More than 33,000 women served in Desert Shield and Desert Storm, with 26,000 in the Army.

Recently, the House Armed Services Committee approved an amendment that would permit, but not require, the military services during combat to place women in assignments such as fighter or bomber pilot, navigator or weapons service officer. This is an important step forward. Giving the services more flexibility in the assignment of their human resources can only make a great force greater.

Attracting the Best

Most importantly, I think I speak for many in the military when I say we want the best person to be selected for the job and we don't want our military readiness to suffer. The focus should not be equal opportunity. During these changing times, the focus must be to keep our best-qualified people and continue to attract the very best. The services can ill-afford to arbitrarily remove half the population from consideration. . . .

We in the military can make much better use of our resources by looking at performance rather than gender.

Should Women Serve in the Military?

No: Women Should Not Serve in the Military

Women Make Poor Soldiers
Women in the Military Harm America's Defense
Children Are Harmed When Mothers Serve in the Military
Women Should Not Support America's Military Goals

Women Make Poor Soldiers

Brian Mitchell

About the Author: *Brian Mitchell is a former U.S. Army infantry officer and intelligence agent. Mitchell, now a reporter for* Navy Times *newspaper, is the author of the controversial book* Weak Link: The Feminization of the American Military, *from which this viewpoint is excerpted.*

The party line in Washington is that all is well with women in the military, that with the exception of a few minor annoyances to be dispelled by the magic wand of policy, sexual integration is proceeding smoothly without degrading military readiness. Women are "an integral part" of the nation's defense, and they can do the job "as well if not better" than their male comrades, say responsible officials, some of whom seem quite willing to believe that women actually make better soldiers than men do.

The proof, they say, is in the women's consistently faster rate of promotion. Women are sometimes twice as likely as men to be promoted. In the spring of 1987, the Army promoted 33 percent of eligible women to the rank of E-7 but only 16 percent of eligible men. DoD-wide [Department of Defense], women are promoted with less time-in-service than men to every grade from E-2 to O-7. Female officers are promoted to rear admiral and brigadier general (O-7) five years earlier than men, on average. Enlisted women can expect promotion to senior NCO [noncommissioned officer]or chief petty officer rank (E-7) two to four years earlier than enlisted men.

There are, however, several reasons for doubting the significance of promotion comparisons.

Higher rates of attrition and lower rates of retention trim much of the deadwood from the women's ranks. In the past, those who survived until retirement were intensely dedicated women who forsook marriage and family for the sake of their careers. Today less dedicated women are favored by promotion systems that emphasize education, test scores, and personal appearance. Women tend to have higher levels of education, they perform well on written advancement examinations, and they often demonstrate greater poise, composure, and eloquence before promotion boards. Of course, promotions are centrally controlled and therefore not immune from manipulation for political or other purposes. The services do, in fact, exert considerable institutional pressure at all levels to safeguard the advancement of women.

The assertion that women in general are performing as well as or better than men is by no means proven. No doubt some women outperform some men, but the many good servicewomen who excel at their jobs do not compensate the services for the problems that women overall have caused them.

> ## "The assertion that women in general are performing as well as or better than men is by no means proven."

The general lack of physical strength among servicewomen bears directly upon their ability to perform assigned duties. Yet to many, the lack of physical strength among women seems hardly worth mentioning. The notion that technology has alleviated the need for physical strength is almost universally accepted. Say the words "modern warfare" and the minds of many Americans fill with images of control consoles and video displays. "There's an awful lot of button-pushing going on out there," says a reporter for *Time* magazine who thinks the physical demands of the military have been exaggerated.

There is, however, no real evidence that technology has in fact reduced the need for physical strength among military men and women. What evidence there is shows that many military jobs still require more physical strength than most women possess. Technology has not affected the way many simple, unavoidable wartime tasks are performed. It has not provided the Air Force with automatic litter-loaders to move wounded soldiers onto MEDEVAC [medical evacuation] aircraft when female loadmasters are unable to do so, nor has it relieved the Army of the task of sorting artillery rounds by hand. What technology has done is made service members able to do more, thereby making more for them to do. Many of the buttons that need pushing are attached to large pieces of equipment that must be hauled with haste back and forth across the battlefield.

Though estimations vary, there is without doubt a significant gap between the physical abilities of men and women. Tests of men and women entering the West Point class of 1980 found that, on average, the upperbody strength of women is 56 percent of the strength of men, their leg strength is 80 percent, and their gripping strength is 69 percent. Even when height is kept constant, women possess only 80 percent of the overall strength of men. When one considers differences in power (the combination of strength and speed) and in work performed within a span of time, both of which factor in the greater lung capacity and endurance of men, the disparity between the physical abilities of men and women appears more extreme. After eight weeks of intensive training, male plebes demonstrated 32 percent more power in the lower body and performed 48 percent more work at the leg press than female plebes. At the bench press, the men demonstrated 270 percent more power and performed an extraordinary 473 percent more work than the women.

It is little wonder then that servicewomen should find so many workaday duties beyond their ability. Even in the modern Air Force, routine tasks are often too much for them. The GAO [General Accounting Office] found that 62 of 97 female aircraft mechanics could not perform required tasks such as changing aircraft tires and brakes, removing batteries and crew seats, closing drag chute doors, breaking torque on bolts, and lifting heavy stands. Female missile mechanics often lack the strength and physical confidence to harness and move warheads and to maneuver large pieces of machinery. Some have trouble carrying their own tool boxes. . . .

Medical Differences

Lack of physical strength contributes to another problem with women in the military: they need greater medical attention. Women in all of the services are hospitalized two to three times as often as men, a difference corresponding to that found in the civilian community. In the 1970s, the percentage of Navy women requiring hospitalization fluctuated between 25 and 30 percent while hospitalization of Navy men declined from 13 percent in 1966 to 11 percent in 1975. When men and women are subjected to the same work requirements and living conditions, as during recruit and cadet training, women's hospitalization rates are significantly higher than men's rates for nearly all diagnoses: mental disorders, musculoskeletal afflictions, acute upper-respiratory infections, medical and surgical aftercare, rubella, infective and parasitic diseases, and digestive, diarrheal, and genitourinary disorders.

"The lack of discipline among men is itself the fault of a feminized force."

In the services at large, differences in military occupation and off-duty behavior mean different rates of hospitalization for the various diagnoses. Men are generally more prone to injury (fractures, lacerations, and dislocations) because of their poorer driving records and greater involvement in hazardous work and athletics, though Navy women in the lower grades assigned nontraditional jobs have shown "considerably higher" rates of injury than similarly assigned men, probably because of their lack of physical confidence, mechanical experience, and upperbody strength. Women generally are still more prone to mental illness, genitourinary disorders, and disease, with pregnancy-related conditions accounting for one third or more of all women hospitalized. Among mental disorders, men show higher rates of schizophrenia, alcoholism, and drug-related conditions, while women show higher rates of neuroses, eating disorders, and "transient situational disturbances."

"Servicewomen place a considerable additional burden on the already overburdened military medical system."

Though many military women deny or downplay the effects of pre-menstrual syndrome (PMS) on the behavior of women, medical experts estimate that 5 to 10 percent of all premenopausal women experience severe PMS-related symptoms, including incapacitating depression, suicidal thoughts, extreme mood swings, self-abuse, and violence. "These are women who suffer chronic, debilitating distress—women who are often unable to take care of themselves or their family," says Nancy Reame, associate professor of nursing at the University of Michigan at Ann Arbor. Most women experience milder symptoms such as bloating, headaches, backaches, irritability, depression, breast tenderness, and food cravings. Roughly half of all women who suffer PMS characterize the condition as "mildly distressing." Only about 10 percent of pre-menopausal women experience no symptoms of PMS. The impact of PMS on unit effectiveness is compounded by the natural, involuntary tendency of women living in close quarters to synchronize their menstrual cycles.

Much of the debate about the medical cost-effectiveness of women versus men has focused on rates of "noneffectiveness" or "nonavailability," the amount of duty time service members miss while receiving medical attention. The medical nonavailability rate for women is consistently 2 to 2.5 times the rate for men. Much of the difference is attributable to pregnancy, but the women's rate exceeds the men's rate for all diagnoses. The women's nonavailability rate is 8.7 times the male rate for genitourinary disorders, 2.6 times the men's rate for morbidity (disease), 1.4 times the men's rate for mental illness, and 3.8 times the men's rate for spurious complaints. Women lose five times as much time as men for attempted suicide but are successful at suicide only half as many times as men.

The significance of the greater medical needs of women has been very effectively suppressed by proponents of women in the military who point out, whenever the subject comes up, that though women lose more time for medical reasons, men lose more time for disciplinary reasons. The greater need of women for medical attention and the greater trouble men cause by undisciplined behavior are quite different problems, however, and the discussion should not end with a simple comparison of lost time.

Lack of Discipline

The lack of discipline among men is itself the fault of a feminized force, a force that fails to instill discipline during basic training because of its be-nice-to-privates approach to attracting and managing troops. Still, a commander has much more control over a unit's disciplinary problems than its medical problems, and rates of nonavailability for indiscipline vary dramatically from unit to unit and from time to time. Since the comparison of nonavailability for all reasons was last made in 1980, rates of indiscipline among men have declined as the services have attracted better quality recruits. The Defense Department no longer knows whether men or women lose more time overall.

In contrast, the medical demands of women in the peacetime force have been relatively steady. Modifications of clothing and equipment have reduced the rate at which women seek medical attention only slightly. Sex education has done little to reduce rates of pregnancy. If the medical nonavailability rates of women change at all, they are likely to increase as more and more women are assigned nontraditional duties for which they have not the physical ability. Nonavailability will also increase if women are employed closer to the fighting in wartime. The services can expect an increase in mental illness and infectious disorders among women. Unsanitary conditions combined with inevitable shortages of such items as sanitary napkins will aggravate genitourinary infections. In Honduras, servicewomen were forced to use sponges and birth control pills when there was nothing else. In future wars, even those poor comforts may be luxuries.

That servicewomen place a considerable additional burden on the already overburdened military medical system is generally admitted, but the weight of the burden is unknown and not likely to become known for political reasons. In 1985, the Defense Department's Health Studies Task Force recommended that the department fund an independent study of the full impact of integration on the health care requirements of the services, at a cost of $780,000. The task force noted that a joint study by the Defense Department and the Veterans Administration would cost less but would be "suspect in the civilian community and among various women's groups" and might "provoke a political controversy." No study, independent or in-house, has ever been done.

Attrition

One problem with women in the military that does receive some attention is the problem of attrition, defined as the failure to complete an enlistment contract. Attrition reduces service strength, increases personnel turbulence, and robs the service of its training investment.

Women consistently attrit at higher rates than men. The difference is most dramatic between male and female high school graduates, the very people the services want most to keep. In 1981, nearly half of all Marine Corps female high school graduates failed to complete their enlistment contracts, more than double the rate for male high school graduates: 48 to 23.5 percent. In the Army, the attrition rate for female graduates was two-thirds higher than for male graduates: 40.3 to 24.8 percent. More recently, attrition among all servicewomen has been 36 percent higher than attrition among male servicemen: 34 to 25 percent. The difference is least in the Navy, in which men see an unequal share of sea duty. As more women are required to go to sea involuntarily, attrition rates for Navy women will soar.

"Pregnancy is perhaps the single greatest obstacle to the acceptance of women in the military."

Defenders of women in the military have often suggested that the combat restrictions frustrate the ambitions of women and thus contribute to their higher rates of attrition, but all evidence shows otherwise. Attrition among women in nontraditional career fields is consistently higher than among women in traditional career fields and studies indicate that women who attrit tend to hold more traditional views regarding the roles of men and women. A Marine Corps study indentified "traditional family and career orientation" as the most important factor among women who attrited. Thus, those inclined toward leaving service are not likely to be persuaded to stay if offered opportunities for nontraditional work, and those who complain about limited opportunities are not likely to leave service because their ambitions are not fully satisfied. As the services push more women into nontraditional jobs, attrition among women will increase.

By far, the largest reason for attrition among women is pregnancy. The services estimate that 25 to 50 percent of women who fail to complete enlistment contracts do so because of pregnancy. Pregnancy and parenthood accounted for 23 percent of all women discharged in 1980. It is estimated that 7 to 17 percent of servicewomen become pregnant each year. As mentioned earlier, the Army found that one-third of the women who became pregnant opted for voluntary discharges under the policy that leaves the decision to stay in or get out in the hands of the woman.

Pregnancy is the only temporary disability that service members can inflict upon themselves without fear of punishment. It is also the only temporary disability that earns a service member the right to decide for herself whether to stay in the service or get out, notwithstanding the desires of her commander or the needs of the service. The 1976 ruling [by a federal circuit court] that pregnancy is like any other temporary disability has been applied only to favor and protect women.

Problems of Pregnancy

The problem with allowing the woman to decide whether she should stay in the service is that the only way the service comes out ahead is if the woman elects to have an abortion. Otherwise, either the woman contributes to the problem of attrition (and still receives military maternity care until six weeks after delivery) or she becomes a burden to her unit. Restrictions vary from service to service, but the typical pregnant service member is exempt from a variety of routine duties and requirements. She must not be made to stand at attention or parade rest for more than 15 minutes (no parades or ceremonies). She must not be exposed to harmful chemicals or vapors (no chemical warfare training, no painting, limited duties in the motorpool). She must not receive routine immunizations (no deployments overseas). She must not remain aboard ship in port past her 20th week and must not go to sea (no sea duty). She must

not be assigned to remote installations where there are limited medical facilities. She must not be assigned duties in which nausea, easy fatigue, sudden lightheadedness, or loss of consciousness would be hazardous to her or anyone else (no flying, driving, diving, or operating large machinery). The Navy bars pregnant sailors from participating in swim tests, drown-proofing, field training, and weapons training. The Army exempts pregnant women from overnight duty and limits their work-week to 40 hours or less, with frequent rest periods. . . .

"The absence of *machismo* among military women is no advantage."

Needless to say, pregnancy is not viewed by many as just another temporary disability, like a hernia or a broken leg. Most men and many women, particularly women officers, view it as a unique indulgence the military is obliged to allow its female members for no good reason. Many of the most dedicated men and women see motherhood and military service as conflicting obligations. Many military men still like to think that they endure the danger and hardships of service so that mothers and children can be safe at home. Whatever they think about equal opportunity, they still find the sight of a pregnant woman heading a formation of troops unsettling. Few people, civilian or military, can escape the notion that pregnancy is inconsistent with the role of the warrior, that the killing spirit and motherly love are necessarily inimical to each other, and that where the two are combined, the one is weakened and the other perverted. The services themselves are extremely sensitive to this glaring inconsistency. When the Army unveiled its new camouflage maternity uniform, it insisted that the uniform is not a battle dress uniform, which it resembles so closely; it is a "maternity work uniform and will be referred to as such." The reason for the difference was not explained.

Pregnancy is perhaps the single greatest obstacle to the acceptance of women in the military among military men. Charles Moskos, professor of sociology at the University of Chicago, after interviewing Army women with their units in Honduras, concluded, "When there are no pregnant women, the incorporation of women into nontraditional roles is greatest." He added, "If there is an absolute precondition of the effective utilization of women in field duty, it must be exclusion of pregnant women."

The services would be more than happy to exclude pregnant women altogether, but their hands are tied. The policy of tolerating pregnant women in uniform, forced upon the military from above, has put the services in an impossible position. The services are duty bound to reduce pregnancies to improve readiness but legally and politically bound to honor pregnant women as fully accepted service members in good standing. They dare not recommend abortion to pregnant women, nor can they actively encourage pregnant women to opt for voluntary discharge, nor can they apply official disincentives to discourage women from becoming pregnant. Their efforts to make life easier for pregnant women only make pregnancy less of a thing to avoid. The services view pregnancy as a serious problem, but many of the women who become pregnant apparently do not.

"Women lack the killer instinct."

The little the services have done to reduce the incidence of pregnancy might have had the reverse effect. Recruits receive a few hours of sex education in basic training, after which they rarely receive more. The lack of additional training probably does more to reduce pregnancy than anything else, because the services have been, and probably always will be, woefully ineffective at discouraging sexual activity through education. Far from discouraging women from having sex, the services' nonjudgmental, safety-first, girls-will-be-girls approach tends to encourage promiscuity, even to the point of advising female soldiers on how to properly have sex in the field environment. Following the scout's motto, a pamphlet entitled "Feminine Hygiene in the Field Setting," published and distributed at Fort Meade, Maryland, advises women to always be prepared:

> Sex does not just happen in the garrison setting. If you are on birth control pills, make sure that you bring enough packs along to last you for the exercise, and an extra pack in case something happens to the pack you're currently on.

It might have been more in the interest of the service to advise women that sex does not *just happen* anywhere and that they have no business making it happen while on maneuvers. Unfortunately, the good of the service has all but been abandoned in dealing with the problem of pregnancy. . . .

Psychological Differences

Underlying all of the problems with women in the military are significant psychological differences between men and women. At one time, all who were interested in the issue of women in the military were eager to analyze the ways in which men and women behave differently. Lately, however, the operating assumption has been that there are no significant differences in the behaviors of men and women, and official research efforts seem intent upon proving the assumption. Sociologists studying academy graduates marvel at the psychological similarities between men and women and minimize their differences. When exceptions are granted, they are usually presented to show that women are in some way superior to men.

Significant differences do exist, however, and few are to the women's advantage. One obvious difference is that the military is still far more popular among young men than among young women. "Women do not grow up with the notion that they're going to be a soldier," explains the Army's chief of personnel. "They need a lot of convincing." The expansion of the 1970s quickly exhausted the small pool of high quality women who were eager to enter the military. Today, the supply of young women bent on military careers barely meets the demand. Army recruiters must approach three times as many women as men for each enlistment. The quality of female recruits is becoming increasingly difficult to maintain, and the services fear that if Congress forces them to recruit more women, they will have no choice but to lower standards further. . . .

Even when men and women in the military make the same choices they often do so for different reasons. Their motivations for entering the military are widely separate. Women are much more likely to list practical, selfish reasons for joining the services. Education, travel, and money rank high on their list. The background review found that women tended to think they could earn more money in the service than in the civilian world, while men tended to believe that they were giving up brighter economic opportunities on the outside by remaining in service. Women simply do not feel the same attraction and attachment to military service that men feel. They are much less interested in military history and world affairs. A 1986 poll by CBS News found that only 25 percent of American women knew which side the United States was supporting in Nicaragua, while 50 percent of the men did. The same disparity exists among members of the military.

"The presence of women inhibits male bonding."

Men tend to give other reasons for joining the military, such as patriotism or love of country, but these lofty ideals usually serve to hide other, less respectable reasons. Most are too embarrassed to confess that they derive a profound sense of personal importance from their role as protector. Navy Lieutenant Niel L. Golightly, a fighter pilot and Olmsted Scholar, is not embarrassed. He writes:

[C]onsider the young man under fire and neck deep in the mud of a jungle foxhole, sustained in that purgatory by the vision of home—a warm, feminine place that represents all the good things that his battlefield is not. Somewhere in that soldier's world view, though he may not be able to articulate it, is the notion that he is here . . . so that all the higher ideals of home embodied in mother, sister, and girlfriend do not have to be here.

Not too long ago, this was conventional wisdom, admitted unabashedly by everyone from Harvard to Hollywood. In a scene from the movie *Operation Petticoat*, the crew of a submarine watches in awe as a group of nurses are brought aboard. The boat's executive officer says to a sailor, "If anybody asks you what you're fighting for, there's your answer." Today the same line might be intended to invite snickers as a caricature of sexism.

Masculine Motives

Many men are attracted to the military by its intensely masculine and deeply romantic character. The uniforms, the rank, the danger, the purposefulness, the opportunity to earn the respect of men and the admiration of women, all contribute to the military's enduring hold on the imagination of men and boys. Such things have inspired many men to greatness, but they too seem embarrassingly puerile in today's world. Progressive society prides itself with having evolved to a higher level where ancient impulses are deplored as childish *machismo* and where the most socially respectable motivations are, ironically, the most material and the most selfish. Young men today dare not confess their captivation with the romance of martial glory, even to themselves. Instead, when asked why they entered the military, they say patriotism. The more thoughtful among them have better answers, but they are equally evasive. Ask a young man entering a service academy today why he wishes to go there and he is likely to answer "to get a good education" or "to pursue a military career." Such answers sound good but tell us nothing about the man.

Women, however, are blissfully unbothered by the psychological complications of masculinity. They are not impressed with physical prowess, they do not relish competition, they are not intrigued by danger, they do not need to prove their manhood, and they see little reason to hide their weaknesses, psychological or physical. One researcher has suggested that women have higher rates of morbidity because they are not as reluctant as men to report feeling sick, perhaps because it is generally more acceptable for a woman to complain of sickness or injury and because the role of the patient is more compatible with the woman's passive, dependent role in society.

The absence of *machismo* among military women is no advantage. In war, physical prowess is important, dangers must be faced, and petty personal concerns cannot be allowed to interfere with greater events. The military quite naturally holds physical infirmity in contempt. It encourages the suppression of personal hurts and stigmatizes those who hurt too easily or too often as "gimps" and "snivellers." Good soldiers pride themselves on avoiding injury, ignoring illness, and enduring pain. They strive never to be found among the "sick, lame, and lazy.". . .

Too Difficult a Task

Unfortunately for the services, most women do not manage or even attempt the conversion to masculinity. Not all are that dedicated, but even among the many dedicated military women the task of conversion is too much to ask. They would be kicking against the goads of Nature by adopting mannish ways, for many fundamental behavioral differences between men and women are firmly rooted in biology.

Many feminists still reject the possibility that sex differences are biologically based and therefore beyond the reach of social reform. Some cite the work of Howard A. Moss of the National

Institute of Health, whose experiments showed that men and women respond differently to even newborn baby boys and girls, unwittingly influencing their future sex differentiation. Moss made no claim that all psychological sex differences are the result of the different ways adults treat babies, but his findings have been accepted as the last word on the subject by feminists who have lost patience with biologically based explanations. The reaction of a female Army colonel is typically dismissive: "Don't give me any of that hormones shit! I've had it up to here with hormones!". . .

"Most women do not manage or even attempt the conversion to masculinity."

Testosterone's effects on behavior are plainly seen in the greater aggressiveness of men, "one of the best established, and most pervasive, of all psychological sex differences," say feminist scholars Eleanor Maccoby and Carol Jacklin of Stanford University. In *The Psychology of Sex Differences*, Maccoby and Jacklin write:

(1) Males are more aggressive than females in all human societies for which evidence is available. (2) The sex differences are found early in life, at a time when there is no evidence that differential socialization pressures have been brought to bear by adults to "shape" aggression differently in the two sexes. (3) Similar sex differences are found in man and subhuman primates. (4) Aggression is related to levels of sex hormones, and can be changed by experimental administration of these hormones.

Traditional socialization, therefore, merely confirms what has been ordained already by biology. It ensures that a child's physical development and psychological development proceed in the same direction, and it teaches boys and girls to make sense of themselves, their bodies, and their relations with the opposite sex.

A favorite feminist theory holds that proper, non-sexist socialization can, over time, correct biology, producing women as psychologically aggressive and as physically capable as men. There is, however, no evidence that the biological contribution to sex differences can be completely overcome without the assistance of modern drugs.

Some feminists argue that modern warriors need not be as aggressive as warriors of the past, or that the lack of aggressiveness offers definite advantages to the modern military. Women make better soldiers, they say, because they are well-behaved, less dangerous to themselves and others, and better suited for many routine tasks that men find tedious. Two Army studies indicate that women are better at routine, repetitive tasks. One, during World War II, found that women performed much better than men when assigned the monotonous task of monitoring a radar screen for an anti-aircraft battery in Nova Scotia. The other, in 1984, found that female officers were quicker than men to decide on a course of action when presented with familiar situations, but slower than men to make up their minds in unfamiliar situations.

"The roots of group behavior among men run deep into our being."

If war were always tedious and routine, women would be better suited for it. But war is not always tedious and routine, though its participants might find periods of both, before and after moments of emergency and upheaval. For those crucial moments, women are ill-suited. Even in peacetime, many military jobs require quickness and daring. Female intelligence personnel assigned to shadow Soviet Military Liaison Mission (SMLM) vehicles have proven too timid to keep up the chase through crowded German towns and on the open autobahn, where speeds in excess of 130 m.p.h. are common. The implications of this example for female fighter pilots are obvious, but Defense officials will not admit that women lack the killer instinct. Proof of their deficiency must await their first actual dogfights with real, all-male enemies.

A Negative Effect on Men

A final problem with women in the military, one which has nothing to do with comparative abilities of men and women, is the impact of the presence of women on the behavior of men. It is not just a problem of morale. The morale of men has hardly been a concern during the integration process. When integration of the academies caused bitter resentment among male cadets and midshipmen, integrators dismissed low morale as sexist irrationality. When Navy surveys showed junior enlisted men aboard integrated ships approving the presence of women, however, integrators heralded higher morale as women's contribution to readiness.

The different responses among men to integration are an indication of the complexity of the problem. On the one hand, the best educated and most intellectual men with a keener appreciation of military ethics and tradition overwhelmingly opposed the presence of women. On the other hand, the less educated, less intellectual, and less career-minded men enjoyed their presence. At the same time, charges of sexual harassment are aimed most often at junior enlisted men, while senior enlisted men and senior officers are more prone to fraternization and usually most outspoken in defense of women. Clearly the integrators are mistaken in believing that opposition to women comes from older men simply because they are old-fashioned and the lowest ranks simply because they are uneducated. Things are not that simple.

The roots of group behavior among men run deep into our being. All-male groups have existed in virtually every known society. Most anthropologists agree that all-male groups produce a peculiar kind of non-erotic psychological bond that men crave and cannot find elsewhere. In some societies, bonds between male friends are stronger and more sacred than bonds between husbands and wives. In his book *Men and Mar-*

riage, bestselling author George Gilder writes:

> The closest tie in virtually all societies, primate and human, is between women and children. But the next most common and strong connection may well be the all-male bond. The translation of the rudimentary impulse of love into intense ties between specific men and women appears to have been emphasized and sanctified later, in the course of creating civilized societies.

Typically, says Gilder, the all-male group is strongly hierarchical, placing heavy emphasis on leadership, loyalty, and excitement. Members are admitted and ranked according to their demonstrated ability to contribute to the group's common purpose. Competition is the key to entry and advancement. It is also a source of excitement. Leaders command the loyalty and respect of inferiors because they best personify the values of the group.

The military is also strongly hierarchical. It begs for leadership, demands loyalty, and lives for excitement. It is this way, first, because it was created by men, and, second, because such characteristics make it effective at making war. The military depends upon men acting as a team at the very moment when every man is under great temptation to seek his own comfort and save his own life. The personal bonds that men form with each other, as leaders, as followers, as comrades-in-arms, often enable ordinary men to perform acts of extreme self-sacrifice when ideals such as duty, country, or cause no longer compel. The all-male condition reinforces all of the military's highest organizational values.

The presence of women inhibits male bonding, corrupts allegiance to the hierarchy, and diminishes the desire of men to compete for anything but the attentions of women. Pushing women into the military academies made a mockery of the academies' essential nature and most honored values.

Women in the Military Harm America's Defense

Jean Yarbrough

About the Author: *Jean Yarbrough is a professor of government and legal studies at Bowdoin College in Brunswick, Maine. She specializes in political philosophy and American political thought.*

The United States is the only major country to consider seriously the question of women in combat. Of the 72 nations that register or conscript citizens for military service, only 10 include women and none places them in combat. Although women are still excluded from combat by law in the Navy and the Air Force, and by policy in the Army, the United States has moved closer to placing women in combat than any other country. Not only have women moved into "combat related" tasks, but the distinction between combatants and non-combatants has been blurred by the inclusion of women in "technical" combat positions, such as missile launch officers, which would be prime targets in a war.

It is true that women have fought in combat in the past. Sexual egalitarians point approvingly to the heroism of Soviet women during World War II and, more recently, to the combat role of women in the Israeli army. But in the Soviet Union, women fought out of dire necessity, not ideological conviction, and in all-female units. The case of Israel is even more interesting. Partly for ideological, mostly for military reasons, Israel sent women into combat in 1948. But they were withdrawn in three weeks. Israeli men proved more protective of the women, jeopardizing their own missions to save them.

Jean Yarbrough, "The Feminist Mistake." Reprinted with permission from the Summer 1985 issue of *Policy Review*, the flagship publication of The Heritage Foundation, 214 Massachusetts Ave. NE, Washington, DC 20002.

And Israeli commanders found that Arab forces fought with greater determination against female units to avoid the humiliation of being defeated by women; as a result, casualties on both sides were higher. If the Israelis could not change the attitudes of their own soldiers toward women, still less could they raise the consciousness of their enemy.

Far more instructive is the present policy of both these countries. Of an estimated 4.4 million member force, the Soviet Union employs approximately 10,000 women, all in traditional female tasks. There is not one woman general officer in the entire Soviet military. Today, Israeli women are drafted, but not for combat. Although they are given defensive weapons training, their function is to free Israeli men to fight.

In the United States, feminists support women in combat for ideological reasons—they regard it as a measure of equity—while some military professionals see it as a measure of expediency. The debate took hold in the early 1970s, when the proposed Equal Rights Amendment seemed to be prospering. The Supreme Court for the first time invalidated a number of sex-based classifications, and the federal courts then extended the principle to the military. Abandoning the judiciary's traditional deference to Congress on military policy, the federal courts greatly broadened the rights of women in the military in a series of cases in the mid and late 1970s.

> ## "In the United States, feminists support women in combat for ideological reasons."

Congress entered the picture when it voted to end the draft in 1973, resulting in a decline in the number of qualified men joining the armed forces. To compensate, the Pentagon sought to attract more women; during the 1970s, the number of women in the military increased by more than 350 percent, to 150,000. In 1975, Congress opened the service academies to women, and the Army began to narrow its definition of combat to routine direct combat and to assign women to positions previously classified as combat. Women were assigned to combat "support" units, in which they would certainly be shot at, and were trained in the use of light anti-tank weapons, M-16 rifles, grenade launchers, claymore mines, and M-60 machine guns. Under pressure from the courts, the Defense Department also revised its regulations so that pregnancy was no longer grounds for automatic dismissal.

Registration Roulette

With the election of Jimmy Carter in 1976, the pace of change accelerated. Two independent studies recommended recruiting more women for reasons of both economy and quality; one concluded the services could perform their mission with one-third female personnel. Field experiments conducted by the Army Research Institute concluded that difficulties attributable to the presence of women in the field were due chiefly to training and leadership problems that could be solved. In response to a court order, Congress enacted legislation in 1978 permitting women to serve on non-combat ships and combat ships for up to 180 days. Co-ed basic training was also launched. The following year, the Air Force opened pilot and navigator positions, and allowed women to become missile launch officers, a position previously classified as combat.

In 1979, in its most controversial move to date, the Pentagon proposed repealing the combat restrictions on women altogether, stressing the military's need for flexibility in meeting their recruitment goals and the desire for equity. According to the Undersecretary of the Air Force, Antonia Handler Chayes, it was a question of "equal opportunity to fight and die for the country."

In the last significant measure of his administration, President Carter called for the registration of 18-year-old men and women. The admin-istration's arguments for registration of women recall the discussion of women warriors in Book V of Plato's *Republic*. Here Socrates, discussing the differences between men and women in combat, facetiously suggests that the differences between the sexes are no greater than between bald and long-haired men. Richard Danzig, a Carter official, when asked in the Senate if the proposal to register women was based on military necessity, replied seriously with a similar analogy: "If you said to me does the military require people with brown eyes to serve, I would have to tell you no, because people with blue eyes could do the job."

In rejecting the proposal, the Senate Armed Services Committee Report called the plan a "smokescreen" that diverted attention from serious manpower shortages in the all volunteer force (AVF). The Report noted that although 95 percent of the job categories were open to women, 42 percent of the total number of jobs were closed to them because of combat restrictions. Since most of the shortages occur in combat positions, registering women would not solve the problem. Indeed, looking ahead to a general mobilization, the Report warned that if the proposal to register women in equal numbers were interpreted to require their induction in equal numbers, it would seriously impair military readiness.

"Congress believed there was a tension between the requirements of equity and a strong defense."

The Report concluded that the proposal to register women was based on equity rather than military necessity, and it rejected the plan for this reason. In passing, the Report also addressed the inherent difficulty of the equity argument. If all women were required to register, but then were not inducted in equal numbers (administration officials testified that the ratio of men to women to be called up was 6:1), or admitted to combat, then the plan would fail to satisfy its own principle of equity. Unlike the administration, Congress believed there was a tension between the requirements of equity and a strong defense. It chose defense; and the Supreme Court upheld the decision not to require draft registration of women.

"The American military has grown increasingly dependent upon women to meet its 'manpower' requirements."

To many feminists and others who view the military primarily as a social institution, this was a serious blow; the subsequent election of Ronald Reagan seemed to foreshadow major cutbacks in many of the gains women had made in the military in the 1970s.

At first, it did seem likely that the Reagan Administration would change policy concerning women in the military. Immediately after the 1980 election, the Pentagon ordered a "pause" in the recruitment of women to assess their impact on military readiness. It temporarily established a ceiling of 65,000 enlisted women in the Army, and held recruitment levels steady in the other services.

In 1982, the Army, in its policy review, *Women in the Army*, (WITA) recommended 1) the development of a "gender neutral" physical fitness test (MEPSCAT) that would have effectively barred most women from the strenuous military occupational specialties (MOS) to which they were assigned, but were performing inadequately, and 2) the closing of 23 additional MOS to women because of the likelihood of routine direct combat. In the same year, the Pentagon ended co-ed basic training for recruits; male and female officers still train together.

In an odd alliance, feminists joined with free market supporters of the AVF in denouncing these moves, and in the end they prevailed. De-spite the administration's opposition to the ERA, it was bound by the imperatives of the AVF to continue to expand opportunities for women in the military, including combat-related MOS. Six months after the WITA recommendations, Secretary of the Army John O. Marsh, Jr. announced that the MEPSCAT tests would be used only as a "guideline" in the classification process, and that female soldiers would not be denied entry into a particular field because of their physical strength. Army officials stress that "closing a career field to female soldiers is not related to the physical standards of jobs or the physical strength of the applicants"; it is "solely a function of the probability of direct combat involvement." At the same time, the Army re-opened 13 of the 23 MOS closed to women for this reason.

Growing Dependence

The American military has grown increasingly dependent upon women to meet its "manpower" requirements in the volunteer force. Defense Department publications regard the increase in women from 173,445 or 8.5 percent of the active force in January 1981 to over 200,000 or 9.4 percent at the end of fiscal 1984 as a "significant improvement." And as the number of women in the military has grown, they have emerged as a powerful interest group. General Jeanne Holm, one of the leading advocates of women's rights in the military, makes it clear that as the number of women increases, the pressure to repeal combat restrictions on women will also grow.

> Sooner or later, if the numbers and proportions of women continue to expand, Congress and the services will have to confront the restrictions imposed by the combat laws and policies and will have to decide whether they should be changed and, if so, how.

Pressure for change comes most from the female junior officers whose careers are most directly affected by the combat exclusion policy. In a report on field exercises in Honduras, Charles C. Moskos notes that among female officers, "about half believed that women should be allowed to volunteer for combat units . . . the remainder said women should be compelled to go into combat units in the same manner as men . . . "

The Combat Exclusion Policy

A memo from Secretary of Defense Caspar Weinberger, written in July 1983, suggests that the Pentagon recognizes the tension between the military's growing reliance upon women and a broad interpretation of the combat exclusion policy. "The combat exclusion rule should be interpreted to allow as many as possible career opportunities for women to be kept open," wrote Weinberger. He warns the service secretaries that "no artificial barriers to career opportunities for women will be constructed or tolerated." In keeping with Weinberger's directive, the Defense Department's publication *Going Strong: Women in Defense* (1984) boasts

> that women in the Army serve in more than 86 percent of the enlisted career fields, and more than 96 percent of the officer specialties are open to women. These fields include non-traditional specialties such as air traffic control, military intelligence, aviation, equipment maintenance and operation, communications, computer repair, and law enforcement.

In the Navy, nearly 10,000 of the 42,000 enlisted women serve in non-traditional areas. One hundred and seventy-two women officers and 3,359 enlisted women serve aboard 32 ships. Ground support and maintenance positions were opened up to enlisted women. In June 1984, the Navy assigned the first woman executive officer aboard ship. In another change, women officers can now be assigned to "mobile logistics support force ships for temporary duty and deployments." As *Going Strong* explains, "this allows women helicopter pilots and women members of explosive ordnance disposal detachments to deploy with their units."

In the Air Force, the following specialties have been opened to enlisted women since 1981: Airborne Warning and Control Systems (AWACS), KC-10 aerial tanker crew, and 26,000 security police positions. More than 300 women officers serve as pilots and navigators of non-combat aircraft, including the mammoth transport aircraft, the C-5A Galaxy. In 1985, women officers were made eligible for assignment as launch control officers in the Air Force's most advanced strategic nuclear missile, the Minuteman II. And on April 30, 1985, Air Force Secretary Verne Orr announced that more than 800 new positions were being opened to women, including the "C-23 and EC-130H aircraft, forward air control post, the airborne battlefield command and control center mission, and some munitions sites."

Despite its initial reservations, the Reagan Administration has been forced by its commitment to the AVF to expand opportunities for women in the military. As long as the AVF continues, the pressure to increase the number of women and to open all military specialties, including combat, will continue to grow, and to pose serious problems for combat readiness.

"As long as the AVF continues, the pressure to increase the number of women . . . will continue to grow."

Morale is difficult to assess because it defies precise quantification. Nevertheless, a number of problem areas have emerged.

1. *Fraternization.* Military policy traditionally prohibits social relations between officers and enlisted personnel in order to maintain impartiality, discipline, and morale. James Webb, a Naval Academy graduate, in a controversial article in *The Washingtonian*, "Women Can't Fight", cites one cadet's opinion of how fraternization has undermined morale at West Point.

> Our squad leaders talk about honor, performance, and accountability. Then before you knew it, they were going after the women plebes, sneaking some of them away on weekends. How can you indoctrinate the women when you're breaking the regulations to date them? And how can you talk about integrity and accountability when you're doing these sorts of things?

2. *Special Treatment.* Even when fraternization rules are observed, both men and women complain of double standards. Men believe that women receive preferential treatment in duty hours, assignments, and sick call. They resent having to assume additional responsibilities because women are pregnant or physically unable to perform strenuous assignments.

"Sexual harassment is . . . especially acute in the military."

But it is not only the morale of men that suffers. In the Honduras exercise, Mr. Moskos, who generally regards the operation as a success, nevertheless notes:

> Men and women ran together, which led to one of the few forms of invidious comparisons between the sexes in the encampment. Initially, the women were mixed in with the men, but this typically led to the women as a group falling behind the men. The procedure was then changed to place women in front of men. This resulted in the whole group running at a slower pace than if the men had run alone. Either way, the women felt they were being regarded as failures, firstly by not being able to keep up with the men, or secondly, by holding the men back.

Finally, even when women soldiers share equally in the hardships of the field exercises, they are never really comfortable with the lack of privacy in sleeping and showering arrangements, and this too can affect morale, especially among the women recruits.

3: *Sexual Harassment.* Although sexual harassment is likely to occur wherever men and women share close quarters and work together, it is especially acute in the military, and has increased as the number of women has grown. One reason may be that the insularity of military life intensifies sexual attraction and conflict. Another may be that the military legitimately cultivates aggressive behavior to a greater degree than civil institutions. Researchers have suggested that some men may find it difficult to restrain their hostile impulses toward women, especially if they disapprove of their having invaded this most masculine profession.

Nor is sexual harassment only a problem between the sexes. In the Honduras exercises, enlisted women mentioned approaches from lesbians. As Mr. Moskos notes, "accounts of lesbians would come up spontaneously in most extended interviews with female soldiers," though the women were less alarmed than male soldiers by homosexual overtures.

The military's policies on sexual matters tend to go off in opposite directions. Reformers want the military to stay out of private matters with regard to fraternization, pregnancy, family matters, and sexual conduct in general, but they call on the military to intervene in private matters involving sexual harassment, and to use the authority they are otherwise unwilling to acknowledge to reform offensive attitudes. The authority these reformers would give the military is broad indeed: the female officers interviewed by Mr. Moskos consider sexual harassment to include "sexual definitions of suitable work, the combat exclusion rule, sexist language, etc." Similarly the Defense Department defines sexual harassment in part as "verbal or physical conduct of a sexual nature," which creates an "intimidating, hostile, or offensive environment." According to this definition, many of the traditional military techniques for instilling courage and a fighting spirit might be regarded as "sexual harassment."

The Service Academies

Traditionally, the service academies have prepared officers for leadership positions, chiefly combat ones. But in evaluating the performance of women at the academies, supporters stress women's academic performance, while minimizing the effect of changes in the physical training curricula. Although the academies initially tried to hold women to the same physical standards as men, with only minimal changes, the disparity in performance between the men and the women necessitated the development of different standards. As General Holm reports:

Women at West Point carry lighter rifles; pugil stick training, in which cadets practice hand-to-hand combat with padded sticks, pits only women against women; and parts of the obstacle course have been adjusted to accommodate shorter people.

In keeping with this view of the academies as essentially academic institutions, West Point publications now stress equal effort rather than equal performance.

> ## "Officers understand that their misgivings about women's performances can adversely affect their careers."

On the other hand, critics insist that the principal task of the academies (which cost the American taxpayer over $100,000 per graduate) is to prepare men for combat leadership. They deplore the shift from leadership to "management," from physical strength to "general excellence," and blame the admission of women for accelerating these trends. At the Naval Academy, physical punishment and verbal abuse of cadets have been abolished. Although this sounds like a sensible reform, and is consistent with the Defense Department's broad definition of sexual harassment, a plausible case can be made that, however brutal, these earlier practices helped to prepare men for the kind of stress and violence they would encounter in combat. Similarly, the Academy has replaced the longstanding practice of peer evaluations with officer evaluations because the officers feared that male cadets would not rate women as effective leaders. Male cadets complain that the leadership evaluation process has been "sterilized" and that women cadets have been singled out for advancement on the basis of their managerial and academic performance. They object that women have not proven themselves effective leaders in ways that matter.

Yet they also know that they dare not say this publicly. Cadets at West Point are rated on their "attitudes toward equal opportunity," and officers understand that their misgivings about women's performances can adversely affect their careers.

Advocates of expanding opportunities for women in the military concede that most women are physically weaker, but they dismiss the issue of strength. They cite studies like the Gates Commission, which maintained that the percentage of ground combat jobs requiring few technical skills had declined and would continue to do so. Future confrontations will require a higher percentage of soldiers skilled in electronic and other technical fields. Also, the advocates say, women recruits are more intelligent and better able to operate such sophisticated equipment. And finally, most of what the Army does requires teamwork. Men can cooperate with women as well as with men if required by their leaders to do so.

Upon closer analysis, these arguments are unpersuasive. The necessity of avoiding a general nuclear holocaust makes it likely that future wars will be limited and improvisational. The Army believes that victory in such contests will depend upon "initiative, depth, agility, and synchronization . . . maneuver and surprise . . . leadership, unit cohesion, and effective independent operations." It further assumes that casualties will be high in combat "support" units, in which women now serve. . . . Victory will depend more on traditional infantry stamina than sophisticated weapons.

Mercenaries for the Privileged

During the Reagan Administration, the overall quality of the armed forces, measured by percentage of the force with high school diplomas and high AFQT scores, has improved dramatically, significantly narrowing the gap between male and female performance. Nevertheless, there are strong indications that this trend may not hold. The proposed Congressional cap on military spending and the decline in the 18- to 20-year-old pool pose severe problems for the quality of the AVF. In testimony before Congress in 1985, Assistant Secretary of Defense Lawrence J. Korb predicted that "recruiting will continue to become increasingly difficult." In this case, the gap between qualified women and men may again widen, as it did during the Carter years. The real question remains—not whether women are more qualified than high school dropouts or mental incompetents to engage in combat specialties, but why we as a nation allow poor, disproportionately black, men and women to become mercenaries for middle and upper class white men.

Adverse Effects

Moreover, although women do pose fewer disciplinary problems, they adversely affect combat readiness in other ways. According to the office of the Assistant Secretary of Defense, "Ten percent of the women in the Army are pregnant at any given time. Over the course of the year, it is estimated that 17 percent of the Army's female personnel will have been pregnant." This creates problems of lost time, child care, and deployability. Although unmarried mothers with dependent children are not allowed to enlist in either the active or reserve forces, they are allowed to remain if they divorce or become pregnant after their enlistment. . . .

Although it is true that many military tasks require teamwork rather than virtuoso displays of physical strength, it is not so clear that men will cooperate with women as readily as with men, or that they will perform as effectively if they do. In the two Army studies designed to measure the effect of women on combat effectiveness, MAXWAC and Reforger, the conclusions, though favorable, are ambiguous. A special team of observers found no differences in units composed of 35 percent women in the MAXWAC study, but noted informally that the "women generally did not perform the field tasks as well as men.". . .

The Defense Department no longer conducts such tests. According to Lieutenant Colonel John Boyer of the Pentagon, "the question of whether women can perform as well as men in combat service support type skills is no longer at issue. It is recognized that women do perform as well as men in these jobs."

Finally, the dispute over quality involves different, frequently unstated, methodological assumptions. On the one side is the technical, or what William J. Gregor of West Point calls the "instrumental" approach to measuring military effectiveness. The instrumental view relies upon supposedly objective quantitative tests—nothing is true until it has been quantitatively measured. But technicians, too, have values—in this case that women can perform effectively in nearly all, if not all areas of the military. And the kind of studies they design tend to give them the answers they want. When the tests do not confirm their values they assume that human nature is malleable, and can be changed through "effective" managerial techniques.

By contrast, the "normative" model recognizes the limits of quantification, and recognizes that ultimately the kinds of questions asked and the methods employed to answer them reflect opposing political philosophies. There is no "value-free" study of women in the military. Certain variables like morale or male bonding are subjective and difficult to measure accurately, but they are nevertheless crucial to any realistic assessment of combat effectiveness. Human nature, which is at once universal and particular, human as well as male and female, is not amenable to unlimited experimentation.

"It is not so clear that men will cooperate with women as readily as with men."

But the trend of recent history and court decisions is to ignore these differences in the pursuit of social equity. The demand for equity has widespread appeal because it is simple and reflects the egalitarian principle of American society. But when applied to military affairs, it is wrong and dangerous. The military cannot and should not try to mirror exactly the principles of democratic society. The military is not a "civic instrument" that reflects social progress. Nor is it a social welfare agency. The relationship between the military and civilian spheres is more complicated. Although the military defends the principles of democratic society, it cannot fully embody them. Its end is victory, not equity; its virtue is courage, not justice; its structure is authoritarian, not pluralistic. In short, although the military defends democratic principles and is shaped by the regime of which it is a part, it is not simply a microcosm of the larger society. The requirements of military life clash with the democratic commitment to equality, natural rights, and consent.

This does not mean that the military can or ought to ignore democratic principles altogether.

The demands of black soldiers are a case in point. Until after World War II, racial segregation was official military policy. Beginning in 1948, and prior to the great court decisions outlawing discrimination in civil society, the services sought to eliminate racial segregation and discrimination. But the situation of blacks and women is not the same. The arguments for segregating blacks were based on longstanding and irrational white prejudice, whereas the case against women in combat is rooted in recognition of genuine physical and psychological differences that are important in battle, such as strength, aggressiveness, and sexual attraction. To the extent that the prejudice against women is based on an appreciation of these natural and desirable differences, it is valid and should influence military policy.

Children Are Harmed When Mothers Serve in the Military

Elaine Donnelly

About the Author: *Elaine Donnelly is an activist in the Michigan Republican Party and a former member of the Pentagon's Defense Advisory Committee on Women in the Services.*

"If we can't win a war without our mothers, what kind of a sorry fighting force are we? Even the evil Saddam Hussein doesn't send mothers to fight a war. And what kind of policy is it for a nation to send both parents, single parents or mothers to war? A shameful and uncivilized policy, that's what."

This impassioned passage was written not by Phyllis Schlafly, or Pat Buchanan, or even Mr. (Fred) Rogers. It was none other than Sally Quinn, the blond *Washington Post* writer, who wrote that she felt downright queasy when she first saw a picture of a uniformed soldier-mother, kissing her baby good-bye as she headed off to war.

Something "snapped" in Quinn, however, when she heard the poignant story of an infant whose parents were shipped out to Saudi Arabia on 48 hours' notice. The little girl, who was carried to Boston in the arms of an airline stewardess, screamed in terror as she was handed over to the "designee"—an aunt she didn't know with four children of her own.

Harvard pediatrician T. Barry Brazelton has expressed outrage over this incident and many others. In a television interview he noted, sadly,

Elaine Donnelly, "Should We Have Mothers in the Military?" *Human Events*, March 16, 1991. Reprinted with permission.

that children whose parents were shipped to Saudi Arabia suffered from severe insecurity and fear that they themselves are to blame. Even non-military children, seeing mothers torn away from babies on the evening news, were terrified that their own mothers might be snatched away as well.

Former "Army brat" Quinn, who was traumatized by separation from her father during the Korean War, argues convincingly that mothers should not be sent to fight a war. She is less convincing, however, when suggesting that children are suffering because of what she calls "feminism gone awry."

The truth is that bedrock feminist ideology has always maintained that men and women are interchangeable in all life occupations—that it really doesn't matter who does the soldiering and who does the mothering. This is the "politically correct" theory that was put to the test—with relentless efficiency—by the Pentagon in "Operation Desert Storm."

What we are witnessing is a massive wartime social experiment which, like many other "enlightened" experiments of the past two decades, is putting children at serious risk. The contrast between theory and reality has never been more clear.

Infants know nothing of binding contracts, international crises, or feminist theories about women in the military. Unlike the children of civilian women in the workforce, they will not even see their mothers for many months.

"Even the evil Saddam Hussein doesn't send mothers to fight a war."

Many child psychologists say that fathers or grandparents can help children left behind, but early, long-term separation from their mothers often causes severe depression, anger and grief which are expressed in a variety of ways. Excessive crying and clinging, nightmares, stomachaches and problems in school are evidence of a lack of trust and confidence that causes children to withdraw from adults and even their mothers when they finally return.

The sight of male soldiers leaving their children behind has always tugged at the heart, but there is an undeniable extra dimension of discomfort surrounding military mothers. In an Associated Press Poll, 64 percent of respondents said they opposed the idea of mothers with young children going to a war zone.

In response to growing political pressures, there was a House Armed Services subcommittee hearing February 19, 1991, on the "parenting issues" of "Operation Desert Storm."

"Early, long-term separation from their mothers often causes severe depression."

Rep. Barbara Boxer (D.-Calif.) testified on behalf of her "gulf orphan" bill, which would permit the exemption of one of two military parents, or single parents, from deployment to a combat zone. A similar bill sponsored by Sen. John Heinz (R.-Pa.) would automatically reassign single parents or one of two dual-service parents, but only from the Persian Gulf theater of operations.

Subcommittee Chair Beverly Byron (D.-Md.) offered yet another bill, which would ignore the usual sex-neutral approach by exempting new military mothers only, for a period of six months.

Rep. Jill Long (D.-Ind.) and Sen. Herbert Kohl (D.-Wis.) suggested an indirect approach, with legislation to exempt military parents from deployment to any post that doesn't have facilities for dependents—defined as minor children, elderly persons or disabled adult children who need special care.

Assistant Secretary of Defense for Force Management and Personnel Christopher Jehn led official representatives of the armed services in declaring that the various parenting bills were "unwarranted and unwise." This is not surprising because the armed forces are, by necessity, regimented organizations. In wartime the field commanders must concern themselves with battle damage assessments, not family damage assessments. Any child-care plan that allows the soldier to be deployed, no matter how disruptive, is considered a "success" in military terms.

A Conflict of Interest

Field commanders must concern themselves with pregnancy rates, however, because pregnancy excuses women from overseas duty. Childbirth offers only a temporary break for the women, however. Because military units cannot afford to remain shorthanded, mothers must return to duty within a few weeks of the birth of their child.

This requirement highlights a classic conflict of interest between children, their mothers, and the military. Congressional proposals so far appear to be sensitive and helpful to the children, but they really have less to do with compassion than careerism.

Special exemptions for single and dual-service parents would, in effect, create a new class of volunteer soldiers who could enjoy all the benefits of the armed services in peacetime, but without the full burdens of service in wartime.

Inter-service confusion, unpredictability, administrative delays and high child-care costs would clearly detract from military readiness, while increasing the level of risk for shorthanded troops.

Instead of these short-term, Band-Aid approaches, Congress and the Defense Department should reevaluate and reverse the liberal recruitment and retention policies that have put military children at risk in the first place. For example:

• The military should make a phased return to the pre-1976 policy of honorably discharging mothers and single parents with custody of minor children. (The policy was changed because the Carter Administration refused to challenge a lower court ruling favoring pregnant servicewomen.) Exceptions might be made for veterans with at least 10 years of service—most of whom have older children instead of infants—but it must be remembered that the military is there to defend the country; it doesn't owe a job to anyone.

• Second, the Defense Department must revisit its 1983 decision—made in response to pressures from the Defense Advisory Committee on Women in the Services (DACOWITS)—that the Army's battery of physical strength tests should be used only as a "recruiting guidance tool." Current dual standards allow and even encourage women to take non-traditional jobs that are known to be beyond their physical strength.

The replacing of double standards and recruitment quotas with an honest equal opportunity qualifying system—matching physical abilities to actual wartime job requirements—would probably reduce the number of women in the military, but not their stature.

When combined with a return to the pre-1976 family policy, the change would help to reduce escalating problems associated with dual-service marriages, pregnancies, single parenthood and costly child care.

"The military is there to defend the country; it doesn't owe a job to anyone."

• Instead of working so hard to recruit women by promising them more than the military can possibly deliver, the volunteer forces ought to reevaluate and change their advertising strategies. It's absurd to be tearing mothers away from babies when there are so many patriotic and physically fit young men striding around in Desert Storm T-shirts. Anyone can be trained to drive a Hum-Vee, but a child has only one mother.

• Finally, the Defense Department must marshal its courage and confront the political force at the root of this problem. The Pentagon's DACOWITS regularly intimidates all branches of the armed forces with persistent and repetitive recommendations promoting careerism for women.

Official attempts to appease DACOWITS have resulted in recruiting quotas, relaxed physical standards, liberalized family policies, and constantly changing definitions of "combat" that clearly circumvent the intent of Congress that women should be kept out of it. DACOWITS is at the center of these problems, and it ought to be abolished.

A Change of Attitude

The Persian Gulf war showed that intelligent, patriotic volunteer women are ready to serve their country with distinction, and their willingness to do their duty is admirable. The loyal family members who care for their children deserve all the moral support and help they can get.

Still, signs are everywhere that attitudes are turning against feminism in the military. A former "gung-ho" Army sergeant, for example, told the *New York Times* that she sacrificed her career because ". . . a mother should be with her children. . . . I hate to say it because it doesn't fit with the whole scheme of the women's movement, but I think we have to reconsider what we're doing."

Indeed, we must. In a three-way conflict of interest between children, their mothers, and the military, children cannot fight their own political battles. Now that this war is over, the full damage to our families must be honestly assessed. If we aren't fighting for our children, then whom are we fighting for?

Women Should Not Support America's Military Goals

Helen Vozenilek

About the Author: *Helen Vozenilek is an electrician in Oakland, California.*

Six women were among the U.S. military personnel who died in the Persian Gulf war. I do not feel joyful about this equal-opportunity employment. Scores of thousands of Iraqis are dead, that country is in total ruin, Arab-Israeli tensions are further heightened and the entire Gulf region is awash in black rain. I do not feel proud that women made up 6 percent of the U.S. military forces that wrought this damage and destruction.

During the eight years of U.S. military involvement in Vietnam, 7,500 women served in the U.S. forces. In eight months, the number of women deployed in the Persian Gulf was more than 30,000. Feminists are ambivalent about their assessment of this 400 percent growth of women in combat. I am not.

Choice is generally the platform around which the discussion of this issue revolves. Should women have the right to serve in the armed forces of the United States? And should women be allowed access to the same positions of power, authority and prestige in the military that men are? When reduced to such narrow terms many of us find ourselves agreeing that, yes, women should have the same access and opportunities that men do. Those who, like myself, have worked to open up vocations traditionally closed to women react almost reflexively to the tearing down of this perceived new barrier.

But in adopting the argument that women should have as much right to fight as men do, we are accepting flawed terms of debate. The issue isn't about choice. It's about the lack of choice, the lack of opportunities. A large percentage of women are in the armed services to get an education, learn a skill, earn a monthly paycheck or gain autonomy from limiting lives and circumstances. These are the realities that shape women's lives and dictate their "choices." The increased number of women in the military has more to do with the feminization of poverty than a democratization of the military.

People of color and people with low incomes are disproportionately represented in the ranks. The volunteer draft enacted in 1973 is an economic form of conscription. Demographics is a telling scale by which to read the military personnel blueprints. While African-Americans make up approximately 12 percent of the U.S. population, they comprise more than 30 percent of the armed forces. Forty-four percent of the women in the Gulf are African-American. This is not a form of economic opportunity.

> ## "The issue isn't about choice. It's about the lack of choice, the lack of opportunities."

We've heard some of the arguments against women in the military before. They include: women aren't strong enough to stand up to the rigors of the battlefield, and women don't do well under pressure. Women warriors throughout history concretely disproved these arguments. And women who do whatever is necessary to protect themselves and their families are ample proof of our capabilities in life-threatening situations.

Then there are the chivalrous arguments expressing horror at the idea of women coming home in body bags. This in a society where

Helen Vozenilek, "Women in the Military: Deceptive Feminist Gain." Reprinted with permission from the April 17-23, 1991, issue of *In These Times*, a weekly Chicago newspaper.

women raped, battered and killed every day are not met with presidential accolades or massive media reportage. Concern for "women and children" reaches a particularly sacrosanct level during wartime, although this gallant concern does not extend to the concern for Arab—or other "enemy"—women.

There's one argument used against women in the military that I don't want to throw out: the notion that war is a male thing. From "kicking ass" locker-room bravado to the concerns about George Bush's masculinity, the machismo of militarism is as pervasive as fallout from a nuclear weapon. We hear this talk a lot on job sites, but now the toys are bigger and deadlier.

I am not interested in us womanizing the battlefield. Sure, we have a lot to teach about conflict resolution, creative means of settling differences and the concept of strength through peace rather than peace through strength. But the armed forces are beyond that point; they share an inherited ideology of violence as the supreme arbiter of right and are not the theater in which to create new scripts or even to amend existing ones. The military is adapting to the presence of women only by considering such important issues as attire, maternity leave and sleeping quarters.

The issue of women in combat came to dominate the headlines after the U.S. invasion of Panama in December 1989. Cpt. Linda Bray led a troop of U.S. soldiers against a Panamanian defense-force stronghold. Her efforts were lauded by many who saw her leading the charge to open combat ranks to women. What got lost in all the discussion was the fundamental issue: what was the U.S. doing invading Panama? We cannot separate Bray's prowess from the diplomacy-by-invasion tactics of the United States.

Media Smoke Screen

I would like a woman who kills a battering spouse to get as much publicity and praise as did Cpt. Bray and the women who served in the Gulf. Then, perhaps, I could begin to believe that this country is interested in promoting a new world order based on fairness and justice for all.

"The armed forces . . . share an inherited ideology of violence as the supreme arbiter of right."

I do not come by my position about women in the military from a pacifist ideology. Taking up arms is sometimes necessary. There are liberation struggles being waged across the world where women take their place in the forefront. And there are liberation struggles to be waged by women in this country, where we can't even get an equal-rights amendment passed, where civil-rights legislation gets defeated and where there are no patriotic shields against poverty, hunger and homelessness. These are the wars that need to be waged by women, not the war to restore an oppressive monarchy or to make the world safe for Exxon.

Tradeswomen often invoke the spirit of Rosie the Riveter—the industrial heroine of World War II—as a model for women gaining recognition and approval for non-traditional labor. I am all for reclaiming symbols and making them our own, but we need to consider the evolution of the original symbol. Rosie the Riveter served a useful function during the war—operating the defense industry while men were at battle. But when the war ended, so did the praise heaped on Rosie as men came back to reclaim their jobs.

How the State Department has dealt with the issue of women in the Gulf force is in itself illuminating. How many times have we seen the U.S. government praise women Teamsters or women welders or women in any sort of non-traditional labor on the homefront? Yet women doing these same non-traditional jobs in the Gulf were praised and held up to the media spotlight. These autonomous, stalwart women were contrasted by the media with inferior Arab women who were enslaved by customs, veils and religious fanaticism. Women's roles in the military were used as coals to stoke the flames of anti-Arab racism. (We were given only fleeting glimpses of Arab women, which I guess was understandable, since they didn't exist before August 2, 1990, anyway.)

Women in the military will play a crucial role in the new world order envisioned by the Bush administration. They will be used to legitimize military solutions and to lend credence to the myth of American equality. Increasingly, we live in an age where image replaces substance and words are used to subvert meaning. The image of being an equal-opportunity employer, both racially and sexually, is now crucial to the military.

"We cannot separate the role of women in the U.S. military from the role of the U.S. military in the world."

In 1990 and 1991, 450,000 jobs have been lost in construction. (While only 7 percent of these jobs are held by women, we can assume that we have been laid off in higher proportions than men.) Instead of spending $100 billion on the Gulf war, this country could have been investing money in massive public-works projects to rebuild our country's infrastructure. What if the same recruitment efforts, the same patriotic hype, the same hoopla that goes into military recruitment went into increasing the percentage of women in the construction force to 11 percent? The money invested in this kind of construction instead of destruction would have much more tangible benefits for the minds and bodies of this nation.

Of course, this is fanciful. The reality in the U.S. today is that the war industry is the government's only concept of a public-works program, just as the Gulf war was its only concept of an energy policy. As the economic situation in this country worsens, the military will increasingly serve as an outlet for women and men who have few other options. And given the history of Vietnam, Grenada, Panama and now Iraq, how can we think that future military engagements will be anything but another finger in the glove of U.S. world domination?

I don't think we should condemn women who are in the military—nor men, given our understanding of economic imperatives. But I think we should condemn their role as global police officers. We cannot separate the role of women in the U.S. military from the role of the U.S. military in the world. To treat the two as unrelated is like clamoring to get front seats in a bus that is careening madly off a cliff.

As feminists watch many of the gains of the last two decades either threatened or rolled back, there is an urge among us to hold on even more tightly to whatever may seem to be an advancement. But women's participation in the U.S. military is not an advancement for us or for the human species. It's a giant step backward.

Chapter 2

Should Women Serve in Combat?

Women and Combat: An Overview

Melinda Beck et al.

About the Author: *Melinda Beck is a senior editor for* Newsweek *magazine.*

Editor's Note: In the 1991 Persian Gulf War, 35,355 U.S. women soldiers were sent to Saudi Arabia. While no women were officially allowed to fight in combat, they performed vital combat support duties such as piloting planes and helicopters, directing artillery, operating prisoner of war camps, and repairing ships. Of the 135 U.S. troops killed in action, five were women. Two servicewomen were held as prisoners of war by the Iraqis.

Clearly, many of the servicewomen in the Gulf found themselves exposed to enemy fire and other life-threatening situations. This fact has led some defense experts to conclude that the line between combat and noncombat positions is indistinct, and it has renewed the debate concerning the role of women in combat. Opponents of women in combat assert that women would weaken the military because they cannot fight as effectively as men. In contrast, supporters argue that women are capable soldiers who are excluded from combat because of sexual discrimination.

The following overview, taken from a Newsweek *magazine article by Melinda Beck, was written in September 1990, as servicewomen were first being deployed to the Persian Gulf. Even though it was written prior to the conclusion of the war, it remains an accurate, revealing account of women in the military. The overview examines the role of women soldiers and the attitudes of many servicewomen and defense analysts concerning the wisdom of allowing women to fight on the battlefield.*

The troops in Saudi Arabia have given this crisis a nickname: the "mom's war." The evidence is everywhere in the heat and dust. Maj. Kathy Higgins pinned up a crayon drawing by her 5-year-old son in her medical evacuation office. A few U.S. servicewomen have torn up photos of their children; looking at them was just too hard. Sitting in a field hospital on the edge of a bustling airstrip, Lt. Col. Carolyn Roaf, a medical officer, said that saying goodbye to her 6-year-old daughter was the toughest thing she had ever done especially after the little girl told her, "Mom, if you die over there, I'm coming to rescue you." Capt. Ginny Thomas left the Air Force in 1987 because she wanted more of a home life. In September 1990 she was back as a reservist, piloting a giant C-141 transport around the Middle East. "I'll be glad when it's over," she said. "But I would be disappointed if I was not over here doing something for my country."

"Women have taken part in every American military crisis since the Revolutionary War."

Women have taken part in every American military crisis since the Revolutionary War. But never before have they served on such a large scale or in such a wide variety of jobs. As the massive deployment in the Persian Gulf continues, women pilots from the 101st Airborne Division are ferrying supplies and personnel in Huey helicopters. Female mechanics from the 24th Mechanized Division are maintaining tanks, handling petroleum and coordinating water supply. Throughout the region, women are working as truck drivers, cargo handlers, intelligence specialists, paratroopers, flight controllers, shipboard navigators, communications experts and ground-crew chiefs. Their precise number in Operation Desert Shield is classified, but one Army personnel expert says women will soon match their overall proportion in the services: roughly 11 percent of the 2 million-member armed forces.

Women are still not permitted to serve in combat positions—by law in the Navy, Air Force and Marines and by policy in the Army. But ever since the Pentagon began recruiting women in large numbers in the 1970s, the services have defined "combat" ever more narrowly, giving women increasingly critical roles. That has caused some confusion in past deployments. In the invasion of Grenada, four female MPs [military police] were stopped at the loading ramp and sent back to their barracks three times while the brass hashed out its policy. This time there was no holding back, the Pentagon said: if women were part of a unit stateside, they shipped out when it was deployed. Only the Marine Corps showed some hesitancy, deliberately delaying a few support units that contained women in the early days of the mobilization. But a Camp Pendleton spokeswoman denied reports that men had actually been substituted for women, and since then, the Marines, too, have sent women to the gulf.

For now, the U.S. servicewomen in Saudi Arabia are doing just what the men are doing: setting up vast military installations in the desert, fortifying supply lines and waiting. If the shooting begins, there are no plans to withdraw the women from the theater—and few illusions that they might not be among the casualties. "Just because you're not in a combat unit doesn't mean you won't be in combat," says Lawrence Korb, former assistant secretary of Defense for manpower. "When they start lobbing SCUDS with chemical weapons, they'll be aiming at everybody." To that end, female troops in Saudi Arabia have been issued protective gear, and are required to carry it at all times, just like the men. They also carry arms and are trained to use them should they come under attack.

Some military experts say the gulf call-up underscores the hypocrisy of Pentagon policies toward women: though they can't serve on the fighting lines, they are in harm's way—particularly in a conflict where the "front line" could be everywhere. "Every military manual instructs you to hit the back supply line first and try to isolate the front line," says Rep. Patricia Schroeder, who chairs the House subcommittee on military installations. "Where are all the women? In the back lines with the supply details, communications equipment and refueling planes."

"Women can train men for missions they can't carry out themselves."

Given the desert realities, some servicewomen are lobbying the military to lift the combat restrictions. "I can fly that F-15 just as well as a man," insists 25-year-old Lt. Stephanie Shaw, who controls flight missions for a tactical air wing in the gulf. "I volunteered for the Army, not the Girl Scouts," echoes Capt. Leola Davis, commander of a heavy-maintenance company that fixes everything from tanks to HUMV jeeps at the Army's First Cavalry Division at Fort Hood, Texas. But the objections to women on the front lines are deeply entrenched, as Schroeder found in 1990 when she proposed legislation calling for a four-year Army test of women in combat posts. The Army rejected the idea. . . .

One of the chief arguments against women on the fighting lines is sheer physical strength. Within the tough, tattooed all-male tanker brigades at Fort Hood, for example, it's an article of faith that women don't have the upper-body strength needed to load 60-pound shells into guns. But brute force is irrelevant in many of the combat jobs from which women are excluded. "On a ship, war is high tech," says one former Navy submariner. "Men aren't any better at video games than women."

Male Bonding

Many military men firmly believe the presence of women on the front lines would disrupt what they call "unit cohesion"—the male bonding that theoretically allows warriors to perform acts of heroism under fire. "I want people on my right and on my left who will take the pressure when the shooting starts," says Brig. Gen. Ed Scholes, who commands the 18th Airborne Corps in Saudi Arabia. "Men simply cannot treat women like other men. And it's silly to think that a few months' training can make them into some kind of sexless soldiers," says Brian Mitchell, a former Army captain and author of a 1989 book, "Weak Link: The Feminization of the American Military." But historian Linda Grant De Pauw, founder of the Minerva Center, which studies women in the military, counters that such objections are mired in old stereotypes of women as victims. "It's like the image they used to have of blacks before they served with them— that they were too cowardly, too stupid or would break their weapons," she argues.

"The decision to allow more women in combat . . . rests with Congress."

Justified or not, the restrictions have created a military rife with anomalies. Women can train men for missions they can't carry out themselves. In some cases, they can command units in which they can't serve. Air Force women can ferry troops and supplies over hostile areas, and refuel jet fighters, but they can't fly the fighters. In the Navy, they are barred from permanent assignment on combat ships such as carriers, destroyers and submarines. But they can serve on repair and supply ships in the same waters. In 1987, 248 women were aboard the destroyer tender Acadia, which came to the aid of the USS Stark after it was hit by an Iraqi Exocet missile. Women also make up a quarter of the firefighters on the sub tender USS Dixon. "If you have women fighting a fire in an enclosed area, that's just as dangerous as a combat zone," says reservist Teresa Smith, a first-class petty officer who would report to the Dixon if called to active duty.

What's more, servicewomen say the restrictions hamper their career opportunities. Army officials boast that 285 of the 331 "military occupational specialties" are open to enlisted women. But in fact, only half the jobs in noncombat specialties are available to women, since some are in tank, infantry or other units that are off-limits. Women officers also bitterly complain that the rules have created a "glass ceiling," since advancement to top ranks often depends on leading combat units. "A number of women say, 'Hey, don't protect me from combat' because the price is too high," says Navy Capt. Susan Canfield, who oversees nine ships mapping the Pacific for antisubmarine warfare.

The lust for more action is not universally shared among U.S. servicewomen, however. At Fort Hood, Chief Warrant Officer 2 Portia Dublar, a crack maintenance technician for the Second Armored Division's aviation brigade, says she has no burning desire to fly helicopters—"I'm perfectly content to fix them." Sgt. Elizabeth Hope, one of the few women deployed in Saudi Arabia who has seen combat before as an MP in Panama, thinks women should not serve in the trenches: "It would simply complicate everything if women were fighting alongside men."

Women in Body Bags

Ultimately, the decision to allow more women in combat, at least in the Navy, Marines and Air Force, rests with Congress, where opposition is most deeply entrenched of all. Much of that stems from the perception that the U.S. public won't stomach its daughters coming home in body bags. Yet historian D'Ann Campbell, teaching at West Point, notes that "women have *always* come back in body bags. The question is, are we going to train them for defense? It will depend on how essential it is for the military to be all it can be."

The U.S. women in Saudi Arabia face a more immediate problem—the clash of cultures with their Muslim hosts. In a country where women can't drive, show their faces or venture out alone, Saudi troops don't know what to make of female GIs wearing fatigues and issuing orders. American women are similarly stunned by the Saudis. Two female paratroopers couldn't help but stare as a Muslim woman in a black veil walked by. "Tragic," said First Lt. Jennifer Ann Wood, who quoted a maxim from her West Point days: "That's a tradition unhampered by progress."

"We have a job to do here and we will do it."

The Saudis have made some cultural concessions. U.S. servicewomen can now discreetly drive vehicles while on duty, and at one air base, they can use a gym during limited hours, though they must enter through the back door. Still, they are not permitted to wear shorts, jog or even shop on military bases unless accompanied by a man. Some American women take the restrictions in stride: "This is their culture. We shouldn't impose our ways on them," said Capt. Susan Beausoleil, a paratrooper with the 18th Airborne Corps. Others aren't so complacent. The Saudis "look at you like a dog—they don't want American women here," griped one Army staff sergeant. That kind of treatment incenses Schroeder, as does the U.S. military's tolerance. "Can you imagine if we sent black soldiers to South Africa and told them to go along with the apartheid rules?" she asks.

Conditions could be worse for the U.S. women. Many are quartered in air-conditioned barracks, mobile homes and schools built by the Saudis. All-male Marine combat units deployed further forward live in sweltering tents without cold drinks or hot meals. Even in rear areas, though, comforts are limited. Women often sleep 24 to a room, on cots only three inches apart. There are occasional shortages of such essentials as sanitary napkins. With nowhere to go after hours, no movies or recreational facilities,

boredom sets in quickly. Many women just work, sleep and do laundry. Deprived of TV, some have rediscovered the pleasures of reading and the art of conversation.

Much of the talk is of spouses and children. Military rules specify that single parents and two-career service couples must designate short- and long-term guardians for their dependents. But most servicewomen never thought such arrangements would actually be used, and the reality is heart wrenching. Sgt. Mary Payette, an antitank weapons specialist, left her 8-month-old son with her sister in St. Paul and can't help but think what would happen if she didn't return. She shudders: "I don't want him calling anybody else Mom.". . .

Fear Is Common

The U.S. women in Saudi Arabia joined the armed forces for much the same reasons men have long flocked to the colors—excitement, travel, patriotism and a chance for skills they couldn't get elsewhere. But many didn't plan on this kind of adventure. Just like the men, they are scared—of the strange, forbidding desert, of an unpredictable enemy and especially the threat of a poison-gas attack. "Anyone who says he or she is not scared is lying to themselves," says Lt. Stephanie Shaw. "I wake up each morning hoping my arrival in Saudi Arabia was just a dream," admits Army specialist Sandra Chisholm. "But we have a job to do here and we will do it."

No one can predict what that job will ultimately entail for the American troops. But the women, more than the men, believe their future in the armed forces is on the line that George Bush has drawn in the sand. If a major war erupts, spreading unisex casualties throughout the theater, it could finally bring down the combat exclusions—or it could so outrage the American public, and its leaders, that women are never again placed so close to the action in so many critical roles.

Should Women Serve in Combat?

Yes: Women Should Serve in Combat

Women Serving in Combat Would Strengthen America's Defense
Women Are Capable of Serving in Combat
The Persian Gulf War Proved That Women Can Serve in Combat
The Combat Exclusion Law Should Be Repealed
The Combat Exclusion Law Is Unconstitutional

Women Serving in Combat Would Strengthen America's Defense

Paul E. Roush

About the Author: *Paul E. Roush is a professor at the United States Naval Academy in Annapolis, Maryland. A retired Marine Corps colonel, Roush served as a combat officer during the Vietnam War.*

The months preceding hostilities in the Persian Gulf Conflict made for some interesting reading. Columnist Mark Shields wrote in the *Washington Post* on November 2, 1990 that those who were urging the use of force in the liberation of Kuwait were bellicose hypocrites! Their sin was the commitment of an army without the commitment of the nation. "If this war is worth Americans' fighting and dying for," he said, "then it must first be worth calling to service the sons of anchormen and of senators, (the sons) of Cabinet members and college presidents, (the sons) of columnists and CEOs [chief executive officers]." Mr. Shields said he wanted a military that was truly representative of the country. In all probability it never even occurred to him that, in his effort to put everyone equally at risk, he had omitted 50% of the population.

His omission was a reminder of the consequences of the combat exclusion legislation introduced in 1948 by Congressman Carl Vinson of Georgia as part of the Women's Armed Services Integration Act. The Act prohibits the service by women on combatant ships or on aircraft with combat missions. By contrast, there is no legislation which prohibits women from serving

Paul E. Roush, "Rethinking Who Fights Our Wars—and Why," speech delivered to the Harvard Law School, April 6, 1991. Reprinted with permission.

in ground combat units. The Army and the Department of Defense employ, as a matter of policy—not law—a direct combat probability code and a risk rule, respectively, to limit the likelihood of exposing women to direct combat.

Combat exclusion rests on a number of assumptions. One is that women would denigrate our ability to wage war. Another is that, even if they enhanced our warfighting, society does not want them in combat. An inferred assumption is that what we are doing now isn't broken and doesn't need to be fixed—the status-quo is just fine, thank you.

Those assumptions suggest a number of questions that I want to explore. . . . First, what are the capabilities of women as warriors? Second, what would be the effect of women warriors on the men warriors who are their potential comrades-in-arms? Third, what is the tolerance of society for women as warriors? Finally, what are some of the consequences of the status quo?

The appropriate response to the assessment of women's capabilities—or men's capabilities, for that matter—is, "Compared to What?" Assessment only makes sense with reference to standards.

> **"Combat exclusion rests on a number of assumptions. One is that women would denigrate our ability to wage war."**

Let me illustrate the standards issue with a personal example. I have a son who is one of about fifty U-2 pilots in the Air Force. He has frequently been cited for his outstanding performance of duty. In April 1991, in fact, he was personally decorated by the Secretary of the Air Force and the Vice Chief of Staff of the Air Force. Years ago, I attended his graduation from flight school. A disproportionate number of the awards at the graduation ceremony were won, not by my son—and he is a very excellent pilot—but by women. Physiologically, they enjoy certain advantages over pilots who are men; the inverse relationship between height and G-tolerance is an example. Women, of course, were not permitted to fly U-2s in those days, but it had nothing to do with ability. They were precluded solely by political decisions springing from an ideological base. Today women are permitted to fly the U-2. What changed? They did not become more capable in the interim. An arbitrary barrier, based entirely on gender, was simply withdrawn. For decades a deliberate choice had been made to give priority to the maintenance of gender segregation rather than to the pursuit of combat effectiveness.

Women Succeed in the Military

I have access to fitness-report data about performance of Naval Academy graduates in the fleet. Our first women midshipmen graduated in 1980. The cumulative record for the ensuing decade shows that women graduates are recommended for accelerated promotion by their rating officers at far higher proportions than are the men who graduate with them. For ensigns, the differential is 76%; for lieutenants, junior grade it is 46%; for lieutenants it is 27%. Also, contrary to the expectation of some of their early detractors, a higher proportion of women graduates is still on active duty at the ten year point than is the case for the men who graduated with the class of 1980.

Sometimes the case against women in combat is based on the factor of reliability rather than performance. Some military men believe that women are pregnant or ill or otherwise absent from duty an inordinate amount of time. It is true, of course, that lost time is an important aspect of the capabilities discussion. When we go beyond perceptions and dwell on data, however, an interesting pattern emerges. Available data show much more lost time for men than for women when all causes are considered. A 1984 Navy study calculated lost time for men and women for each year of their first enlistment. Lost time events included hospitalization, confinement in a brig, and desertion or other unau-

thorized absence. During the first year, days of lost time for each 100 men was 2.5 times that for each 100 women. During the second, third, and fourth years, lost time rates for men exceeded rates for women by factors of 5.0, 4.1, and 3.5, respectively.

Another important aspect of the capabilities equation is leadership. The issue is not the superiority of one gender over the other but the fact of gender differences. An accumulating research base is showing that men and women are likely to employ different approaches to leadership. Women are more likely than men to encourage participation, to share power and information, to work actively at enhancing the self-worth of others, and to project enthusiasm. Their tendency is to focus on collaboration rather than competition and to emphasize process as well as task.

Another way of expressing the differing leadership preferences is to speak of transformational versus transactional leadership. Each gender uses both but the former is preferred by many women and the latter comes easier to many men. The transformational approach attempts to have the follower set aside his or her own self-interests in service of the larger interests of the group. Transactional leadership is essentially an agreed-upon exchange in which the leader satisfies an interest of the follower in exchange for a follower behavior that promotes an interest of the leader.

"A deliberate choice had been made to give priority to the maintenance of gender segregation."

We recently completed a study of leadership styles at the Naval Academy involving over 1300 midshipmen. Followers reported anonymously their responses to the practices of midshipmen leaders. The most common leadership approach was transactional, specifically management-by-exception. Followers reported that they were less likely to make extra effort for leaders who led that way. When leaders, whether men or women, used transformational practices—charisma, individualized consideration, intellectual stimulation—the followers reported that they wanted to put forth extra effort.

Impact on Men

So far I have talked about one of the ways in which women are sometimes alleged to denigrate our ability to wage war—namely the capabilities they bring or fail to bring to that undertaking. The second part of the allegation has to do with how their presence on ships or aircraft with combat missions would affect the men beside whom they would be engaged in combat. A *New York Times* article of 15 March 1991 reports the perspective of cadets at the Citadel, one of two state-supported, single-sex colleges in the nation. The Citadel perspective is that hazing is a necessary and sufficient precondition for bonding; hence, the requirement to practice hazing is put forth as a rationale for the exclusion of women from the college—the argument of military necessity. If the basic assertion were true—if bonding is dependent upon hazing—it means our armed forces must go into combat without the capability to bond, since hazing is an impermissible and counterproductive practice. Congressional legislation which prohibits hazing at the Naval Academy defines hazing as unwarranted assumption of authority resulting in cruelty, indignity, humiliation, hardship, or the deprivation or abridgement of rights. Those qualities hardly represent the kind of leadership to which the nation wants to subject its sons and daughters. In my view, hazing is the adolescent version of child abuse. It has the same dynamic; victims perpetuate the abuse on subsequent generations.

Interference with male bonding has been a persistent objection to repeal of the combat exclusion legislation. While it should not come as a surprise that male bonding occurs in all-male units, it's difficult to respond to the notion that women can't, don't, or won't bond, and that their presence precludes males from bonding with each other. The assertion is a little strange, given the history of extremely effective bonding among guerrilla and assorted revolutionary groups, many of which include a high proportion of women fighters. A current example comes from the nearly three-decade war—apparently just concluded—between Eritrea and Ethiopia. Of the 45,000 Eritreans in the field, fully 35% of the front line troops are women. A *Washington Post* article from May 29, 1991 asserted that about a third of the front line fighters of the other major rebel unit, the Tigrayans, are also women. Some of the Marines in my Combined Action Group in Vietnam fought against women combatants, and they saw no evidence that mixed-gender Vietnamese could not bond. Mixed-gender police teams and fire-fighters everywhere are able to bond, to rely on one another in life threatening situations. Whatever one believes about their political views, it seems absurd to argue that women in feminist groups do not bond.

"Women are more likely than men to encourage participation, to share power and information, . . . and to project enthusiasm."

In fact, the bonding process is no great mystery. It requires three elements: organization for a common goal, the presence of (or potential for) danger, and a willingness to sacrifice. Not one of those elements is gender-specific.

In the racially charged era of the Vietnam War there was sometimes a bonding problem between black and white males for whom exposure to the enemy was not imminent. All that changed, of course, when the firing began. Inter-racial bonding suddenly became very "do-able." It is disingenuous to state that it would be otherwise with inter-gender bonding. Given the option to "bond with this woman or die," most men I know would bond. Even bigotry has its limits.

Recycled Arguments

The attempt to retain the combat exclusion laws is also based on the appeal to tradition, the loss of which is purported to have negative consequences for the intangibles which cause units to prevail in the face of overwhelming odds. My response to that line of reasoning is that I have heard it before—when we were attempting to bring about racial integration in the military. There are, of course, traditions that must be preserved at all costs. There are others that are simply not worth preserving.

In the building where I work are pictures of all Naval Academy graduates who have been awarded the Congressional Medal of Honor. Not one of them is black. Does that mean that whites perform better in combat than blacks? Could it possibly mean that most of the years during which our tradition accumulated were marked by systematic, invidious exclusion on the basis of race? When I was a midshipman, one of my 1300 classmates was black. After I graduated and reported to Quantico, there was one black lieutenant in my Marine Corps Basic School company. He, of course, could not be served in Quantico restaurants—twenty-five miles from our nation's capital. On road trips my black teammates on the Quantico Marines football team sat in the bus while the rest of us ate in style. We tolerated and participated in a tradition as old as the nation. We did it without any sense of guilt, because we made the facts fit our beliefs. We told ourselves and one another that our actions would support combat readiness and that to contravene tradition would degrade combat readiness. We argued that blacks would not perform well in combat. They were not qualified. They were not intelligent enough. They would break and run in time of danger. They were not psychologically equipped to lead whites in combat. Whites were not psychologically equipped to accept orders from those whom the culture had designated as less-than-equal. The arguments we are hearing now with regard to women are precisely analogous.

Some men argue that women cause them extra work. Heavy toolboxes or oversize fittings, couplings or other equipment require more physical strength than some women can muster. It is well to remember that the equipment we use in the military was designed to accommodate the strength of men. It could have been made even larger and heavier and more difficult to manipulate so that most men could not handle it either. It could also have been designed so that women could use it effectively. It doesn't make much sense to blame the victim. Let's design it right in the future.

"Mixed-gender police teams and fire-fighters everywhere are able to bond."

You may recall that I pointed out a few minutes ago that men have quadruple the lost time rate of women during their first enlistment. The studies which I cited to make that point represent only the tip of the iceberg. True lost-time statistics should not be limited to time charged to physical absence. They should include, as well, time taken from productive work by the entire infrastructure which has to deal with disciplinary problems, the overwhelming proportion of which are caused by men. That infrastructure includes all involved in counseling, from the immediate chain of command to chaplains, psychologists, substance abuse counselors, and so forth. It includes . . . commanding officers, witnesses, trial lawyers, legal clerks, Judge Advocate General reviewers. Then there is the entire force involved in incarceration—the people who operate the brigs and stockades—plus the medical personnel charged with repairing the damage wrought by substance abuse or violence. Finally there are the recruiters and trainers who have to compensate for unanticipated losses. If the true costs were counted, there is not the slightest doubt that the lost-time rate for males would exceed that for females by an order of magnitude of immense proportions, perhaps by a factor of ten or more. . . .

"There are, of course, traditions that must be preserved at all costs. . . . Others . . . are simply not worth preserving."

Occasionally it is pointed out that men will take risks in combat on behalf of women that they would not take for men, thereby diluting the cohesion and combat effectiveness of the unit. It is certainly true that men sometimes take extraordinary risks for other *men* in combat. We generally confer on them decorations of valor for such behavior. On the other hand we have been reasonably good at teaching our leaders the circumstances under which they should and should not put their ships and aircraft in harm's way. Given the absolute accountability of a ship's commanding officer for everything his or her command does or fails to do, I am reasonably sure the issue can be adequately addressed.

If there is concern about excessive risk-taking by military men on behalf of military women, there has been even more hand-wringing about how the public would react to women coming home in body bags, or—God forbid—becoming prisoners of war [POW], thereby subject to rape and other unspeakable horrors. Well, some came home in body bags and some were POWs. The public took it in stride. There was no outcry. It was one more case of a non-issue being exploited by those who want to retain the combat exclusion laws. Interestingly, about the same time the POWs were released, so was a press release which pointed out that in excess of 100,000 rapes were officially reported in the United States in 1990, with more than ten times that number on file in rape-crisis centers. The fact of more than a million rapes in 12 months with hardly a ripple of public notice seems to me to be a far more accurate indicator of the level of national outrage over this issue than is the alleged concern over women POWs.

Expectations for Women

Finally, it is worth considering the opportunity costs of doing business as usual. The answer to the question, "Will bad things happen if we stay with the status quo?" is that bad things will *keep on* happening. We will continue to forfeit 50% of the brain power available to us in combat, including, especially, the propensity of women for the natural exercise of transformational leadership. Second, we will continue to transmit expectations of second class status and sub-optimal performance for women in the military. Unfortunately, expectations habitually translate into reality. Third, we will continue to reinforce bigotry as a learned behavior. The combat exclusion legislation mandates unequal treatment solely on the basis of gender—with no compelling evidence of military necessity. Fourth, we will continue to invest in the counterfeit currency of hazing as a surrogate for leadership in our training and education. Hazing, I might add, diminishes both the practitioner and the recipient. It is a lose-lose arrangement—an equal-opportunity, moral vacuum. Fifth, we will continue to model hypocrisy in the programs designed to promote equal opportunity and to counter sexual harassment. The Navy's most recent study on the subject labels sexual harassment pervasive throughout the service.

The combat exclusion legislation is a major contributor to every one of these problems. The price for its retention is too high. We will fight better when it is gone. The status quo is not a tolerable option. Combat exclusion is more than an anachronism. It is an affront to our basic system of values. Our oath, as military members, is to the Constitution, but combat exclusion degrades our commitment to the principles the Constitution enshrines. It creates moral eunuchs of us all.

Women Are Capable of Serving in Combat

Lorraine Dusky

About the Author: *Lorraine Dusky is a contributing writer to* McCall's, *a monthly women's magazine.*

Should women serve in combat?

It's a question the Panamanian invasion has left lingering in the air. When the shooting was over, it was clear that women had been in combat—hundreds of them, in fact, had operated in the combat zone.

Captain Linda L. Bray, of Butner, North Carolina, commanded a platoon that engaged Panamanian soldiers in a firefight at an attack-dog compound near Panama City. Two female helicopter pilots rushing troops into combat came under heavy gunfire. Lieutenant Lisa Kutschera and Warrant Officer Debra Mann both have been nominated for the Air Medal, the first women so honored. Private First Class Christina Proctor captured an enemy soldier, and Staff Sergeant April Hanley directed a unit of soldiers near the Vatican embassy, where Noriega holed up for 11 days.

Yet officially, these women should not have been where they were, since women are barred from serving in combat positions and are restricted to "support" jobs. But the distinction between combat and noncombat jobs has increasingly blurred as the nature of combat has changed. This was demonstrated nowhere more clearly than in the invasion of Panama.

Today women serve on missile crews in Europe and as Marine security guards at embassies abroad, and are ready to launch nuclear ballistic missiles from capsules 65 feet underground. They can be found on Navy sea-lift command ships, filling a variety of dangerous, theoretically noncombat roles, from aerial refueling to serving on repair ships assigned to dangerous waters.

Yet the ban against women in combat remains. And as long as it does, women are denied equal opportunity in the military because promotion often hinges on command experience in aircraft, fighting ships or tanks—and without it women's careers are limited. Based on the Panama experience, at least one woman has filed a sex discrimination complaint charging that a male soldier was selected over her despite her expertise as an intelligence analyst in that country.

Representative Patricia Schroeder has introduced legislation to conduct a four-year experiment to integrate women in all units—including combat—in the Armed Forces. She pointed out that the Army's commercials portray women handling communications. "Assuming that our enemy is intelligent, that woman would be the first hit in a strike," she told Congress. "It's always smart to destroy your enemy's lines of communications first. So let me see if I've got this straight. Army policy allows women to be shot first, but they can't be the first to shoot. The logic eludes me."

> **"As for courage in the face of danger, women in Panama proved they were up to the task."**

But Secretary of Defense Dick Cheney has said the Pentagon has no intention of dropping the combat exclusion of women; Pentagon officials say any change in policy will have to come from Congress; and Congress is filled with men who are leery of voting to send women into combat. "No politician wants to see that 30-second negative ad that accuses him of putting your mother into combat boots," Schroeder says, acknowledging that her legislation may not win enough support even though others before her have recommended that the ban be lifted. The Pentagon's own committee assigned to study the matter recommended a test similar to the one proposed by Schroeder, and in the fall of 1989 a report from the General Accounting Office to Congress called combat exclusion "the greatest impediment women face" in advancement in the military.

"It is time for the ban on women in combat to be lifted."

Currently women are eligible for slightly more than 88 percent of all military job classifications, but in reality only about half of the more than two million jobs are open to women. And a spokesperson for the Pentagon admitted that some jobs are closed to women so that men who are overseas in combat positions can be rotated to stateside.

As long as the Armed Forces' nearly 230,000 females are officially barred from combat, the debate over what constitutes "combat" will continue. Is a woman in combat if she is driving a jeep bringing soldiers to a war zone? If she is securing public buildings while sniper bullets are flying nearby? In a modern battlefield, the action shifts—no matter where you are, you are a target.

Further complicating the issue is that each branch of the Armed Forces has its own criteria and risk threshold. Women in the Army, for instance, could build airstrips and clear debris during combat, but women in the Navy would probably be barred from those jobs. Women may be medics at a general support hospital, but not be assigned to infantry aid stations on or near the front; Air Force women may fly the planes used in airdrops into combat zones, but not the jet fighters protecting them.

Other countries have already come to the conclusion that the distinctions barring women from combat are no longer valid. Although Israel no longer assigns women to combat units, Canada and Sweden have dropped nearly all restrictions preventing women from being fully integrated into its Armed Forces. However, rigorous physical tests required by both countries will keep most women out of the infantry, where strength could be an issue.

Critics contend that using women in combat will mean that more people will be killed in war, since women lack the brute strength needed in rugged combat jobs. Women Marines, for instance, are not allowed to toss live grenades because supposedly they cannot throw them far enough to avoid injury.

Yet recent Army studies indicate that women's strength develops quickly through training. And as Meredith Neizer, head of the Pentagon's committee on women, notes, "Modern war is fought in a variety of arenas, and the slight physical differences don't have to play a role." Intelligence and technical skills are certainly critical to today's soldier, and in general women in the Armed Forces are better educated than their male counterparts.

Women Proved Themselves in Panama

As for courage in the face of danger, women in Panama proved they were up to the task. Women were in the platoon that moved into the narrow streets of Panama City shortly after the invasion for a nighttime raid. "Not one woman washed out," their commanding officer, Lieutenant Colonel Mike Sullivan, has said. "I don't know how many females I have in my battalion. I can only tell you that the women are doing the same job as the men. If you're talking about going to the chin-up bar and doing push-ups, probably the females can't do as many. But when you're in combat, you don't do chin-ups and push-ups."

The infantry—where risk and physical strength are factors—appears to be a stumbling block to the passage of Schroeder's bill. Some urge that instead of pushing for women in the infantry, more jobs should be opened to them where strength is not critical, such as serving as a jet-fighter pilot or on an attack submarine. Pilots, for instance, need intellectual acuity and finger dexterity, not brute strength.

"It is time for any barrier to women's full acceptance in the military to be shed."

But arguing over whether women can serve in every single job in the military clouds the real issue—public sensitivity over female casualties of war. Even the military knows that the combat exclusion would not protect them: "In war, we expect women to be casualties in direct proportion to the numbers in which they serve," notes Army spokeswoman Paige Eversole. Nearly 11 percent of the Armed Forces are made up of women.

And as long as the military accepts women into its ranks—indeed, advertises for them, showing them in combat situations—placing artificial barriers to their advancement is spurious. The arguments that they are not up to the task sound like the old chestnuts once raised about women in journalism, medicine, law, any number of jobs that time has shown they can fill competently. . . . It is time for any barrier to women's full acceptance in the military to be shed. It is time for the ban on women in combat to be lifted. It is not as if women have not died fighting for their country. A few fought in the Revolutionary War. One of them, Margaret Corbin, is buried at West Point.

The Persian Gulf War Proved That Women Can Serve in Combat

Jeanne M. Holm

About the Author: *Jeanne M. Holm, author of* Women in the Military: An Unfinished Revolution, *is a retired major general in the United States Air Force.*

Of all the new realities brought home to Americans by the nightly news from Saudi Arabia, none was more startling than seeing a U.S. soldier in full battle gear, M-16 slung over the shoulder, and discovering that "he" was a "she."

For most people, this was the first full realization that wives, sisters, daughters and mothers would actually be sent off to a combat theater to serve side-by-side with men in the tough, dirty, risky jobs of war. That some became casualties and prisoners of war was perhaps the biggest surprise of all.

Even more than events a year earlier in Panama, the Persian Gulf War spotlighted the new roles women have assumed in the armed forces and refueled the simmering debate over women in combat.

Operation Desert Storm was the first large-scale test of the all-volunteer force and the troops performed superbly. This war was also the first true test of what former Chairman of the Joint Chiefs of Staff John Vessey has called the "coeducational military." It too succeeded far beyond most expectations.

"Women have made a major contribution to this [war] effort," said Defense Secretary Dick

Jeanne M. Holm, "Women in Combat: The New Reality," unpublished paper. Reprinted with permission.

Cheney: "We could not have won without them." Commanders in the field echoed similar sentiments.

More than 33,000 women served in the gulf, 6 percent of the U.S. forces—the largest wartime deployment of American military women in history. They did just about everything on land, at sea and in the air except engage in the actual fighting, and even there the line was often a fuzzy one.

They piloted and crewed planes and helicopters over the battle area, serviced combat jets and loaded laser-guided bombs on F-117 Stealths for raids on targets in Baghdad. They directed Patriot missiles, drove trucks, ran prisoner-of-war facilities, refueled M-1 tanks on the side of the road and guarded bases. They served on naval replenishment and repair ships, fleet oilers, and hospital ships off shore.

The women shared the same risks as the men with whom they served and 21 paid the ultimate price.

According to their commander, General Norman Schwarzkopf, his American women had performed "magnificently."

But all the praise of women's performance cold not mask the conflicts and confusion generated by the rules governing women's roles in combat. The confusion surfaced in all the services but was most apparent in the Army where the policies on women's assignments are so complicated as to be almost incomprehensible to the people in the field.

> **"The Persian Gulf War spotlighted the new roles women have assumed in the armed forces."**

For years politicians and military leaders have claimed that military women are excluded from combat by law and service policies. Anyone following news out of the gulf could easily see it wasn't so. In the real world theory and reality parted company.

Women are not supposed to be frontline troops or assigned to direct combat units. But in modern war there are no fixed positions or clear lines in the sand, and rear areas are as vulnerable to attack as are forward positions. Moreover, distinctions between support and combat units have blurred to a point that the illusion of "safe havens" has all but disappeared.

"In the real world theory and reality parted company."

Female soldiers are concentrated in combat support units located in rear areas on the theory that they will be less vulnerable to direct enemy fire. But support troops in the rear areas are prime targets for long-range artillery and surface-to-surface missiles. Soldiers watching an incoming Iraqi Scud must have thought they were in combat no matter what the military calls it.

Being in the rear area in a noncombat unit provided little protection to the soldiers of the 14th Quartermaster Detachment when a Scud missile slammed into their barracks near Dhahran, Saudi Arabia, killing 28 of them. Specialist Adrienne L. Mitchell was one of three women to die in the attack—the first U.S. enlisted women ever killed in action.

Specialist 4 Melissa Rathbun-Nealy, a truck driver, was captured near the Saudi-Kuwait border, thus achieving the dubious distinction of being the first American enlisted woman to become a prisoner of war [POW], and the first female POW since World War II.

Army women are banned from the direct combat branches, namely infantry, armor, and cannon artillery. Patriot missile units are not classified as combat but the soldiers, male and female, who shot down incoming Scuds thought it was a distinction without a difference.

Women are not permitted to fly the Army's Apache attack helicopters—but female pilots of the 101st Airborne Division's Screaming Eagles flew Black Hawk and Chinook helicopters loaded with supplies and troops 50 miles into Iraq as part of the largest helicopter assault in military history.

Army flight surgeon Major Rhonda Cornum was in a Black Hawk helicopter on a mission into Iraq to rescue a downed F-16 fighter pilot. The chopper was shot down over enemy territory killing five of the eight soldiers aboard. Major Cornum survived the crash with two broken arms and was taken prisoner by the Iraqis.

Air Force women are not permitted to fly F-15 or F-16 fighters but they were at the controls of the KC-135 jet tankers that refueled the fighters in mid-air during attack missions. Women were directing the massive air traffic over the battlefield aboard Airborne Warning and Control Systems (AWACS) aircraft. They also flew giant transports delivering troops and supplies. All of these combat operations were lucrative targets.

Navy women are banned from permanent assignment to combat ships such as destroyers, battleships, and aircraft carriers. But female sailors were aboard combat logistics support ships that provided essential supplies, repair and ammunition to the American fleet during gulf combat operations. Support ships were no less vulnerable to Exocet and Silkworm missiles or floating mines than the combat ships.

By Marine Corps policy, female leathernecks are banned from all combat jobs and units. But more than 170 of them were assigned to the 2nd Forward Marine Support Group dug into the desert near the Kuwait border when the ground attack kicked off. Neither they nor most of their male comrades had ever faced combat before but they were all prepared to do what they had been trained for. According to the Corps' Commandant, General Alfred M. Gray, Jr., they were all superb marines.

Today's Volunteer Military

The superb performance of America's armed forces during Operation Desert Shield/Storm is a total vindication of the all-volunteer force which many had predicted would not be up to the challenges of war. One reason for uneasiness was the heavy reliance on women. They have been described by some detractors as the military's "weak-link" and by others as a "social experiment."

"Female pilots . . . flew Black Hawk and Chinook helicopters loaded with supplies and troops 50 miles into Iraq."

If there is a weak link in today's armed forces it was not discernable during the gulf war. They are being described as the finest, most professional forces in our nation's history. More than 11 percent are women, by far the largest female representation in military history, up from one percent just twenty years ago.

The growing use of women in defense was not an experiment but a military manpower necessity—the need to achieve a quality force of volunteers and the inability to do it without women.

When the draft ended the numbers of women expanded from a token 45,000 to 230,000 with an additional 150,000 more women in the reserve components. The Coast Guard, under the Department of Transportation, has another 4,300 women on active duty and in its reserve units.

Once confined to a few selected shore bases and traditional jobs, women now serve at nearly every U.S. military installation in the world and aboard Navy and Coast Guard vessels deployed afloat. They can be found in nearly every non-combat job on land, at sea and in the air. They are so integrated into the units and ships' crews that the U.S. could not have gone to war without them and their involvement in combat was inevitable and unavoidable.

Contrary to popular mythology (perpetuated by the military itself) there has never been a blanket law excluding women from combat. There are two statutes which prohibit women from serving permanently aboard combat ships of the Navy and from flying in aircraft of the Navy and Air Force when "engaged in combat missions." They neither state the underlying objectives nor define "combat missions." They do not apply to the Army nor do they directly address the subject of combat, per se.

In the absence of any other statutory guidelines, Army and Defense Department leaders have devised a set of policies to comply with what they perceived to be the law's "intent." At best, this process has been imprecise, since the original laws, passed in 1948, were designed for a set of assumptions entirely different than exist today about the military and women's roles in it. No one at that time contemplated that women would ever constitute more than 2 percent of the armed forces (as in World War II) or that they would be used in any roles even remotely involving combat operations. The matter was not even debated by the lawmakers.

At that time it was common, accepted employment practice to bar women from risky jobs for their own protection; e.g., police officers and fire fighters. Such policies have since been discarded or overturned by the courts. Only in the armed forces are they still tolerated under the guise of women's best interest and military necessity.

A Risky Profession

The very concept of protection within the military is a contradiction. The military is, by definition, a risky profession. No matter how recruiters may try to mask its true nature, waging war can be dangerous to your health. Taking the military oath is like taking marriage vows—it's for better or for worse. It is the obligation of the services to make this clear to every potential recruit before taking the oath. Any man or woman who volunteers must be prepared to accept that reality or find another line of work.

What little protection the rules provide for women is at the expense of their opportunities for challenging jobs and experiences that enhance career advancement, particularly to the senior officer and enlisted grades. It is also at the expense of military personnel flexibility and efficiency. They waste precious talents and reduce women's ability to contribute to the military mission.

A recent Navy study has identified the most insidious effect of the combat exclusion:

> In the view of all Navy members . . . the law profoundly influences both the acceptance and the quality of treatment accorded to women since they are perceived to be distanced from the heart of the organization and its primary mission-achieving units.

There is hardly a woman who has ever served in the armed forces who does not identify with that observation. Most military men today would also acknowledge its validity, while not necessarily espousing the cure.

Repeal Exclusion

The only cure is repeal of the combat exclusion laws. The only serious attempt to do so was proposed by the Carter Administration in 1979. During Congressional hearings the proposal was abruptly scuttled by the opposition of Navy and Marine Corps leaders.

Many arguments raised against repeal were defused in Panama and the gulf war. But the most frequent one that still survives is that repealing the laws would remove all legal constraints resulting in women being assigned to direct combat positions for which they lack the necessary qualifications. The argument is usually couched in ground combat terms, the infantry specifically. The example is chosen for maximum emotional impact because it evokes images of hand-to-hand combat—an idea which offends most people.

It is a specious argument on several counts: first, the law does not apply here, the rules are set by the Army; second, the overwhelming majority of women (and most men) would not volunteer to be "grunts" even if they could; and third, the physical requirements would exclude all but a handful of women.

The bottom line in military personnel utilization is that *no* individual, male or female, should be allowed or required to fill any job he or she cannot perform satisfactorily in war for whatever reason. All the services have aptitude tests and physical standards to prevent just that.

Moreover, Desert Storm demonstrated how dramatically technology has altered the personnel requirements of the military in the forty years since the exclusion laws were enacted. Today's military depends much less on brawn in favor of smart, educated, technically trainable people. As a lieutenant colonel in Saudi Arabia observed: "You can't have space-age hardware without space-age personnel." This technological shift clearly accommodates the use of women.

In any case, the fact that the vast majority of women could not qualify for most ground combat duties even if they wanted to, does not justify continuing laws which exclude qualified women from assignments to combat aircraft or ships.

When it comes to flying in combat or serving on combat ships, physical capability is not the issue—the law is. The Air Force's chief of personnel, Lt. General Thomas A. Hickey laid it out during Congressional testimony in March 1990. He acknowledged that there is probably not a combat job in the Air Force that women cannot do. "They can fly fighters, they can pull Gs, they can do all those things," he said. "They are physically [and] emotionally capable," adding that "the issue is if you [Congress] want us to to put them there, just change the law and the Air Force will do that."

"If there is a weak link in today's armed forces it was not discernable during the gulf war."

When Air Force women pilots were surveyed on the subject, overwhelmingly they responded that they are capable and willing to go into combat. "I can fly that F-15 just as well as a man," said Lt. Stephanie Shaw, who controlled missions for a tactical air wing in Saudi Arabia.

As for the element of risk, women pilots call it a "red herring" used to keep them out of high-performance aircraft. Capt. Debra Dubbe, who flew as a navigator on a refueling tanker during the Grenada invasion, believes there is no difference in women or men taking risks—or dying. A graduate of the Air Force Academy, Dubbe says: "I signed up to be an officer, and if it means having to die, that's what I agreed to do."

Effect on Readiness

A fear often expressed is that assigning women to combat units and ships would adversely affect efficiency and readiness. One version of this argument is that the presence of women would distract the men and destroy the "male bonding" that is essential to an effective fighting team. Yet in Panama and the gulf war, combat support units, ships and aircraft with women assigned performed their missions well and team bonding did occur.

The argument raises obvious questions: If a destroyer tender can do its job with women in her crew, why not a destroyer? And, if a tactical air base ashore can perform its combat mission of launching aircraft with women in a wide variety of jobs, why not an aircraft carrier with the same mission and many of the same jobs to be done?

The last defense of the combat exclusion policies is that they reflect the will of the American people. While that was undoubtedly true when the statutes were written, social attitudes and laws on women's employment are light-years from the 1940s. A poll conducted by CBS and *The New York Times* following events in Panama showed that 72 percent of the American people favor women in combat. The media coverage of the deployments to the Persian Gulf has further heightened public awareness of women's ability to perform in a combat environment.

Very probably, the public is far more sophisticated on these matters than the Pentagon and Congress are willing to acknowledge.

In efforts to force the issue, it has been proposed that the services test and study the use of women in combat assignments. However, it is not clear what useful purpose a test would serve since the results are easily predictable and the Canadians have already done it. Any objective test will show that, overall, women do as well as men, sometimes less well—sometimes better. It is more a matter of individual rather than inherent gender differences.

The Canadians came to that conclusion when they tested gender-free assignments. As expected, they found that very few women are able to qualify for and perform jobs that require considerable physical strength, particularly in the infantry. But women excelled in other areas. Before the tests were even completed, Canada made the decision to open all but the infantry and a few other ground combat jobs and to continue testing performance in those. The only assignments still off-limits are submarines and, according to a Canadian spokesman, that may change as new submarines come on line. There is no reason to believe that a U.S. test would produce different conclusions.

"The very concept of protection within the military is a contradiction."

Sociologist Charles Moskos makes the point that the problem with such a test "is not that it will prove women cannot fight, but that it will prove they can." He was right, of course, but he might have added that an objective test would also prove that many men cannot. In any case, a test leaves unresolved the core political policy question of whether women *should* be assigned combat roles.

To date, five NATO [North Atlantic Treaty Organization] nations have faced the issue and made the decision to allow women in combat: Canada, Denmark, Norway, Greece, and the Netherlands. Also, Great Britain has opened positions on combat ships of the Royal Navy.

Whatever conclusions are drawn from the

gulf war, women's place in the U.S. armed forces has been permanently altered and universally recognized. It is time for leaders in the Pentagon and Congress to bite the bullet and get rid of old laws and policies that both the military and women have outgrown.

"Today's military depends much less on brawn in favor of smart, educated, technically trainable people."

The Pentagon still prefers to pass the buck to Congress on questions of repeal saying if you want us to open combat assignments to women then you repeal the law and we'll do it. That may be the politically expedient posture to assume considering the volatile nature of the issue both within and outside military circles.

There is evidence on Capitol Hill and within the Pentagon of growing interest in reviewing the exclusion statutes in the light of the Persian Gulf experience. If they are not soon repealed, the courts may act as they have on other laws and practices aimed at "protecting" women from risk in employment.

Without the legal constraints the Secretaries of Defense and the services would be able to set the ground rules on the utilization of all military personnel based on legitimate service requirements and individual capabilities.

In the final analysis, it is a matter of tapping the best talents available from a shrinking pool of young potential recruits to do the jobs required by the military . . . a military that grows technologically more demanding each day.

It is also a matter of equity, or reverse equity, if you will. Sooner or later the question boils down to this: Is it right to expect military men to face the risks of combat while attempting to protect the women who take the same oath, draw the same pay, get the same training, and wear the same uniform?

Today, an increasing number of women are saying: NO. So are growing numbers of men. A young female enlisted paratrooper who had landed in Panama with the 82nd Airborne laid it out in simple terms: "If they are going to let us wear the uniform then they ought to let us defend it. Otherwise, don't let us wear it."

The spirit of many of the women on duty in the gulf was expressed by Captain Ginny Thomas, a reserve pilot flying a C-141 transport in the theater. "I'll be glad when it's over," she said. "But I'd be disappointed if I was not over here doing something for my country."

Military Women

Military women have proven that they are ready, willing and able to accept the risks and responsibilities that go with the oath they have freely taken. They have earned the right to be treated like members of the first team rather than as a protected sub-class on the fringes of their profession. As citizens, they deserve the opportunity to be all they can be.

The Combat Exclusion Law Should Be Repealed

Patricia Schroeder

About the Author: *Patricia Schroeder, a Democrat from Colorado, is a member of the U.S. House of Representatives. Schroeder has sponsored legislation permitting women to serve in combat.*

The latest Army recruiting commercial portrays a female soldier operating a communications van during field maneuvers. Army Sergeant 1st Class Georgiana Cleverley, a communications specialist, told the *New York Times* that she would have seven minutes to live before the first bomb landed on top of her antenna. In other words, because of the Army's combat exclusion policy, women can be the first killed in a battle. But they cannot hold a combat job.

For reasons lost in the vapors of legislative history, Congress passed a combat exclusion law in 1948 that prohibited the Air Force, Navy, and Marine Corps from permanently assigning women to combat positions. The Army, however, was allowed to "assign, and detail the duties" of Army personnel as it saw fit. We can only guess that the combat exclusion law was intended to protect women in the military from harm, ensure a combat-effective force, and reflect public opinion. In fact, the law fails on all three counts.

First, the Army evaluates the jobs they open to women in terms of their theoretical proximity to the battlefield. However, the realities of modern warfare, whether missiles or guerilla tactics, make it difficult to define a field of battle. Mili-

Patricia Schroeder, "Be *All* We Can Be," statement before the U.S. House of Representatives Armed Services Committee's Subcommittee on Military Personnel and Compensation, March 20, 1990. Public Domain.

tary personnel, regardless of their position, are likely to be exposed to danger. Contemporary battle doctrine calls for striking first at the supply lines instead of the front lines. While women are barred from assignment to the jobs that are most likely to face direct combat, they are assigned to support and service support positions that bring them into the battlefield on a regular basis. Sgt. Cleverley spelled it out: combat exclusion policy is obsolete if the goal is to protect women by confining them to support roles.

Some military reluctance to assign women to combat is based on assumptions about women's physical capabilities. General M.R. Thurman, of the Southern Command in Panama, remarked at a Senate hearing that "the routine carrying of a 120-pound rucksack day in and day out on the nexus of battle between infantrymen is that which is to be avoided and that's what the current Army policy does." In fact, few men dash around in combat with a 120-pound pack. There have been debates about how far women can throw a grenade or carry a wounded soldier, or how fast they can run. The real issue is training. Some women can indeed carry as much weight, throw as far and run as fast as some men, and some women exceed some men in physical strength and endurance. Such athletes as pitching ace Kathy Arendsen, who throws a softball 96 miles per hour, underhand, and Florence Griffith Joyner, who runs the 100 meters faster than O.J. Simpson ever ran while competing for USC [University of Southern California], would scoff at the "girls can't throw" argument. These women demonstrate that trained individuals can do anything.

"Women can be the first killed in a battle. But they cannot hold a combat job."

Second, the combat exclusion law weakens the military. Excluding women from combat jobs requires a larger pool of male volunteers to ensure a combat ready force. In an effort to attract enough men to meet the rotational needs created by excluding women from combat positions, the Army set lower recruiting standards for men than women. Only 65 percent of all men are required to hold high school diplomas instead of GEDs [general equivalency diplomas], while all women must be high school graduates. As the pool of males eligible for military services shrinks, the military will have to look to women, who now make up almost 11 percent of the military, to fill the gap. The military should, as a good employer, aspire to fill the infantry with the most qualified soldiers available, male or female.

"The combat exclusion law weakens the military."

Third, the combat exclusion law neither reflects public opinion nor everyday realities during peacetime or wartime. Many opponents of allowing women in combat claim that the American public simply isn't ready to see women wounded or killed. Female police officers face life-threatening dangers every day. One woman faces the terror of rape every three and a half minutes. In the murder capital of the nation, Washington, D.C., death is a daily companion for many women. And yes, women have even experienced war firsthand. In both World War II and Vietnam women came home in body bags. More than 10 million women and children have been killed in 150 armed conflicts since 1945.

Public opinion polls dispute the claims of women-in-combat opponents. In a 1982 poll, taken by the National Opinion Research Center, 84 percent of the American public supported keeping or increasing the proportion of women in the services, and 62 percent were in favor of allowing women to be fighter pilots. In January 1990, *New York Times*/CBS News reported that 72 percent of Americans believed that "women members of the Armed Forces should be allowed to serve in combat units if they wanted to."

We are not protecting women or the American public, nor are we maintaining a more combat-effective force by excluding women from combat jobs. We are denying women the chance to further their careers by opting for a combat assignment. Most importantly, we are denying the military the skilled and qualified personnel that they need, where they need them. It is time for military service to be based on qualifications, not gender.

The Combat Exclusion Law Is Unconstitutional

Kathy L. Snyder

About the Author: *Kathy L. Snyder is a law student at the West Virginia University College of Law in Morgantown.*

Law and policy restrict women in the United States Military from serving in positions that would require them to engage in direct combat. The Women's Armed Services Integration Act of 1948 excludes women from Air Force and Navy vessels and aircraft that might engage in combat. The Army and the Marine Corps also exclude women from combat through their official established policies. The result of these statutes and policies is the exclusion of women, on the sole basis of gender, from over twelve percent of the skill positions and thirty-nine percent of the total positions offered by the Department of Defense. There has never been a direct challenge to the constitutionality of these laws and regulations banning women from combat. The closest the United States Supreme Court has come to deciding the issue was in *Rostker v. Goldberg*, where the constitutionality of a male-only draft registration was upheld. The statutes and policies excluding women from combat positions should be repealed by Congress or declared unconstitutional. . . .

The Fourteenth Amendment's Equal Protection Clause insures that no state can deny any person "the equal protection of the laws." Although the Fourteenth Amendment's Equal Protection Clause is not applicable to the federal government, the United States Supreme Court

Kathy L. Snyder, "An Equal Right to Fight: An Analysis of the Constitutionality of Laws and Policies That Exclude Women from Combat in the United States Military," *West Virginia Law Review*, vol. 93, Winter 1990-91. Reprinted with permission.

has held that the Fifth Amendment's Due Process Clause prohibits the federal government from making unreasonable classifications. Thus, the Fifth and Fourteenth Amendments guarantee that people who are similarly situated will be treated similarly by federal and state government. . . .

The traditional arguments raised in defense of excluding women in combat . . . are either invalid or based on unacceptable, outdated stereotypes. These reasons fail to show that restrictions on women in combat substantially relate to maintaining an effective military force or to any other important governmental interest. . . .

"The laws and policies excluding women from combat violate the Fifth Amendment."

The number of positions from which the military excludes women varies from eighty percent in the Marine Corps to four percent in the Air Force. Overall, the combat exclusion laws and policies restrict women from thirty-nine percent of the total positions in the Department of Defense. The combat exclusion laws even close off job opportunities to women that do not involve combat. The military functions on a rotation basis, whereby men can be rotated out of "combat-ready" posts when needed. As a result there are limits on the numbers of women who can be accepted into the military for even clerical and administrative jobs. [A July 18, 1981 *New Republic* article states that] "Military statistics show that female volunteers . . . are easier to recruit, more mature, better educated, more quickly promoted, more inclined to re-enlist, and less inclined to have drug or disciplinary problems than their male counterparts." Yet despite manpower shortages, the limits set on the number of women that can be accepted are forcing recruiters to turn away qualified women. Therefore, the combat exclusion laws result in some women being completely restricted from the military.

The laws and regulations banning women from combat not only restrict them from the military completely because of the rotation system, but also deprive them of promotions. Promotions normally require officer experience in a major command or extensive sea or flight experience. Because women lack experience in combat positions, the exclusion laws and policies are keeping women out of top military posts. These combat restrictions severely limit the careers of women who join the military.

The laws and policies excluding women from combat violate the Fifth Amendment's Due Process Clause by denying women their fundamental right to engage and advance in their chosen occupation. The statutes and policies intentionally discriminate against women as a class. The explicit basis of the classifications is gender and the statistics cited above show the discriminatory effect that the statutes have had in denying women promotions and employment.

A Violation of Civil Rights

Restrictions that exclude women from combat are not only unconstitutional, but they may also violate Title VII of the Civil Rights Act of 1964, as amended by the Equal Employment Opportunity Act (EEOA) of 1972. The EEOA added the term "sex" to the list of traits that employers may not use to discriminate for employment purposes. Congress also amended Title VII in 1972 to include "military departments." Whether Title VII applies to the uniformed military, however, is not yet settled. . . .

The exclusion of women from thirty-nine percent of the total positions in the Department of Defense illustrates that the combat restrictions have had a negative impact on employment of women in the military. The appropriate congressionally-mandated standard in a Title VII case is whether the classification is a "bona fide occupational qualification reasonably necessary to normal operation of that particular business. . . ." [According to the court's decision in *Satty v. Nashville Gas Co.*]. . . . Gender does not deter-

mine who can perform capably as a soldier. Therefore, being a male should not be a bona fide occupational qualification for military combat. As long as the statutes excluding women from combat endure, however, being male is apt to remain a BFOQ, and the courts are unlikely to rule that the restrictions violate Title VII.

"Gender does not determine who can perform capably as a soldier."

Other countries around the world do not find the idea of women in combat shocking. In *Rostker v. Goldberg*, Justice William Rehnquist pointed out that "[n]o major country has women in combat jobs in their standing army." That statement is no longer true. In 1989, Canada accepted women in all combat forces except on submarines. Canada is the fifth NATO [North Atlantic Treaty Organization] country to employ women in combat positions along with Belgium, the Netherlands, Norway and Denmark. Sweden also dropped its ban on women in combat in 1989. The number of women joining the military rose sharply in Australia when they became eligible for most combat positions in May 1990. Although rigorous physical tests still keep many women out of the infantry, these countries allow women to serve in most combat positions. With more categories of military jobs becoming open to women in the United States, "combat duty is the last hurdle," [according to a January 15, 1990 article in *U.S. News & World Report*]. Americans must show that they believe in the idea of equal rights themselves if the United States is to continue as a leader for equality in the world.

The Panama Invasion

The United States' invasion of Panama in December 1989, known as "Operation Just Cause," provided tangible proof that women are capable of performing well in combat. During the invasion, 174 women in Army military police and combat support units fought snipers and provided security. Women commanded two of the Army Military Police units. One of those units, commanded by Captain Linda Bray, came under enemy fire at a Panamanian guard dog kennel. Two other women piloting "UH-60 'Blackhawk' helicopters came under heavy fire as they shuttled soldiers into combat during early hours of the invasion," [according to *Minerva's Bulletin Board*, Spring 1990]. Several rounds of fire struck Warrant Officer Debra Mann's helicopter, damaging it so badly it had to be grounded. In all, almost 800 women took part in the Panama operation, becoming the first American women to engage hostile troops in modern combat.

Senseless Results

Operation Just Cause also provided at least one example of the senseless results of the combat exclusion laws. Sergeant Rhonda J. Maskus is a paratrooper and intelligence analyst stationed at Fort Bragg. She specialized in Panamanian intelligence for two years and spent three months working on the invasion plans. However, when officials requested an intelligence analyst from her section, the officers in command sent male soldiers with no special expertise on Panama in her place. Incidents of this type serve not only to perpetuate the inferior status of women but also hinder the country's military effectiveness. In times of crisis the person most qualified for the job is the one to send, regardless of gender.

Now that women have successfully engaged in combat, the reasons for maintaining the restrictions become even less convincing. Nevertheless, Brian Mitchell, author of *Weak Link* argues that the use of female soldiers in Panama proved nothing because "[t]he sorts of things they were doing could be done by a twelve-year-old with a rifle." His argument seems rather weak though, since it is hard to imagine twelve-year-olds piloting helicopters and driving trucks to transport troops under enemy fire. The invasion proved that women not only can survive combat, but can be substantial contributors to its success.

The United States is currently engaged in a military conflict with Iraq as a result of the Iraqi invasion of Kuwait on August 2, 1990. The government has classified the exact number of women who are or will be taking part in the Operation, but a Cable News Network (CNN) report estimated that over 27,500 United States military women are in the Persian Gulf area. Never before have women served in such large numbers or in such a wide variety of positions in a major military operation. The women are serving as pilots, mechanics, truck drivers, intelligence specialists, paratroopers, flight controllers, shipboard navigators, communications experts and in many other crucial posts.

Operation Desert Storm illustrates the hypocrisy of the combat exclusion policies. Before the fighting began, the Pentagon told reporters that should active hostilities commence against Iraq, chances were that the women sent to Saudi Arabia with their units would come under fire. Iraq has not yet utilized chemical weapons but there is little doubt that if they do, military women will be among the casualties. These women are training men for missions they themselves are not permitted to carry out, commanding units in which they cannot serve and are working alongside the men under hostile fire without being classified as serving in direct combat.

"Being a male should not be a bona fide occupational qualification for military combat."

The Kuwait crisis could prove to be the final factor in determining the fate of the combat exclusion laws and policies. As the authors of one *Newsweek* article stated:

> [W]omen, more than the men, believe their future in the armed forces is on the line that George Bush has drawn in the sand. If a major war erupts, spreading unisex casualties throughout the theater, it could finally bring down the combat exclusions or it could so outrage the American public, and its leaders, that women

are never again placed so close to the action in so many critical roles.

Although the fighting has just begun, Operation Desert Storm has already undoubtedly provided significant insights into the importance of women in the United States Armed Forces. . . .

"Other countries around the world do not find the idea of women in combat shocking."

The statutes and policies restricting women from combat should be repealed by Congress or declared unconstitutional. The restrictions violate the Fifth Amendment's Due Process Clause and Title VII by purposely discriminating against women. The traditional reasons given for the exclusion of women from combat are outdated and inaccurate. There is no substantial relationship between the restrictions and any important governmental objective. Thus, the statutes and policies fail to meet the standards set forth in the Craig test.

The military should not lower standards for combat readiness, nor should women receive special treatment. Neither, however, should the United States government ban women per se from the chance to achieve those standards merely because of gender. Arbitrarily banning qualified women from positions they are capable of performing harms not only military effectiveness, but also the quality of the American society as well. Until women obtain the opportunity to assume their equal share of societal obligations they will never achieve equal rights as citizens.

Should Women Serve in Combat?

No: Women Should Not Serve in Combat

Allowing Women in Combat Would Weaken America's Defense
Combat Is Not an Appropriate Role for Women
Equality for Women Does Not Justify Placing Them in Combat
The Persian Gulf War Proves Women's Inability to Serve in Combat
Medals on Our Blouses? Neither Women nor Men Should Fight in Combat
The Combat Exclusion Law Is Necessary

Allowing Women in Combat Would Weaken America's Defense

Brian Mitchell

About the Author: *Brian Mitchell is a former U.S. Army infantry officer and intelligence agent. Mitchell, now a reporter for* Navy Times *newspaper, is the author of the controversial book* Weak Link: The Feminization of the American Military.

Lies can't live forever, as we have seen in Eastern Europe. One result of the U.S. invasion of Panama may be that Americans will finally learn the truth about women and the military.

It didn't take long for the truth to come out of Panama. First came a report that a female officer had led American soldiers in an assault against a "heavily armed" attack dog kennel, capturing the kennel after an intense three-hour firefight that left three Panamanians dead.

But that report was grossly exaggerated. The kennel was lightly held; the shooting lasted only 10 minutes; no one was killed or injured, and the female officer was not present during the shooting.

Later, we learned that not all women who participated in the invasion acquitted themselves with honor. Two female truck drivers were accused of tearfully refusing to drive a company of Rangers to the site of the fiercest fighting. Both had to be replaced with male drivers.

For many years, politicians in Congress and the Pentagon have led the American people to believe that women perform well in the military, so well that the Pentagon's official position is that there are no military reasons why women should not serve in combat.

But actions speak louder than words, and the actions of most Pentagon officials support a continued exclusion of women from many combat jobs. They may say that the combat exclusions have no military basis, but they haven't asked Congress to repeal the exclusions. The reason they have not asked for the elimination of exclusions is because there is, in fact, ample evidence that women do not perform many military jobs as well as men, and women cause problems that can only degrade combat effectiveness.

Physical limitations make it impossible for many women to live up to the boast that they perform as well as men. The Marine Corps does not train women to throw hand grenades because a test of female Marines found that barely half of them could throw a hand grenade far enough not to kill themselves. A 1982 Army study found that barely 10 percent of Army women possess the strength to perform 75 percent of Army enlisted jobs, yet half of the Army's enlisted women were assigned to those jobs. Any attempt to ensure that men or women have the strength to complete their assigned jobs would have the inconvenient result of keeping a lot of women out of a lot of jobs.

> ## "Not all women who participated in the invasion acquitted themselves with honor."

Even when women are assigned jobs they can do well, they pose problems that detract from their overall effectiveness. At any time, about 10 percent of servicewomen are pregnant and are not eligible for deployment overseas and emergency duty. They are also prohibited from performing a variety of routine duties to avoid jeopardizing the health of their child or themselves.

Pregnancy is one reason women require much more medical attention than men. Women are also more prone to many diseases, espe-

Brian Mitchell, "Should Military Women Serve in Combat?" *The American Legion Magazine*, May 1990. Reprinted by permission, *The American Legion Magazine*, © 1990.

cially infections of the genitourinary tract, a special threat in field environments where sanitary conditions are less than optimum. Women are also more likely to seek medical attention for spurious ailments and emotional distress because of unfamiliar situations.

"Women in general are less aggressive, less physically daring and less inclined to take necessary risks than men."

Because the U.S. military is responsible for providing emergency medical care to its members anywhere in the world, the greater medical needs of women pose a significant, unnecessary burden. All in all, women are hospitalized two to three times more than men and miss work for medical reasons more than twice as often as men. Ten years ago, when drug abuse and disciplinary problems were much more common in the military, men and women missed work about the same amount of time. Since then, rates of drug abuse and disciplinary problems have drastically declined, but the medical needs of women have not changed, thus, any comparison of lost time would likely show that women lose more time overall.

Women are about eight times more likely than men to be single parents. Single parents require more childcare and are less available for emergency duty, overtime and deployment. And they are more likely to think twice about risking their lives, knowing that their children depend upon them alone.

Women in general are less aggressive, less physically daring and less inclined to take necessary risks than men. Their presence among men in close quarters will inevitably lead to extra-professional relationships that disrupt morale and discipline, distract commanders from the mission at hand and threaten the stability of military families.

Perhaps most pernicious of all, the deceit employed to deny the evidence and to sustain the myth that women perform just as well as men in the military poses a serious threat to the honor and integrity of the services.

Those are a few of the military reasons for keeping women out of combat. We should also consider the effect of using women in combat on American society. The dirty, little secret of the pro-combat crowd is that if the laws barring women from combat are repealed, then women will no longer be exempt from the draft. In the 1981 case of *Rostker vs. Goldberg*, the U.S. Supreme Court established the combat exclusions as the only legal basis for the draft exemption. This means that repealing the combat exclusions would obligate all young American women to wartime military service—even combat service—ostensibly for no better reason than to provide a tiny measure of extra peacetime opportunity to a handful of the military's most ambitious women.

Men and Women in Combat

But greater opportunity for military women isn't really what the proponents of combat for women want. Instead, they want to use the military to create a brave, new, androgynous world in which differences between men and women are ignored and suppressed.

If that is what the American people want, then so be it. But let's at least be honest about what we're doing by integrating the battlefield, and not hide behind the lies about how women are just as good for the military as men.

On the other hand, if what the people want is the best defense the nation can muster, then let's admit the differences between men and women and return to a proven policy that keeps women from combat and limits their role in the military.

Combat Is Not an Appropriate Role for Women

James G. Bruen Jr.

About the Author: *James G. Bruen Jr. is on the editorial advisory board of* Fidelity, *a monthly magazine of conservative Catholic opinion.*

On December 20, 1989, Army Captain Linda Bray, commanding officer of the 988th Military Police Company, led a platoon in a three-hour firefight in Panama against troops loyal to General Noriega at the guard-dog kennel near his headquarters. Her platoon killed three Panamanian soldiers in the fight.

At the White House, President Bush's press spokesman, Marlin Fitzwater, briefed reporters on the battle for the dog kennel defended by Panamanian Defense Forces:

"It was heavily defended. Three PDF men were killed. Gunshots were fired on both sides. American troops could have been killed. It was an important military operation. A woman led it, and she did an outstanding job."

Capt. Bray's exploits ignited fierce debate on the role of women in the military and in combat in particular.

"The myth that women soldiers can't fight was a casualty of the invasion of Panama," opined *USA Today*. "The combat ban should be lifted. It was based on outdated taboos and on fighting a different kind of warfare than today's. The opposition will say anything to perpetuate the myths that discriminate against women in the military. They'll say women are too weak. Truth is, when her troops were pinned down by hostile fire, Capt. Bray crashed the kennel gate in a jeep."

"U.S. law clearly prohibits the assignment of women to military combat. In our invasion of Panama, the Pentagon openly flouted this law by assigning women to combat duty," rejoined Phyllis Schlafly. "Bray's survival of a three-hour gunfight does not in the least prove that she could endure a war."

Feminists, led by Rep. Patricia Schroeder, agitated for legislative repeal of the combat exemption that applies to women. "This distinction between combat and noncombat units is really a joke," said Schroeder.

The *New York Times* of course said it saw both sides of the argument as it endorsed a trial of women in combat roles. The more conservative *Washington Times* also temporized: "Human nature, as discomforting as it may be to feminist ideologues, places real limits on the types of roles that women ought to play in the military. . . . This is not to say that women ought to be prohibited entirely from combat or from taking on dangerous roles in wartime."

Truth is, though, that Capt. Bray's exploits are a myth. The firefight at the kennel lasted ten minutes, not three hours. No Panamanian soldiers were killed. And, most damning of all, Capt. Bray wasn't even there when the fighting began. By the time she got there, there weren't any enemy troops.

> ### "Most of what we hear about the performance of women in the U.S. Army is grossly exaggerated."

Apparently the proponents of women in combat were willing to say anything to perpetuate the myth. As Mrs. Schlafly noted: "The real lesson we learn from the use of women in the Panama invasion is that most of what we hear about the performance of women in the U.S. Army is grossly exaggerated even to the point of falsehood." After the truth was revealed, the

James G. Bruen Jr., "Women at War with Themselves," *Fidelity*, October 1990. Reprinted with permission from *Fidelity*, 206 Marquette Ave., South Bend, IN 46617.

White House's Fitzwater brushed off inquiries about the accuracy of his earlier press briefing by saying he had got his information from newspaper accounts.

In June 1990, the Panamanian in charge of the police dogs charged that Bray's unit unnecessarily killed up to 25 caged dogs in the attack on the kennel. Perhaps Bray, feminist symbol and heroine, more appropriately deserves to be a symbol for animal rights activists.

"[Women] are agitating for equal opportunity to fight less important battles . . . while their children are left to their own defenses at home."

But myths die hard. Especially when feminists want to use them to force a result. The deployment of American troops in the Persian Gulf and Saudi Arabia in August 1990 reignited the debate about women in combat, and Capt. Bray's example was dragged out again. *USA Today* still insisted that "Army Capt. Linda Bray, as a military police officer, led an assault on a Panamanian canine unit." And the *Independent* was still maintaining that she "took part in some of the fiercest fighting around General Noriega's headquarters."

USA Today, enamored with its "truth is" format, kept up the late summer assault: "Those who want to keep women out of combat argue that they aren't as strong as men, can't run as fast or throw hand grenades as well. Truth is, it's a matter of training. Kathy Arendsen of Holland, Mich., throws a softball 96 mph, underhand, and Florence Griffith Joyner runs faster than O.J. Simpson."

So what? The proponents of women combatants are erecting strawmen to blow over. My 12- and 14-year-old daughters play softball too, and while they aren't as exceptional as Arendsen or Griffith Joyner, they throw a ball pretty well and run fast too. Does that mean my adolescent daughters should be eligible for military combat? Does that mean they should be eligible for the draft, the probable result of opening combat duty to women?

Physical ability isn't the only issue involved in deciding whether to expose women to combat. It shouldn't even be the primary issue. Some women undoubtedly are capable of performing well in combat. After all, the Catholic adolescent woman warrior is not unknown in history. In obedience to heavenly voices and visions, St. Joan of Arc led the armies of France to victory over the English at the siege of Orleans. And there are probably combat roles that many women could perform better than most men. The question is not whether women can perform satisfactorily in combat. The question is why should they. As far as I know, although many apparitions are now being alleged throughout the world, no one is today claiming private revelation that St. Joan of Arc's example requires opening military combat to all women.

Whether Capt. Bray single-handedly killed three Panamanian soldiers while she alone captured the kennel or whether instead she was far away while her platoon massacred 25 caged dogs isn't particularly important to resolution of the question of whether women should be in combat. If she wasn't there, she could have been. If she didn't pull a trigger, she could have. She may only be 5-foot-1 and 100 pounds, but that's big enough to tote and fire an M-16. And it's big enough to stop an enemy bullet or stray friendly fire. Public opinion about women in combat may be expressed loudly when television news first shows the injured, maimed, wounded, and dead women shipped home after combat.

A Military Orphan

Bill Brown's parents, Nat and Ronna, are among the troops President Bush sent to Saudi Arabia to "defend our way of life." Bill is six years old and lives in Georgia; his parents are assigned to an Army tank unit that is in Saudi Arabia. Army spokeswoman Capt. Barbara Goodno explained that "dual service" couples can be deployed but they are required to have a plan delineating who'll care for their kids. Right now, the Browns' plan is working: grandma is caring for Bill in New York. According to grandma, Bill likes to read Bible stories. But, one bomb and his parents are both dead, and Bill Brown is an orphan. Who'll replace his parents then? Who could replace a generation of moms killed in combat? Government day care centers?

"Women have something better and more important to do than go off to war: bear and raise children."

Bill Brown's separation from his mother isn't an aberration. In 1989 they were separated for a year while Ronna Brown was in Korea. And grandma also had little Bill in July 1990 while his parents were in California receiving desert training.

Staff Sgt. Faagalo Savaiki of the 501st Signal Battalion at Fort Campbell, Kentucky, was also deployed to Saudi Arabia. When he went to the Middle East, he left a note explaining how to use the bank's automatic teller machine and instructing his kids to pay certain bills. Other than that, his 13- and nine-year-old sons and his 12-year-old daughter were on their own: they didn't even know how to do their laundry. When the children were discovered, the state put them in a foster home and charges were brought against Savaiki. And where was the mother of Savaiki's children? According to the police, the youngsters' mother divorced Sgt. Savaiki and went to Hawaii just before he went to Saudi Arabia.

Mrs. Brown and Mrs. Savaiki (or whatever names they go by) typify the real problem: the willingness of American society and American women to leave children motherless. The *Washington Times* editorialized that "Bill Brown and other American children like him, whose mothers are hunkered down in the Saudi desert or swabbing the decks of a warship in the Persian Gulf, can be justly proud of the sacrifices their moms are making." But the primary sacrifice those women make is the sacrifice of their children on the altar of the women's choice to do something other than raise their children. That's nothing to be proud of.

Millions of American mothers routinely abandon their children. Some put their children in day care; some leave them through divorce; others are assigned to Saudi Arabia. They think they have something more important to do than raise their children; that can be left for others. These modern American women are prepared to do battle in the business world or in the Saudi desert; they'll live or die for the free market. But they are deserters in the battle between good and evil over the souls of their children. They are agitating for equal opportunity to fight less important battles in Central America and the Middle East while their children are left to their own defenses at home. Most don't even seem to know that that battle for their children is being fought or that they should be in the front line.

Saying Goodbye

Deep down, though, they know where they should be. As *People* magazine wrote of Air Force Major Jane Fisher in its mid-September 1990 cover story, "Mom Goes to War:"

> But nothing in her experience could ease the pain of saying goodbye to her family and the uncertainty of not knowing when she might return. "It was tough," she said before leaving. . . . "All I could say to Mary Jean is that Mommy's going on a big airplane and is going to be gone a while. And Jayson, who remembers the time I left before, knew from television and newspapers that something was not good. He asked me, 'Mommy, what if you die?' I said, 'Well, I die.' I had to laugh. It was kind of funny. I just hope they can understand that I have to do this," she said quietly, "and I don't know how to express it." She begins, very softly but unashamedly, to cry.

Or, as *Newsweek* put it in its mid-September 1990 cover story, "Women Warriors": "A few U.S. servicewomen have torn up photos of their children; looking at them was just too hard."

It's already too late to prevent American women from military combat roles. Defense Department spokesman Pete Williams said there wasn't any discrimination in Operation Desert Shield: "Units deployed were not given any directions not to take women." According to *Newsweek*, "The troops in Saudi Arabia have given this crisis a nickname: the 'mom's war.'" Our country has evaded the question of why should we expose women to combat: since they can do the jobs, they are assigned jobs that will expose them to enemy fire despite a technical ban on women in combat. "Ever since the Pentagon began recruiting women in large numbers in the 1970s, the services have defined 'combat' ever more narrowly, giving women increasingly critical roles," deadpans *Newsweek*. The women may not be in combat units, but they will be in combat. In effect, American children are already vying, to paraphrase the Viet Nam era lyrics of Country Joe & the Fish, to be the first one on their block to have their mom shipped home in a box.

But the law should nevertheless continue to exclude women from combat. Not only because the exalted honor of being capable of being a mother means women should be protected as much as possible from the horrors of war. And not just because their children need them. But also because law has a teaching function. For example, although it may be impossible to prevent all abortions even if all were made illegal, the fact that American law has become permissive towards abortion has encouraged the acceptance of abortion. If it's legal, it's acceptable. Similarly, if the use of women in combat isn't technically prohibited, it will become more accepted and routine. And, of course, if the law remains in place, perhaps it will be enforced through a court-martial of those responsible for putting women into combat situations or as a result of public reaction to dead and mutilated mothers.

Motherhood

Ultimately, though, the point is that women have something better and more important to do than go off to war: bear and raise children. It's a point that should shape our country's laws and that should guide the consciences and hearts of all people, not just women. Of course, though, this point is unpopular today: it also argues against women in the armed forces, women in the workforce, daycare, contraception, extramarital sex, abortion, permissive divorce laws, and all the other non-negotiable demands of feminism. Motherhood is the most noble human calling. Unless we reinstitute respect for motherhood, women will continue to search futilely for something else to fulfill them, children will continue to suffer, and our society will continue its descent.

Equality for Women Does Not Justify Placing Them in Combat

Richard D. Hooker Jr.

About the Author: *Richard D. Hooker Jr. is a captain in the U.S. Army and a social science instructor at the U.S. Military Academy in West Point, New York. A 1981 graduate of the academy, Hooker served in the invasion of Grenada. He has a doctorate degree in foreign affairs from the University of Virginia in Charlottesville.*

The issue of women in combat, thought to be resolved by the demise of the Equal Rights Amendment and the conservatism of successive presidential administrations in this decade, is riding the crest of continuously evolving social mores and changing views of sexual politics. Changes in definitions of sex roles and the removal of many traditional barriers to women in the US Army and the other military services insures that this emotional and confrontational issue will not go away soon.

This article contrasts the Army's commitment to affirmative action with the exclusion of women from combat roles. Current policies may provide grounds for challenges to the combat exclusion rule, while some evidence suggests that combat readiness and full gender integration may not be fully compatible goals. A reassessment of current policies may be needed to clarify the relationship between the twin priorities of maximum combat readiness and maximum opportunity for women. The answers to these and related questions may profoundly af-

Richard D. Hooker Jr., "Affirmative Action and Combat Exclusion: Gender Roles in the U.S. Army," *Parameters*, December 1989. Reprinted with permission.

fect not only the long-term nature of military service in the United States, but the civil-military relationship itself.

Current Army assignment policies for women are based on Title 10 of the US Code, Section 3012, which gives the Secretary of the Army the authority to set personnel assignment and utilization policies for all soldiers.

Unlike the Navy and Air Force, there are no statutory restrictions that prohibit the employment of female soldiers in combat. However, in an effort to ensure a measure of consistency with sister services, Army assignment policies parallel those in the rest of the Department of Defense by restricting women from serving in positions requiring routine exposure to direct combat.

Current policies concerning women in the Army are a product of the rapid expansion of women in the force beginning in the early 1970s. Two significant events were primarily responsible. The first was congressional approval of the Equal Rights Amendment (ERA) in March 1972. The second was the end of the draft in 1973, which caused an immediate decline in the number of qualified males joining the force. Though ratification of the ERA ultimately foundered, legislation was passed in 1975 opening the service academies to women, and soon after the Women's Army Corps was disestablished and women were integrated into male promotion lists.

> ## "The army has lived up to its promise to provide equal promotion opportunities for women."

In 1977 the Secretary of the Army issued a combat exclusion policy prohibiting assignment of women to the combat arms. Problems were quickly identified, since women in some other specialties often collocated with combat units and were exposed to virtually identical measures of risk:

The rapid growth of women in the Army took place without adequate planning and analysis.... There was no established policy of putting the right soldiers in the right jobs based on physical capacity to meet the job requirements. Also, the Army had not made a thorough analysis of where women should serve on the battlefield.

In May 1981 the Army implemented a temporary leveling-off of female accessions at 65,000—the so-called "Woman Pause"—"to permit a review of policies and programs and to determine the effect use of women may have on combat effectiveness and force readiness." A policy review group was established to study these issues. Its report was issued on 12 November 1982, establishing the Direct Combat Probability Coding system that is still in use. Many of the assumptions and conclusions outlined in the 1982 Women in the Army Policy Review continue to guide Army policy today.

"Sexual role differentiation remains central to our way of life."

US Army policy in 1989 is that "women will be assigned in all skills and positions except those which, by doctrine, mission, duties of the job, or battlefield location involve the highest probability of direct combat with enemy forces." Direct Combat Probability Coding (DCPC) is the mechanism used to assess and identify those positions closed to women. The DCPC process assigns each position in the Army a ranking from P1 to P7 based on the probability of *routine* engagement in direct combat. Only those positions coded P1 are closed to women. This policy, which is periodically reviewed and updated, is referred to informally as the "combat exclusion" rule. In 1988 the DCPC process was amplified through the "risk rule":

The risk rule states that *noncombat* units should be open to women unless the risk of exposure to direct combat, hostile fire, or capture is equal to or greater than that experienced by associated *combat* units in the same theater of operations.

At the present time, approximately 750,000 positions in the Total Army can be filled by either sex. Eighty-seven percent of enlisted military occupational specialties (MOSs), 91 percent of warrant officer positions, and 96 percent of officer specialties are open to women. As of the end of the third quarter of FY [fiscal year] 1989, females comprise 11 percent of the active force, filling 11,110 officer positions out of 91,443 overall, 435 warrant officer positions out of 14,971, and 72,389 enlisted positions out of 654,537. Today, women are represented in every career management field except infantry, armor, and special operations.

Compensating for Past Discrimination

The promulgation of a unified promotion system has been accompanied since its inception by an affirmative action program designed to compensate for the effects of "past personal and institutional discrimination" which may have operated to the disadvantage of female soldiers. This program encompasses minority as well as female-specific promotion and assignment issues. It is intended to counteract the effects of latent or residual discrimination by ensuring that female soldiers enjoy promotion and assignment potential commensurate with their representation in the force. Board instructions include the following guidance to panel members:

[Discrimination] may manifest itself in disproportionately lower evaluation reports, assignments of lesser importance or responsibility, etc. Take these factors into consideration in evaluating these [soldiers'] potential to make continued significant contributions to the Army. . . . The goal is to achieve a percentage of minority and female selections not less than the selection rate for the number of [soldiers] in the promotion zone (first time considered category). . . . [P]rior to adjournment, the board must review the extent to which it met this goal and explain reasons for any failure to meet this goal in the report of [soldiers] recommended for promotion.

But what exactly is meant by "affirmative action"? The concept is both an outgrowth and a response to the Civil Rights movement of the 1960s. Affirmative action goes well beyond the establishment of equality of opportunity to insure equality of *result*. In the interest of vigorously moving to correct past injustices, the federal government in general and the armed forces in particular have embraced the *preferment* of insular groups which in the past have suffered from institutional discrimination.

As a group, women in the Army have enjoyed greater promotion success than men for almost a decade. Individually, some less-well-qualified candidates have inevitably been selected for promotion and command—an unavoidable price, perhaps, of a necessary and just commitment to the achievement of parity, but one with unpleasant side-effects just the same. It is this phenomenon that gives rise to the charge of reverse discrimination, most keenly felt by individuals who believe they possess equal or superior qualifications but nevertheless lose out to female or minority peers for promotion or command selection. Although personnel managers avoid using the term "quota" in favor of "goal" or "objective," board results consistently confirm that promotion rates for women meet or exceed the targets set by Department of the Army. At least from an institutional perspective, the Army has lived up to its promise to provide equal promotion opportunities for women by implementing an aggressive and comprehensive affirmative action agenda.

"Females lack the aggressiveness and psychological resistance to combat-generated stress."

Affirmative action has generated a momentum all its own. While some advocates are critical of policies that inhibit career opportunities for women in *any* way, expansion of career fields and access to previously closed opportunities and positions in the last decade has been im-

pressive by any standard. Few Western military establishments come close to matching the level of participation of American women in the armed forces, as the figures cited above demonstrate. Pressures continue to build, nevertheless, for realization of a gender-neutral Army in the near future. . . .

Maintaining Perspective

Few issues in the areas of civil rights and civil-military relations are as value-laden or as controversial as those involving the role of women in the armed forces. Advocates on both sides find it difficult to address these issues calmly and without emotion. Nevertheless, objectivity and balance are needed to maintain an appropriate perspective on this most difficult of issues. What are the dominant arguments defining the continuum of debate on gender roles in the US Army and in the military as a whole?

Proponents of a gender-neutral military establishment envision the participation of women in all phases of military life, to include membership in and command of "combat" organizations such as maneuver battalions and brigades, naval warships, and fighter and bomber squadrons. They rely heavily on legal arguments borrowed from the civil rights and feminist movements to attack gender distinctions as inherently discriminatory or violative of fundamental constitutional guarantees of equal protection and due process. One central tenet is lack of opportunity for promotion to the highest grades, traditionally reserved for officers possessing combat specialties. Another is a declining pool of eligible male volunteers, which can be offset by recruiting larger numbers of females into previously closed specialties.

Because expanded roles for women in the military have been accompanied by defensive weapons training as well as doctrinal requirements for transient exposure in forward areas, it is often argued that traditional distinctions between combat and non-combat or combat support roles have become blurred or are no longer meaningful. Technological advances in nuclear and conventional weaponry, accompanied by a proliferation of rear area threats, buttress this claim. Integrated military training in precommissioning schools, in officer and enlisted initial entry or basic courses, and in many service schools is often cited as proof that no practical distinctions exist between male and female performance in basic combat tasks.

Although these individuals and organizations do not always claim to represent the views of the majority of women in the United States, they insist that the right of *individual* women to pursue fulfilling and rewarding careers in the military cannot be abridged by "traditional" views of sexual roles which overstate sex differences and devalue female strengths and capabilities. Differences in physical capacity or behavior patterns are believed to be largely irrelevant or distorted by bias in the structure of test instruments or interpretation of test data. Sexual issues that do not lend themselves easily to this interpretation can be solved, it is argued, by the application of better, more equitable leadership and training programs. Finally, advocates for gender neutrality in the military posit an irrebuttable presumption that opposition to their views is proof of sexual bias. Thus they can frequently seize the moral high ground and force their opponents to respond reactively and defensively.

> "Assignment of female soldiers without regard to their physical ability to do the job can only . . . damage . . . successful integration of the female soldiers affected."

It is important to note that this perspective is not confined to fringe elements or to small but vocal groups operating on the periphery of the policy-making apparatus. Many women (and not a few men) in each service support a more gender-neutral approach, a point of view that tends to dominate service literature on the subject. Their views enjoy widespread currency and sup-

port in the academic, media, and legal communities. This movement is no mere exercise in advocacy. It represents a powerful and broad-based constituency with considerable prospects for eventual implementation of its views.

Opponents of combat roles for women focus on two essential themes. The first is the effect on readiness and efficiency of sexually integrated combat units and the impact of a female presence in the "fighting" components. The second is the social impact of female mass casualties which would surely follow commitment of a fully integrated military force to combat under modern conditions.

Views of Traditionalists

For "traditionalists," the argument that physical, psychological, or social/cultural differences are irrelevant to military efficiency is risible. They cite medical evidence that documents male advantages in upper body strength, cardiovascular capacity, lean muscle mass, and leg strength to demonstrate significant differences in physical capacity. Physiological research suggesting a higher incidence of injury in training for women augments this thesis. Emphasis on the *aggregate* effect of women in the force is stressed, for while the physical capacity of individual females may equal or exceed that of the male mean, they are sparsely represented among the population. Reduced physical capacity, primarily a factor in tasks requiring heavy lifting or stamina, is predictable when females are compared to males according to this view.

For this school, psychological, social, and cultural factors are inextricably embedded in the physical differences between the sexes. They are much harder to quantify, but it is argued that their influence is nonetheless profound. While sexual roles have been greatly redefined in the last 25 years, sexual role differentiation remains central to our way of life. Combat exclusion proponents insist that sexual behavior traits, whether genetic (inherited) or environmental (learned), cannot be wished away. Their potential impact on the performance of combat units must be factored into the equation.

Crime statistics are often used to demonstrate that female participation in violent crime is dwarfed by that of males—implying much higher levels of aggression for men. Biomedical and genetic research supports the hypothesis that sex role characteristics are by no means purely environmental or social/cultural products. These and other studies are believed to complement what is perhaps the most strongly held normative assumption of all: that in the aggregate, females lack the aggressiveness and psychological resistance to combat-generated stress of males and are therefore less suited for the rigors and demands of extended combat.

An important factor, not to be overlooked according to advocates of more traditional roles for female soldiers, is the effect of female presence on the fragile psychological basis that is the foundation of cohesion and esprit in traditionally all-male combat units. Thus it is argued that sexual integration of these units, even with females screened for physical capacity, would destroy or impair fighting efficiency by introducing elements such as protectiveness, sexual attraction, social role inversion, and leader/follower conflict based on gender stereotypes, among others.

"It is dangerous to assume . . . that physiological, psychological, cultural, and social distinctions . . . are meaningless on the battlefield."

While this assumption is dismissed by combat exclusion opponents as sexist, or at most curable with good leadership and proper training, it is frequently asserted by combat veterans familiar with the unique psychological stresses and demands of the battlefield. They insist that the psychological "chemistry" of combat units is regulated and defined by adherence to and reinforcement of the traditional sex roles of warrior

and protector. To dilute this crucial but delicate balance by adding females merely to promote feminist values of full equality—values that do not reflect the aspirations of women as a group—would destroy the sexual identity that lies at the root of the combat ethos.

Affirmative Action

Affirmative action in its broadest sense commits the armed forces to policies that ultimately collide with the combat exclusion rule. Because no official attempt is made to articulate the basis for excluding women from combat beyond vague references to "the implied will of Congress," it is difficult from an institutional perspective to mount a reasoned defense against those who move for full sexual integration of the military. Indeed, evolving policies on women in the Army already embrace most of the arguments of those who advocate a gender-neutral force.

For example, current policy does not restrict females from any career field or position because of physical requirements. Although the 1982 Policy Review recommended "matching the soldier to the job" on a gender-neutral basis using physical demands analysis during medical screening, such testing is conducted on an "advisory" basis only—leaving final determination of acceptability to recruiters already pressed to fill recruiting quotas:

> [Physical capacity] testing is done at the MEPS (Military Entrance and Processing Station) and we don't even get involved. The same test is given regardless of the MOS . . . [and] in two years I've never had a recommendation for a rejection yet. The bottom line is, if they have the minimum smarts and can pass the physical, I sign them up. That's what I get paid for.

In 1976, the General Accounting Office notified Congress of emerging concerns that women were being assigned to positions "without regard to their ability to satisfy the specialties' strength, stamina, and operational requirements." Company-grade commanders of integrated units report identical problems in the force today—13 years later:

Although I had upwards of seventy women in my unit I could not employ many in the MOSs they held due to their inability to perform the heavy physical tasks required. So I used them in headquarters or administrative job. . . . Complaining to higher headquarters wasn't really an option. These things were considered "leadership" problems.

Assignment of female soldiers without regard to their physical ability to do the job can only degrade unit readiness and damage both self-esteem and successful integration of the female soldiers affected.

Current policy also admits of no potential impact on readiness or efficiency because of other gender-related factors. Of 19 areas identified as possible areas of concern, only pregnancy made the cut as a female-specific issue. The rest, which included fraternization, assignment and management of military couples, sole parenting, sexual harassment, professional development, attrition and retention, and privacy and field hygiene issues, among others, were classified as "institutional" matters and referred to appropriate Army staff agencies for resolution. In short, they were dismissed as having little relevance to the formulation of over-arching policies governing utilization of women in the Army.

It would be unfair as well as inaccurate to say that all of these factors pose insurmountable problems that cannot be coped with in many, if not most, unit environments. It is just as inaccurate, however, to say that they are irrelevant to combat readiness and efficiency. Perhaps no bright line exists to show where fairness and equity should give way to prudence and necessity. Still, the question must be asked—and, more important, answered.

Conclusions

In the military as elsewhere, resolution of competing claims involving constitutionally protected rights is an exercise in line-drawing. Here the first imperative for any armed force—the maximum possible level of combat readiness and efficiency—stands in potential conflict with bona fide institutional desires for equal opportunity. Evolving policies have predictably attempted to define these twin imperatives as mutually supportive, not mutually exclusive. Since the end of the Vietnam War, the US Army has repeatedly demonstrated its commitment to the fullest possible range of opportunities for women in the force. Yet nagging contradictions persist.

If, for example, it is the implied will of Congress that women not serve in direct combat, then doctrinal proliferation of females in forward areas in the absence of a clear delineation between combat roles and support roles confuses the issue. Congress and the courts may find it impossible to sustain what may *appear* to be an increasingly artificial distinction. Risk of death or capture is, after all, a function of position on the battlefield as well as unit mission.

"It is the implied will of Congress that women not serve in direct combat."

Despite judicial support for ever-broadening female participation in the military, a healthy deference to the leading role of the executive and legislative in military matters still exists. By dismissing most gender-related factors as irrelevant to military efficiency, defense policymakers have reduced the arguments against total gender-neutrality to one: popular opinion. As the record shows, popular opinion often carries little weight with federal judges concerned to protect individual freedom and opportunity. There must be substance to the combat exclusion rule or it will surely fall.

The organizational structure of military units is highly flexible and can adapt to many of the changes that necessarily accompany the expansion of women in the Army. This should not be confused with a priori assumptions equating equal opportunity with gender-irrelevancy in terms of battlefield performance. The price of error, however well-intentioned, could be fatal.

Expanded opportunities for women have enhanced the quality of the service, binding it closer to the lives of the people and aspirations of the society it serves. The contributions and professional dedication of female soldiers serving throughout the force now make sex-based distinctions in many areas unsustainable. Many barriers have fallen, revealed as discriminatory obstacles without a rational basis. To the extent that sexual integration and overall combat efficiency are found to be in harmony, there can be little excuse for restricting female participation.

Sexual Differentiation

Sexual differentiation nevertheless remains a fact of life. The differences between men and women can be muted, compensated for, and even exploited to enhance military performance—up to a point. It is dangerous to assume, however, that physiological, psychological, cultural, and social distinctions rooted in gender are meaningless on the battlefield.

There is a substantive and important difference between those units whose primary purpose is direct, sustained ground combat and those which support them. In combat, ground maneuver units will continue to suffer the heaviest casualties, place the heaviest demands on the physical abilities of soldiers, and endure the highest levels of psychological trauma and stress. At the sharp end of the force, sexual differentiation may matter very much indeed. The combat exclusion rule reflects this basic premise.

The Persian Gulf War Proves Women's Inability to Serve in Combat

Human Events

About the Author: Human Events *is a weekly newspaper of conservative political and social opinion.*

The U.S. military deployment to the Persian Gulf has dealt a body blow to a key tenet of the radical feminist agenda: that male and female soldiers should be treated exactly alike, with the same expectations and demands applied to each indiscriminately.

Perhaps the last thing dogmatic feminists anticipated was widespread opposition to their propaganda from female soldiers themselves.

Nevertheless, a cascade of news articles and television broadcasts has recently made clear that women in the gulf, especially those who are mothers, think the idea of sending them to a potential war zone is a terrible one.

Perhaps the most impressive of these recent articles was written by *New York Times* reporter Jane Gross. Gross quotes one discharged female soldier, former Sgt. Lori Moore of Ft. Benning, Ga., as saying, "I hate to say it [that women belong at home with their children], because it doesn't fit with the whole scheme of the women's movement, but I think we have to reconsider what we're doing." Although Moore, whose husband is stationed at Ft. Benning, described herself as a "gung-ho careerist," she accepted a slightly tainted general discharge rather than deploy with her unit to the Persian Gulf and leave behind her three children, aged 3, 2 and nine months. "We're [The Army] mission-oriented," explained Moore, "and our mission is combat. Sending my kids [to relatives] was just part of the job—until they left. Then I was overwhelmed with guilt.

"I asked the good Lord, what is going on? Why am I feeling this way? What did I do to my family?

"And what I came up with is [that] a mother should be with her children. I had to pursue that, because if I didn't I couldn't be at peace. . . .

"I produced these kids, and I needed to take responsibility for them. I'm afraid the children are the unsung victims of Operation Desert Shield. There is no question that women can do this [deploy to a potential war zone]. The question is whether we should."

Similarly, Sgt. Twila Erickson-Schamer, about to be deployed to the gulf, now wonders how she could ever have believed that she could be "a soldier and a mother at the same time."

"There are so many feelings," she told Gross. "How can I possibly sort them out? I have tried to convince myself that it's going to be okay and displayed that attitude to other people.

"If I didn't, I'd be in a constant state of emotional breakdown. I'd be crying all the time."

Many reports have also come from female soldiers already deployed to the Persian Gulf that suggest that mothers in combat zones have a more difficult time performing their military duties.

"Women in the gulf . . . think the idea of sending them to a potential war zone is a terrible one."

Spec. 4 Robin Williams told the Colorado Springs *Gazette-Telegraph*, "It's like this: I'm a woman and a mother before I'm a soldier. . . . Out here I think more about my family than my job. And, yes, that could affect my performance

Reprinted, with permission, from "Female Troops Desert Feminist Ranks," *Human Events*, December 22, 1990.

if things got intense here."

At long last, a few within the armed forces have begun to stand up to the powerful feminist lobby. Maj. Brady Lawrence, chief of human resources at San Francisco's Presidio Army base, says the "dismay among mothers proves the wisdom of barring women from combat ."

"Do we really want to open up the field," Lawrence asked Gross, "if we're having the problems we're having now?"

"Mothers in combat zones have a more difficult time performing their military duties."

Human Events contacted Elaine Donnelly, a former member of the Defense Advisory Committee on Women in the Services (DACOWITS, increasingly a feminist enclave) and asked her about the fast-changing attitudes of female soldiers about serving in war zones while separated from their children.

Donnelly said that it was mainly enlisted women who were now paying the price for this social experiment and she cautioned, "Army officials will declare Operation Desert Shield a success if their numerical objectives are reached—regardless of the long-term effects on children, families or society at large.

"But no one knows how far-reaching the real damage could be. Imagine the trauma to a young child whose mother comes back mangled or killed."

Donnelly questioned the continued existence of DACOWITS, "unless they use this new information to reassess their policy of pushing for more women in more roles in the service, even in the combat arms. . . . But feminists never admit mistakes and feminist ideology is in the driver's seat at DACOWITS."

Donnelly predicts that because of publicity about the hardships, both physical and psychological, endured by women in the gulf, future enlistments in the all volunteer armed forces will

drop. She also fears the possibility of women being drafted—even for combat units—some day.

"If we have to reinstitute the draft," reasons Donnelly, "and if women are already in the combat zone, then there will be no legal basis to exclude them from the draft."

Even if we should avoid that worst-case scenario, however, Donnelly believes that our present policies regarding women in the military will continue to create problems for our society.

"The more numbers of women in the military you have," Donnelly explains, "the more you're going to multiply the horror stories that you've already got. It's a natural progression: When you have a higher percentage of women, you have more fraternization between the soldiers. Then you have more marriages, then you have joint spouse assignment problems, then you have pregnancy problems, then you have child care problems.

"All of these things kind of grow geometrically. We need to decide if this is the kind of military that we want.

"We used to have essentially a bachelor army; now we have a family force. Are we going to wind up with child care centers in Saudi Arabia?"

No Sympathy for Feminists

Brian Mitchell, author of *Weak Link: The Feminization of the American Military,* shared many of Donnelly's concerns with us.

"We should have known," said Mitchell, "that young mothers sent to the other side of the world where they may die in the desert were going to react this way.

"I have sympathy for the ones who have come to their senses, but not for the radical feminists and military leaders who presented them with a pollyanna vision of simply doing a different, non-traditional kind of job. Nobody pointed out to them the kinds of physical dangers and psychological pressures they might someday find themselves facing."

Mitchell has concluded that we should have a military in which women are not expected to deploy at all, serving instead in garrison units here in the U.S., perhaps in non-deployable finance and personnel units.

"This means women will be limited to very few jobs in the military," Mitchell continued. "We need a much-reduced female presence in the military because you cannot really solve the problems of deployability."

"We need a much-reduced female presence in the military."

Mitchell hit hard again and again at the military leaders who have, by his lights, ignored the welfare of children in military families.

"How can any of this be good for them?" asked Mitchell. Referring to the problem of so-called joint assignments in which both a husband and a wife are sent overseas, Mitchell warned, "You could have children orphaned because of a political imperative to use women in the military in the same way that you use men."

Mitchell predicted that six months to a year after everyone is home from the Persian Gulf, and after the hurrahs and congratulations, studies will be prepared for arguments against heavy reliance on women in the military.

"The military has not been able, politically, to do this until now. Now at least they have an operation, an experience they can point to and say, 'This is not good.'"

From sources within the Pentagon itself, as well as some in the Persian Gulf, Mitchell reports he has heard that at least three female soldiers have been sent home for being charged with prostitution. Pregnancy rates are said to be even higher than the 10 percent of military females that are normally pregnant at any given time.

"All sorts of problems are cropping up," Mitchell said. "Women are not as effective, partially because they require more medical attention."

Pro-Family Forces

Problems such as those pointed to by critics like Donnelly and Mitchell provide a ready storehouse of ammunition for pro-family forces in the Congress. Reform is clearly needed if we are to avoid a tragedy.

Some no doubt will resist all evidence, all common sense. Rep. Patricia Schroeder (D.-Colo.), a long-time proponent of women in the combat arms, scolded, "We have to be careful we don't start talking about 'Mommy Tracking.'"

In truth, what we really need to be careful of is "Mommy Burying."

Medals on Our Blouses? Neither Women nor Men Should Fight in Combat

Mary E. Hunt

About the Author: *Mary E. Hunt, a Roman Catholic feminist theologian, is co-director of the Women's Alliance for Theology, Ethics, and Ritual (WATER). WATER is a nonprofit institute in Silver Spring, Maryland, which explores religious issues from a feminist perspective.*

Women in combat came to public attention during the U.S. invasion of Panama in late 1989. The situation in the Middle East raises the question of their presence once more. The result of the discussion is a no-win situation for women, damned to discrimination if they cannot fight and damned to combat if they can. This reality presents a dilemma for religious feminists who believe in the equality of women but reject combat as a solution to global conflict. The dynamic is reminiscent of the struggle for equality in the board room though we may reject capitalism, equality at the altar although we may reject patriarchal religions, and so forth.

Little did I dream that the Persian Gulf War would emerge, adding analytic data to my earlier concern. At this writing, thousands of U.S. servicewomen are baking in the desert and dodging missiles along with their male counterparts. Some may come home in body bags. . . . The issues take on even greater urgency than they did following the Panama incursion when

Mary E. Hunt, "Medals on Our Blouses? A Feminist Theological Look at Women in Combat," *Waterwheel,* a quarterly newsletter of the Women's Alliance for Theology, Ethics, and Ritual, vol. 3, no. 3, Fall 1990. Reprinted with permission.

no one really raised the question until a U.S. victory over a weak opponent was assured. This time such a victory is not as likely. Ironically, tabloid stories of grandmothers going off to war and style section accounts of husbands left behind struggling to find the diapers are the flimsy substance of the current public debate. Will women simply fight and talk about it later?

There are more than 225,000 women in the U.S. combined armed services making up 11% of the total; estimates of their numbers in the Middle East indicate that they are probably about 10% of the total there. Officially they are in non-combat roles, but the threat of chemical warfare and the rigor of the conditions in Saudi Arabia render that distinction dubious if not moot.

What begs analysis is whether this is a feminist achievement or a patriarchal ploy. Is it proof that women can and should do anything men do, or a good example of how even feminism can be coopted to serve the end of patriarchal power structures?

On the one hand, I urge women's equality in and access to all avenues of society. On the other hand, I oppose combat almost without nuance. Thus I am left in a kind of feminist limbo, having to sanction, at least implicitly, something that I oppose in the name of affirming something that I support.

"I urge women's equality in and access to all avenues of society."

I embrace the notion of women in the military with all of the enthusiasm I reserve for women in the episcopacy, and perhaps a little less. While I understand that cosmetic changes alter the aesthetic, I am not persuaded that they finally change structures at all. Rather, I suspect that in certain instances, as in the case of women in hierarchical leadership in sacramental churches, such additions of women to the structures may serve to maintain rather than to dismantle those structures. The Roman Catholic Church, like the military, is hierarchical by design, de facto and de jure excluding women from leadership and decision-making roles, and using outmoded reasons for doing so that mask the real issue, namely, whether this model of religion, like this model of military, is good for anyone, male or female.

Alleged Equality

My basic worry about women in combat is the liberal claim that equality demands it. I wonder if there aren't really places, the combat-ready military for one, where alleged equality is really the diminution of the human spirit, beginning with women's and including men's, hence reinforcing rather than shifting the power equation.

Many issues call for attention. Inevitably the point is raised about women's competence and suitability for combat. In 1991 this sounds like a pitiful pedestrian concern about women's strength and spunk when evidence is plentiful that some women, as some men, are more than qualified for combat. Since modern warfare is based more on technology than brute strength, and since some women's physical strength surpasses some men's, this issue no longer commands sustained discussion except to point out how dated it is.

Politely speaking, combat does not require the highest mental, physical or spiritual capacity known to humanity. Just as some men are not physically and/or psychologically suited for combat, neither are some women. The point is that one qualified woman would be enough to justify inclusion of women in combat on the grounds of equal access, just as one Afro-American, one Hispanic and/or one Asian-American man was, in principle, sufficient to integrate the ranks.

Asking the question, "Should women be in combat?" borders on the disingenuous. It presumes that women are not in combat and that it is an ethical question asked by those who would protect women's virtue out of concern for women's well-being. The fact is that women are in combat already, virtue or no. It is time to reframe the question to reflect the reality.

Captain Linda Bray led her troops in Panama to a dog kennel where enemy troops were alleged to have been hiding. Gunfire was exchanged. This is combat by any definition, and Captain Bray is a woman. Hence my claim that women are engaging in combat is proved albeit by an incident that was embarrassing to the military when it handed out combat medals. The question would be usefully reframed as "What does it mean that women are in combat?" this being the concern of those who stress strict equality; or "Should anyone be in combat?" or "How can we avoid combat?" These questions, virtually absent from public debate, are kept at bay by continually asking the wrong "should" question.

Another issue is whether war is really a male construct, something that women will imitate when given the chance but would probably not come up with on their own. I am increasingly leery of any brands of feminism that make earth mothers of all females, positing certain qualities of harmony and well-being to women, while saddling men with the blame for aggressive, bellicose behavior. I have seen enough pacifist men and been involved in enough feminist battles to know the difference.

"One qualified woman would be enough to justify inclusion of women in combat on the grounds of equal access."

Still, at times when men have held sway, which would be most of recorded history, conflicts have been solved by fighting rather than developing consensus. Women, on the other hand, have been responsible for a range of anti-war efforts, prominent recent ones including the Jeannette Rankin Brigade during the Vietnam War, the Greenham Common and Seneca Peace Encampments against nuclear weapons, the Madres de Plaza de Mayo and other groups of relatives of disappeared persons in Latin America, the leaders of which are usually women.

The most persuasive case for women advancing in the military, something that combat hastens, is the practical case in terms of employment and future benefits. While it is true that combat is a sure route to decorations and promotions and for this reason women should have access, such arguments miss another point; namely, the erosion of military benefits at a time when those who sign up are disproportionately poor, people of color, and lacking in basic educational skills.

"The Catch-22 for women in the military . . . is that they must conform to a norm in which what is feminine is inferior."

The G.I. Bill, long considered a ticket to higher education after military service, now requires that military personnel contribute financially during the time served in order to be eligible afterwards. This is something many women who struggle to make ends meet on a military salary, especially if they have children, cannot afford and/or do not think they will ever use. Hence they lose out from the beginning due to inadequate counseling and the economic disadvantage with which they began their service. So much for an equal opportunity employer in an unequal society.

Likewise, many military training programs that attract women have little transfer value outside the military.

The much touted military discipline, "guaranteed to make a man out of you," is similarly dubious for women. Hazing and harassment that bonded men to other men in the homosocial environment that used to be the military in "the good old days" has not been redesigned to take into account women's ways of bonding.

Sexual harassment is common. Abuse, even rapes have been reported. The notorious case of a woman student at the U.S. Naval Academy, Gwen Marie Dreyer, being chained to a urinal by eight of her male classmates, then photographed for their pleasure just before the Army-Navy football game, touched off an investigation of that institution. The Committee on Women's Issues, including Sen. Barbara Mikulski (D-Maryland), found that "there are structural impediments to assimilation of women" at Annapolis and that "breakdown in civility and discipline contributes to sexual harassment at the academy." It is reported that "low-level sexual harassment can pass as normal operating procedure" among some students and faculty.

The Catch-22 for women in the military, and especially for women in combat, is that they must conform to a norm in which what is feminine is inferior. Recruits are taunted with the epithet "girls" if they do not perform properly. It is one thing for a young man to have stereotypically masculine traits ingrained into him, quite another for women. Women must choose between participating in the implicit degradation of all women by tolerating the abusive macho practices, or distinguish themselves as feminists or be accused of being lesbians because they maintain their integrity as women in a system in which being a woman under any circumstance is wrong. This dynamic leaves me pessimistic about rapid changes in military life even if women enter combat, and fearful that women who do will be victimized by enemies on both sides, including their would-be comrades. Who would want her daughter in such a situation?

Gender-linked Patriotism

Even patriotism is gender-linked in a patriarchal society. While for men the ultimate expression of loyalty to one's country is to serve honorably in the military, in combat if necessary, women are given a very different message. To serve in the military, other than as a nurse or in some other support position, is at best anomalous, at worst invading men's territory, in short unpatriotic. It never occurs to people that groups like Women's International League for Peace and

Freedom, Women Strike for Peace and similar groups express a kind of patriotism that both women and men would do well to imitate. Rather, the gender-bound nature of patriotism, like every other gender-bound dimension of society, is kept under wraps until women cross the gender line as in the case of combat. Then it rears its ugly head, confusing those who do not perceive the message and punishing those who do.

This analysis, while only hinting at the complexity at hand, helps to highlight the feminist dilemma around women in combat. It is further complicated by the problems that such women face when they seek combat positions in a society in which fundamental equality in other arenas is denied.

Impact on Children

The major impact is on children who, despite feminists' best efforts at shared responsibility, are generally cared for by women. While there are cases in the current "Operation Desert Storm" where both parents are on duty with children being left in the care of grandparents, future combat for women may mean increasing problems for children especially if, as is the case with many, the mother is a single parent.

It does not follow that women should not be in combat, but that men ought to assume an equal role in child rearing. Such not being the case, women's entrance into combat, and the injuries and deaths that will inevitably result, will bear disproportionately on children. Our society seems reluctant to equalize such responsibilities outside the combat situation, and/or to develop adequate support structures for most children. Perhaps women's increased participation in the military will have the unexpected side benefit of hastening the day when men assume their fair share of child-rearing.

This difficult scenario admits of no easy feminist solution. Involved are not only deeply held beliefs about the inferiority of women, but also economic, political and racial structures that guarantee that the impact of such beliefs will be felt most profoundly by young, poor women of color who will be the first female cannon fodder when combat is officially opened to women, and the ones to suffer most economically if it is not.

I suggest three preliminary moves toward resolving the question from a feminist perspective. First, it is important to insist on reframing the question, beginning with acknowledging that women are in combat and then asking whether *anyone* should be. Women have learned that how such questions are framed, indeed who frames the questions, determines the answers.

We can redirect the analysis to question whether anyone, male or female, is usefully dispatched to combat at a time when nuclear, chemical and even some conventional weapons virtually assure mass destruction. We are not talking about hand-to-hand combat with national security at risk due to women's lack of upper body strength.

A second feminist ethical move is to take the debate to where women are, to listen to their perceptions, and to theorize out of that base. This kind of grassroots, participatory ethical model avoids the pitfalls of dogmatic liberal feminism wherein mostly white women in no danger of combat make decisions for those who are faced with the choice. More important, it avoids the pitfalls of patriarchy by educating women to listen to one another instead of to the conventional wisdom, especially in this kind of life/death situation.

> **"The gender-bound nature of patriotism . . . is kept under wraps until women cross the gender line as in the case of combat."**

Women's lives have always been considered expendable in a patriarchal society, so there is reason to think that once combat is open to women it would serve the interest of society to fill the ranks with women. Such a sinister plot may seem more the stuff of a Margaret Atwood novel than of a civilized country, but the U.S. track record on abortion, for example, seems to indicate that women's well-being is a low priority. As in the abortion case, I trust women to make responsible decisions as women have made throughout history. Opening combat to women and then coping with the massive numbers of women who conscientiously object would be a strong statement. Support for such a move will be garnered by inviting women to discuss these matters and then to strategize creatively on the basis of their discussions. I would bet on this or another equally creative option as an alternative to gung-ho militarism from most women.

"Women's lives have always been considered expendable in a patriarchal society."

A third feminist move is to broaden the ethical umbrella to include men in the company of those who, in the name of equality, stress peace, justice and cooperation. This is perhaps the most promising strategy because it accomplishes two goals at once. On the one hand, it models equality by insisting that whatever solutions we hope to implement will have to include women and men working together (in sharp contrast to the military decisions about women in combat that are made by all-male combat-trained soldiers). On the other hand, it offers an alternative to the "equality at any price" liberalism that would tolerate women in combat in order to achieve that goal. It takes account of the reality of unequal power dynamics for women and men that assume that equality is impossible in patriarchy and that women will always pay disproportionately for their rights.

This strategy is also practical since it gives peace groups a concrete "both-and" goal. Both gender equality and peace can be pursued through creative educational programs, counseling for women and men about alternatives to military service that will result in job skills and express their patriotism. Children of both genders can see Mom and Dad resisting participation in a military machine that would happily take both of them. And even men and women in the military can consider their role in preventing future wars. Obviously this is a long term, perhaps unachievable goal, but it sets a trajectory for educational programs, lobbying, resistance efforts, tax withholding and other effective strategies that women and men can engage in together before it is too late.

The Combat Exclusion Law Is Necessary

Phyllis Schlafly

About the Author: *Phyllis Schlafly is a well-known conservative writer and activist who publishes the monthly newsletter* The Phyllis Schlafly Report. *Schlafly supports traditional family values and traditional roles for men and women.*

Present [U.S.] military policy is based on the feminist notion that there is no difference between motherhood and fatherhood, and that after maternity leave, the new mother is fully deployable to anywhere in the world. After all, she voluntarily enlisted, so she is supposed to make daycare arrangements for her baby.

This is the policy which the American people watched in amazement when they saw press photos of nursing mothers of six-, 10-, and 12-week-old babies—plus mothers of two and three preschool children—being shipped out to the Persian Gulf war. Some were women on active duty; some were women called up from the reserves after completing their term of enlistment.

The sending of these mothers out to fight a war shows that the military has acquiesced in the feminist fallacy that having a baby is no more incapacitating than breaking a leg; i.e., after six weeks or so, the person is fully deployable.

Pregnancy and motherhood are simply not compatible with military service. It is wrong to pretend that a woman who is pregnant or has a baby is ready to ship out to fight a war. She is not ready, and she should not be paid as though she were ready.

It is ridiculous even to discuss women in combat until the military comes to grips with the pregnancy and motherhood questions. The present policies are contrary to combat readiness, common sense and respect for family integrity.

When the press photos of mothers tearfully saying goodbye to their infants hit the press, the feminists responded by seeking a gender-neutral legislative response. They tried to divert public discussion to problems of single parents and of dual-career military parents deployed to the gulf. But pregnancy and motherhood are not gender-neutral situations, and we should not pretend they are. Human experience recognizes that the mother of a six-week-old baby can never be combat-ready like the father of a six-week-old baby.

The military has consistently concealed how many mothers of babies were deployed to the gulf war. The public is entitled to know this figure. Instead, the military has released only the figure of "single parents" and asserts that there are more single parent fathers than mothers.

It is evidence of the dishonesty of the military that one statistic lumps together both mothers who have recently given birth and have custody of small children along with fathers who do not have custody at all. The pretense that this is the same problem is a fantasy propagated by childless feminists.

"West Point has dual standards for males and females."

We need an investigation of the stress that the gulf war placed on mothers and on their children when women with babies under age three were deployed to the gulf war. How did these mothers perform on the job when they were yearning for their babies at home?

In addition, our society has an obligation to be concerned about the harm caused to the babies by sending their mothers out to the gulf war. It is a national embarrassment that the Pentagon acquiesced in the feminist delusion that

Excerpted from Phyllis Schlafly, "Women in Combat Will Weaken the American Military," speech given at The Heritage Foundation, June 1991. Reprinted with permission.

driving a jeep in the Middle East was more important than a mother taking care of her own baby.

The Affirmative Action Quota Problem—Repealing the combat exclusion laws so that women officers can fly planes in military combat would mean affirmative action quotas for women in an occupation in which they cannot compete equally with men. We know this would be the result because of the mountain of evidence that women are not performing equally with men in military service today.

"The qualities that make [men] good soldiers . . . are conspicuously absent in women."

We can thank the recent Virginia Military Institute (VMI) trial for providing us with proof about how affirmative action functions for female cadets at West Point. Those who are suing VMI to force it to admit women and to feminize its curriculum called as their witness Col. Patrick Toffler, a West Point spokesman, who was supposed to testify that sexual integration is a success at the U.S. Military Academy. During five hours of cross-examination under oath, he revealed a lot of things that West Point has heretofore concealed.

Col. Toffler admitted that West Point does not require the same physical performance of female cadets that it requires of male cadets. He admitted that West Point has dual standards for males and females; that women cadets do not pass the same physical tests as men, and that if they perform the same task, the women are given higher grades. Female cadets are allowed to hold leadership positions based on their padded scores.

Toffler admitted how the training has been changed—"modified," he called it—to accommodate what the female cadets are physically capable of doing and so that they would not be "psychologically discouraged"; e.g., a number of

events have been eliminated from the obstacle course "which require considerable upper-body strength;" cadets now run in jogging shoes instead of in boots; a lighter-weight rifle has been substituted; judo is allowed to substitute for boxing; and the forced march carrying a heavy pack has been eliminated.

Col. Toffler admitted that West Point has a sexual quota system for the admission of women cadets and for their assignment after graduation (such as to the engineers). "Those quotas have got to be met," he said. The women cadets do not compete with the men, but compete only against each other for designated female quota slots.

Toffler admitted that to accommodate the women who cannot perform as well as the men, West Point has changed from equal training of all cadets to "comparable or equivalent training." This is a concept that if men and women exert equivalent effort, they will be ranked as though they had achieved equal performance. An example is the pull-ups, which women lack the arm strength to do, so they are required only to exert "comparable effort" to do a "flexed arm hang."

No Free Speech

Col. Toffler admitted that no free speech is permitted about the performance of women at West Point. Female cadets are allowed to correct their superiors who use such words as "chairman" instead of "chairperson," but men are not permitted to make any negative statement about women in the military.

The *New York Times* reported on May 26, 1991, that it is a "career-killer" for a man to utter anything negative about the performance of women. Toffler even said that the cadets are given sensitivity training to help promote acceptance of the sexually integrated program.

This situation is similar to affirmative action for minorities, which has been taking place for years while authorities have been denying it and covering it up.

When a student at Georgetown University exposed the truth about minority quotas for admission to law school, he narrowly escaped expulsion because the authorities did not want their practice known. The American public has just discovered that for the last 10 years the government has been engaging in a process called "race norming," i.e., falsifying the employment test scores of minorities and then deceiving prospective employers.

"It is a 'career-killer' for a man to utter anything negative about the performance of women."

Thanks to Col. Toffler's sworn testimony, we know that West Point has been engaged in a similar practice—we might call it "sex norming"—and then hiding it from the public.

We can also reasonably infer that the practice at West Point is carried on also at the Naval and Air Force academies. We can also reasonably infer that the same practice would obtain if female officers were admitted into the highly demanding and competitive program for flying combat aircraft precisely because the prime candidates for these jobs would be the female Academy graduates who have enjoyed affirmative action benefits ever since they entered the military.

The Problem of Who Makes the Combat Decision—The congressional news release issued after the Schroeder amendment was passed in a closed House Armed Services Committee meeting explained it thus: "The committee action would not require the services to place women on combat missions, but would give them the option by lifting the statutory prohibition that exists today for the Air Force and Navy."

"Allow" and "option" are certainly very different words from "assign" and "require." It is probable that, when the House Armed Services Committee passed the Schroeder amendment, the members thought they were merely giving the military the discretion to open some combat jobs to women.

However, this plan to pass the buck from Congress to the Armed Services was knocked into a cocked hat when Assistant Secretary of Defense for Manpower and Personnel Christopher Jehn gave a written response to questions from the Senate Armed Services Committee in which he stated that if Congress gives the Defense Department the authority to allow women to serve in combat jobs, the Department of Defense will "be obligated" to use that authority. It is one thing to "allow" the Defense Department to open some combat jobs to women, and it is something else to mandate the assignment of women to combat jobs and missions, just like men.

The Problem of Enlisted Women Versus Female Officers—All this push for women in combat is coming only from the female officers. Enlisted women do *not* want repeal of the combat exclusion laws. The women officers are seeking their career advancement at the expense of the enlisted women who would get the heavy and dangerous work without any of the glamour of piloting planes.

Repealing the combat exclusion laws would betray the enlisted women because they signed up when the law assured them they would be excluded from combat.

Prof. Charles Moskos of Northwestern University interviewed scores of women who served in the Panama invasion, and he did not find *any* enlisted women who favor repeal of the combat exclusion laws.

A Gender-neutral Society

The two laws which would be repealed by the Schroeder amendment do not cover the Army, which maintains its combat exclusion policy by Army regulation. However, this Army policy is clearly tied to and grounded in the legislative policy established by Congress through the combat exclusion laws that apply to the Air Force, Navy and Marines. The repeal of those laws would cut the constitutional ground out from under the Army policy.

The oft-stated goal of the radical feminists is a

totally gender-neutral society, and the military is the cutting edge. Their three-step scenario to achieve this goal starts with repealing the combat exclusion laws, while telling the public that this change would apply only to women who volunteer.

Step number two will be to make the draft registration law gender neutral, while reassuring the public that a draft will never be reimposed.

Step number three will be to impose some kind of conscription or universal military service, thereby inducting young women along with young men.

"Sending moms to battle is not acceptable to any Americans except the radical feminists."

Most advocates of repealing the combat-exclusion laws admit that they seek a reimposition of the draft. That may seem unlikely, but then who would have guessed that any congressmen would have voted to send women into military combat? The radical feminists would then be able to use the raw power of government to force us toward the gender-neutral society which is their long-time goal.

The Problem with Advocates' Arguments—The advocates of assigning women to military combat assert that American attitudes have changed. On the contrary, an Associated Press poll of February 1991 reported that the American public by a 2-to-1 vote thinks that the military policy of sending mothers to the gulf war was wrong. Sending moms to battle is not acceptable to any Americans except the radical feminists who are over military and childbearing age and haven't any daughters.

The advocates of assigning women to military combat assert that the 33,000 women who served in the Persian Gulf proved that women can and should serve in combat.

First of all, by any historical standard, the gulf war was not real combat; it was, as one soldier described it, "a turkey shoot."

During the entire six-week war, with some 540,000 Americans in the region, only about 100 U.S. troops died from hostile fire as compared to more than 100,000 enemy deaths—a precedent-shattering ratio of 1,000 to 1.

The few U.S. servicewomen who were killed in the gulf war prove only that women in a war zone can be killed, which was always obvious. These deaths certainly do not prove that units comprising both men and women can survive successfully when engaging in combat. Combat occurs when a unit must keep fighting while members of the unit are being killed by enemy fire. Even the mini-invasion of Panama provided more combat than the gulf war.

We do not know what the gulf war proved about the performance of servicewomen there because the military would not tell us. The American public got only the news which the military chose to give us, and, as reported by the *New York Times*, military policy permits no negative comment about the performance of women.

The Problem of the Feminist Attack on American Culture—The combat exclusion laws are a rational legislative recognition of fundamental differences between men and women. The combat exclusion laws have been fully supported by the American people through all the wars of this century. The armies and navies of every potential enemy are exclusively male, and no women diminish their combat readiness.

Fighting wars is a mission that requires tough, tenacious and courageous men to endure the most primitive and uncivilized situations and pain in order to survive, plus determination to kill enemies who are just as tough, tenacious and courageous, and probably vicious and sadistic, too.

Masculine Character

Men are attracted to serve in the military because of its intensely masculine character. The qualities that make them good soldiers—aggressive, risk taking, and enjoyment of body-contact competition—are conspicuously absent in women. Pretending that women can perform equally with men in tasks that require those attributes is not only dishonest; it corrupts the system.

Only a tiny minority of American women choose a military career at all, and of those only a tiny minority are agitating to get combat jobs (in peacetime, of course), namely, the officers. This little group of ambitious women should not be allowed to impose their peculiar views of gender neutrality on our nation.

The whole idea of men sending women, including mothers, out to fight the enemies is uncivilized, degrading, barbaric and embarrassing. It is contrary to our culture, to our respect for men and women, and to our belief in the importance of the family and motherhood. And furthermore, no one respects a man who would let a woman do his fighting for him.

Chapter 3

Does Discrimination Harm Women in the Military?

Women's Experiences in the Military: An Overview

Charles Moskos

About the Author: *Charles Moskos is a professor of sociology at Northwestern University in Evanston, Illinois. Two of his most recent books are* The Military *and* A Call to Civic Service.

Editor's Note: The armed forces fully integrated women into their ranks in the mid-1970s. Since then, military laws and regulations have been aimed at eliminating discrimination based on gender. In spite of this official policy, many observers believe that military women are still victims of discrimination, sexual harassment, and disrespect.

According to Dorothy and Carl J. Schneider, authors of Sound Off! American Military Women Speak Out, *the military woman "must waste the energy that men can save for their jobs or their pleasures in proving herself, in smashing stereotypes and overcoming prejudice."*

Others believe the armed forces have fulfilled their promise to eliminate discrimination against women. As evidence, these people point to the women who have reached the top levels of the military. In 1990, there were three women brigadier generals in the army, three women rear admirals in the navy, and two women brigadier generals in the air force. In the opinion of a woman army captain interviewed by writer Fern Marja Eckman, "If you want equality, then join the army."

Because discrimination may prevent military women from serving to the best of their ability, the issue of gender discrimination is of crucial importance to all those concerned with the effectiveness of America's armed forces. Does discrimination harm women in the military? The following overview by Charles Moskos shows the variety of experiences women have in the United States Army.

At 0055 hours on December 20, 1989, U.S. Army helicopters lifted off from Howard Air Force Base, in Panama, to carry infantry across the Panama Canal. Their mission was to assault Fort Amador, one of the few strongholds of the Panamanian Defense Forces [PDF] to offer resistance to the American forces that had invaded Panama as part of Operation Just Cause. Two of the helicopter pilots ferrying the troops were women: First Lieutenant Lisa Kutschera and Warrant Officer Debra Mann. Their Black Hawk helicopters, officially designated transport, not attack, aircraft, carried troops into what turned out to be "hot" areas, where the PDF was firing on helicopters. For their participation in the assault Kutschera and Mann (and their male counterparts) would be awarded Air Medals—a much coveted decoration. . . .

"Some eight hundred female soldiers participated in the invasion of Panama."

All told, some 800 female soldiers participated in the invasion of Panama, out of a total of 18,400 soldiers involved in the operation. Probably about 150 of the women were in the immediate vicinity of enemy fire. Owing to the publicity that women performing hazardous duty attracted, the once-dormant issue of the ban on women in combat units suddenly came awake.

Title 10 of the U.S. Code precludes women from serving aboard combat vessels or aircraft. Although there are actually no statutory restrictions on how Army women can be deployed, the Army derived its combat-exclusion policy from Title 10 and prohibits women from joining direct combat units in the infantry, armor forces, cannon-artillery forces, and combat engineers.

Adapted from Charles Moskos, "Army Women," *The Atlantic*, August 1990. Reprinted with permission.

The Army's formal definition reads as follows: "Direct combat is engaging an enemy with individual or crew-served weapons while being exposed to direct enemy fire, a high probability of direct physical contact with the enemy's personnel, and a substantial risk of capture."

Although many obstacles to women's participation in the military have been overcome, the line that excludes women from combat units has not yet been crossed. None of the women who participated in the Panama invasion, even those who came in harm's way, were assigned to combat units. Rather, they were serving as military police, medical and administrative staff, and members of transportation, communications, maintenance, and other support units.

The issue of women in combat highlights the dramatic recent changes in the role of women in the military. Visitors at most military installations today will see women in numbers and roles unthinkable at the time the Vietnam War ended. Some 230,000 women now make up about 11 percent of all military personnel on active duty. Each branch of the military has a distinctive history with respect to women. The Air Force, which is 14 percent female, has the highest proportion of jobs open to women, mainly because none of its ground jobs involve combat. Although women are precluded from piloting bombers and fighter planes, they fly transport planes and serve on the crews of refueling planes, such as those that took part in the 1986 U.S. raid on Libya. The Navy, which is 10 percent female, did not allow women on ships other than hospital ships until 1977, but today women sailors serve aboard transport and supply ships. The Marine Corps is only five percent female, because a high proportion of its members serve in the combat arms. The Army, which is 11 percent female, has the largest total number of women (86,000), and is the vanguard service insofar as the role of women is concerned

My research as a military sociologist has allowed me to observe at close hand the changing face of the Army since my days as a draftee, in the late 1960s. The account that follows, which briefly surveys the life, the sentiments, and the aspirations of women in the U.S. Army, draws upon my observations of Army units around the world but is based mainly on interviews with soldiers of every rank who participated in the invasion of Panama, including most of the women soldiers who were closest to the shooting.

Some Background

When the second world war broke out, the only women in the armed services were nurses. But manpower needs caused the precursor to the Women's Army Corps (WAC) to be established in May of 1942, followed shortly thereafter by the Navy's WAVES (Women Accepted for Voluntary Emergency Service) and the Coast Guard's SPARs (from "*Semper Paratus*: Always Ready"). Women were allowed into the Marine Corps in 1943, and, refreshingly, these volunteers were called simply Women Marines. Some 800 civilian women who served as Air Force service pilots flew military aircraft across the Atlantic. The Women in the Air Force (WAF) was created in 1948, after the Air Force had become a separate service.

"The issue of women in combat highlights the dramatic recent changes in the role of women in the military."

The Women's Armed Services Integration Act of 1948 gave permanent status to military women, but with the proviso that there would be a two-percent ceiling on the proportion of women in the services (excluding nurses). No female generals or admirals were to be permitted. For the next two decades women averaged only a little over one percent of the armed forces, and nearly all of them did "traditional" women's work, in health-care and clerical jobs. During the Vietnam War some 7,500 women served in Vietnam, mostly in the Army. The names of eight women are engraved on the Vietnam Veterans Memorial, in Washington, D.C.

Starting in the 1970s a series of barriers fell in relatively rapid succession. On June 11, 1970, women were promoted to the rank of general for the first time in U.S. history. The new generals were Anna Mae Hayes, of the Army Nurse Corps, and Elizabeth P. Hoisington, the director of the WACs. Women first entered the Reserve Officer Training Corps on civilian college campuses in 1972. Much more traumatic was the admission in 1976 of the first female cadets into the service academies. Today one of seven entrants to West Point is female, although, if truth be told, most of the male cadets are not yet reconciled to the presence of women.

A Glimpse of Daily Life

Congress abolished the WACs in 1978, leading to the direct assignment of women soldiers to non-combat branches of the Army. Today 86 percent of all military occupational specialties (MOSes) for enlisted personnel are open to women. . . .

I flew down to Panama shortly after the invasion and, with the Army's permission, talked to scores of soldiers and investigated their living conditions. The enlistment motivations of the men and women I spoke to differed in important respects. For the typical male, economic realities were predominant. Most admitted to having seen few job opportunities in civilian life. The decision to enlist was usually supported by family and friends. For many of the men, joining the Army seemed to be the path of least resistance. The women soldiers were much more likely to have entered the military for noneconomic reasons. They also seemed to be more independent and adventurous than the men. Often they had not received much encouragement from their parents to join the service. Many of the men, and even more of the women, were attracted by the Army's postservice educational benefits. For the women, joining the Army was the result of a decision to "do something different" and get away from a "boring" existence in some backwater community. . . .

Many of the women had spent time on field maneuvers, living in tents. Since most of the women were assigned to combat-support functions, they were often able to live in large general-purpose tents. Work sections sleep together in one tent during field exercises whenever possible. This is true whether sections are male-only or mixed-sex. Women drape blankets over a rope between the main tent poles to gain some privacy, although someone on the other side can easily peer over the top. In mixed-sex tents the men generally display some regard for privacy, although not always as much as the women would like. Most of the women sleep in gym clothes or their BDUs (battle dress uniforms), as fatigues are now called. Others become acrobats and manage to change clothes inside their sleeping bags. Almost all the women said they would prefer to sleep in a mixed-sex tent with workmates rather than in a female-only tent with strangers.

"The enlistment motivations of the men and women I spoke to differed in important respects."

Personal cleanliness and hygiene are of much greater concern to women than to men in the field. Even under the tense, busy circumstances of Panama, the women tried to bathe once a day. One young female soldier insisted (wrongly) to me that Army regulations guarantee women a shower at least once every three days. How to wash became almost an obsession for women in the field. One method was to post a guard outside a tent and take a "bird bath," using a can of hot water. One unit moved garbage cans inside the tent for the women to use as stand-up bathtubs. When outside shower facilities were all that was available, women often showered in their BDUs. Female soldiers are expected to plan ahead and provide their own sanitary napkins or tampons. In Panama tampons had to be drawn from the medical-supply system rather than the regular quartermaster system. This created problems for some women in the early days of the invasion. But once life began to return to normal, tampons (and women's underwear) could be readily bought at the post exchange. All in all, menstruation did not seem to worry the female soldiers I spoke with, and it was never invoked as an excuse for absence from work.

Sexual Harassment

Sexual harassment is one of the issues most frequently discussed by women in the military. Enlisted women and female officers differ on this matter in important ways. Enlisted women, like most men of any rank, define sexual harassment mainly in terms of sexual propositions and actual touching. One female sergeant put it this way: "Sexual harassment is making unwelcome advances the second time." Enlisted women also tend to see sexual harassment in almost fatalistic terms, something that "goes with the territory" and is often brought on by the behavior of the woman. But they do not consider every advance to be harassment. Fraternization between men and women among enlisted personnel in the Army (and among Army officers) is as common as it is among students at a coeducational college, and is accepted as normal if it occurs among soldiers (or officers) of the same rank. Most women soldiers who have boyfriends have boyfriends who are soldiers, and the women who are married are far more likely to be married to soldiers than married male soldiers are.

Female officers understand sexual harassment in much broader terms, to include sexist remarks, sex-based definitions of suitable work, the combat-exclusion rule, and so on. Women officers see sexism in the military as something that requires constant vigilance. One lieutenant told me that she found it a "welcome challenge to deal with male chauvinists on a daily basis."

Another form of sexual harassment was mentioned by the enlisted women: approaches from lesbians. The true incidence of lesbianism (and of male homosexuality) in the military is un-

known. There are indications that lesbianism is more widespread in the armed forces than is male homosexuality. Defense Department statistics, whether they reflect selective prosecution or not, show that women are discharged for lesbianism almost ten times as often, proportionately, as men are discharged for homosexuality. Accounts of lesbianism were offered spontaneously in most of my extended interviews with female soldiers. My general impression was that lesbianism causes much less alarm among women soldiers than homosexuality does among the men. Whereas male soldiers expressed disdain for homosexuals with sardonic humor if not threats of violence, the women were more likely to espouse an attitude of live and let live.

"Women officers see sexism in the military as something that requires constant vigilance."

That enlisted women must face being characterized by many men in the military as either loose or lesbian is an unfortunate reality. These attitudes decline markedly when men and women work together over the long term. Such situations also seem eventually to bring out the best in the men. But sex-related issues by no means pervade the everyday existence of female soldiers. The most common topics of concern and conversation, for both sexes, appear to have little to do with sex. They have to do with the work of the Army and with the good and bad of military life.

Family Issues

The army's noncommissioned officers [NCO] inhabit the middle ground between the enlisted ranks and the officer corps. If women sometimes occupy an ambiguous position within the military, female NCOs occupy the most ambiguous position of all. One reason is that there are not many of them: only four percent of all senior sergeants are women.

One Sergeant First Class I interviewed, a personnel specialist, joined the Army in 1972. She told me, "I wanted to see the world, and I sure have—Korea, Germany, and now Panama. I was glad to see the WACs go. There were too many cliques and too much politics. The real problem now is that the female NCO is never taken as seriously as the male. Every time we are reassigned to a new unit, we have to prove ourselves all over again. Our credentials aren't portable like the men's."

Like many female NCOs, this woman admits to having few close friends in the military. "If you get too close to the men, they think you're having an affair. If you hang around with women, they think you're a lesbian. Let's face it, you can't really be one of the boys. The kind of insults men throw at each other a woman can't do, unless she wants to cross an invisible line of respect." The sergeant finally brought up the matter of marriage, which weighs heavily with female careerists in the Army: "I never married," she said, "because I just couldn't think of having children and making a go of an Army career." Only 60 percent of female senior NCOs are married, and of those only half have children. A military career works powerfully on military women to keep them single and childless.

"A military career works powerfully on military women to keep them single and childless."

Above the rank of noncommissioned officers in the Army is the officer corps, where today one lieutenant in six is female—but only one colonel in thirty. Only three of the Army's 407 general officers are women. Women officers feel the same pressures not to marry or raise children that female NCOs do—pressures that male soldiers do not feel. Many women officers believe that the demands of an Army career preclude having children, and they leave the service. Others make the Army a career, deciding to stay

childless. A female helicopter pilot told me, "Having no children is the sacrifice I make to keep flying." In 1989 among male senior officers 94 percent were married, and 90 percent of these had children; among female senior officers only 51 percent were married, and only half of these had children.

A small but growing group of junior female officers, however, seems to have devised a form of planned parenthood that can accommodate both family and career. It works like this. First, aim to be a company commander, an important "ticket to be punched" on the way up the promotion ladder. Company commanders are usually captains with six or seven years in service, people in their late twenties. Company command is a high-pressure job, but it is often followed by a slack time, such as an assignment to an ROTC position or a staff job in a headquarters command. Women officers are coming to regard this period as the most opportune to have a child.

Senior Officers

Almost all junior officers today are commissioned right after college. This contrasts with the biographies of today's senior women officers, who entered as WACs, often after some work experience. Brigadier General Evelyn "Pat" Foote, who was one of the Army's most senior women officers when she retired, in 1989, was well known in the military for being an outstanding and confident professional officer who spoke her mind. She joined the Army at age thirty after a string of white-collar jobs in which, she told me, she always seemed to be "somebody's girl Friday." In her nearly three decades in the Army, Foote served as the commander of a WAC company, as a public-affairs officer in Vietnam, as a faculty member at the Army War College, and as the commander of the Military Police Group in Mannheim, West Germany. She concluded her career as the commanding general of Fort Belvoir, Virginia. She has never married.

Foote espouses a philosophy that is embraced by most senior women officers, at least in private. They hope for a future that harks back to an era when women soldiers, in the main, were unmarried, had no children and few outside distractions, and were more committed to military service than their male counterparts. By now, of course, this is simply too much to expect of female career soldiers.

Foote recognizes that many Army women have been able to combine a military career, marriage, and children. She is adamant that there is little place in the Army for single pregnant women and single mothers. Certainly having pregnant soldiers in deployable units is "the height of folly." In 1988 eight percent of the total female enlisted force bore children; some 15 percent of all enlisted Army women are single parents. Before 1975 pregnant women were routinely discharged from the Army. Today, although pregnant women are ineligible for enlistment, they can remain in the Army if already enlisted. No one knows for sure, but informed sources believe that about a third of pregnant soldiers elect to have their babies and stay in the Army; the women are granted a six-week maternity leave. Another third have abortions and remain in the Army. The remainder leave the service after delivery. . . .

What About Combat?

The various arguments for and against women in combat are complex, and the issues involved are not subject to easy empirical resolution. Whether the propensity of most males to be more aggressive than most females is due mainly to body chemistry or to cultural conditioning is a matter of controversy; so is whether male bonding is chemical or cultural. There are social realities that need be considered, however. We should not forget, for example, that combat troops live, bathe, and sleep together for days and weeks on end. No institution in American society forces men and women into such unrelentingly close contact. That women could be killed or captured in war is a specter raised by those who oppose letting women into combat units. Is this really an issue? Female police offi-

cers have died in the line of duty without raising any particular outcry. On the touchy matter of prisoners of war, we have seen at least a symbolic change. In 1988 President Ronald Reagan signed an executive order revising the Code of Conduct for POWs [prisoners of war]. What formerly began with "I am an American fighting man" was changed to the gender-neutral and less bellicose "I am an American."

What we do know a lot about are differences between the sexes in physical strength and endurance. Statistically speaking, average female upper-body strength is 42 percent less than average male upper-body strength. Looked at another way, the statistics mean that on the average the top fifth of women in lifting capacity are the equal of the bottom fifth of men on the same measure. This means that any work requiring heavy lifting or carrying a great deal of weight—the burden of the combat soldier—puts women at a serious disadvantage. Opponents of the combat-exclusion rule point out that much of modern warfare is technological and "push-button" and does not require the brute strength of the combat soldier of old. There is some truth to this. But women are already allowed in almost all areas of technological warfare, including holding the launching keys of nuclear missiles. The irreducible fact remains that physical strength and endurance are still the hallmarks of the effective combat soldier on the ground; indeed, such qualities may be more important in the future, when we make use of rapid-deployment forces, whose members must carry most of their equipment on their backs. . . .

> ## "Many Army women have been able to combine a military career, marriage, and children."

For all this it is probably the case that most senior female officers privately second the views of General Foote on the subject of women and combat. Foote favors opening all roles to women in the Army, even in the combat arms. Being a woman per se should not, she says, be a disqualification for any military job. Of course, Foote recognizes the differences in strength between men and women. She acknowledges that few women belong in the infantry, and probably not many more belong in the armor or artillery, but says that certainly some could perform well in those roles, and there is no good reason to exclude women from combat aviation. Her basic position is this: "Never compromise standards. Be sure that anybody in any MOS can do everything required in that MOS.". . .

"No institution in American society forces men and women into such unrelentingly close contact."

How female officers and enlisted personnel variously gauge their future Army career opportunities makes for differing views on women in combat. Female officers see their career opportunities as diminishing as they become more senior. Without a chance for command assignments in combat units, the women officers believe, their careers are limited, especially by comparison with men's careers. Although a government study released in 1989 showed that women are promoted at a rate similar to that for men, the fact remains that the combat-exclusion rule precludes any significant number of women from becoming generals, or even full colonels. Among the female officers I talked with in Panama, about three quarters believed that qualified women should be allowed to volunteer for combat units and about a quarter said that women should be compelled to enter combat units, just as men are. A female military-police officer expressed the sentiments of most: "If a woman has the capability and gumption to enter a combat unit, I'd say go for it. Few of us could make it in the infantry. God forbid that the Army shoehorn women into the infantry to

meet some kind of quota. But a woman is as brave as a man, and we shouldn't be kept out of jobs we could do, no matter what the danger. Military women are their own worst enemy by accepting a lowering of physical standards. If we kept standards up, if we kept pregnant women out, then any woman in any MOS would be assigned wherever she was needed when the balloon goes up."

Women's Expectations

Enlisted women, on the other hand, are less subject to career disappointment, because their expectations are not high to begin with. Inasmuch as they generally did not see themselves in long-term Army roles, the women I spoke with thought of their service in Panama as a one-time-only adventure. Enlisted women foresaw their eventual life's meaning in family, in work outside the military, or if in the military, in relatively sedentary and routine jobs. Among the enlisted women I interviewed in Panama, about three quarters said that women should not be allowed in combat units and about a quarter said that women who were physically qualified should be allowed to volunteer for combat roles. None of the enlisted women favored forcing women into combat assignments. One female driver gave a typical enlisted woman's response: "I'm old-fashioned. I want to be treated like a woman. I don't want people to think I'm a man. I certainly wouldn't want to be in the infantry. A normal woman can't carry a rucksack that the guys can. Even if we could, the guys would hate us for being there. And, let's face it, we would probably make things harder on everybody all around. No way."

There is one area where the combat-exclusion rule is questioned by most women and some men: piloting helicopters. The skills required to fly a utility helicopter to transport soldiers into hot zones are not really all that different from those required on gunships such as Cobras and Apaches. In Panama the skills of the female pilots were acknowledged by all to be at least the equal of those of the male pilots. Even the

British high command, that most traditional of general staffs, is studying the possibility of allowing women to train as pilots for Harriers, the jump-jet fighters that saw so much action in the Falklands War. Were women to be assigned to U.S. gunships in future hostilities, however, they would almost surely suffer casualties. Even in the small, short war in Panama four helicopters were shot down and many more were hit by enemy fire.

Two things came out loud and clear in my Panama interviews. One is that the worst thing for a woman officer is to be removed from an assignment she has trained for simply because there is danger. A helicopter pilot told me how she felt on invasion day when she was denied a flight assignment that she thought was her due: "I was insane with anger. After nine years of training they left me out. It was the ultimate slam." The second point is that not a single woman, officer or enlisted, said that she would volunteer to be an infantry rifleman. Surely, somewhere in the U.S. Army, there are women who would volunteer for the infantry. But they were not in Panama.

An Unresolved Issue

Women in the military have been a troublesome issue for feminists. Feminists have also been troublesome for women in the military. Most feminists clearly want women to share equally the rights and burdens of service, but many of them abhor the combat role of the military profession and much of the basic direction of American foreign policy, which the military profession serves. That many of those who opposed the Panama invasion also advocate combat roles for women is indeed ironic. Female officers are understandably distrustful of much of the civilian feminist agenda, with its not-so-veiled anti-military content. Even as they chart new ground in opportunities for women, female officers are unquestionably less liberal politically, on average, than their civilian counterparts.

Where mainstream feminists and senior women officers come together is in their wish to do away with, or at least punch holes in, the categorical exclusion of women from direct combat roles. They see the exclusion as somehow precluding women from full citizenship. Following the Panama invasion and the reports of women in combat, the push to remove the last barriers to women's full participation in the military gained new momentum. Representative Patricia Schroeder, a senior Democrat on the House Armed Services Committee, proposed legislation to set up a trial program to test the suitability of women for the combat arms. Such a program had been recommended in 1989 by the Defense Advisory Committee on Women in the Services. In April 1990 the Army announced that it would not initiate such a trial program. But the Army's decision will not put the issue to rest. As long as there are women in the military, the pressures to end the combat-exclusion rule will remain.

Does Discrimination Harm Women in the Military?

Yes: Women in the Military Are Harmed by Discrimination

Women Experience Discrimination in the Military
Discrimination Makes Women Soldiers Ineffective
Combat Exclusion Promotes Widespread Discrimination in Society

Women Experience Discrimination in the Military

Dorothy and Carl J. Schneider

About the Authors: *Dorothy and Carl J. Schneider taught college courses for two years on American military bases for the University of Maryland's Far Eastern Division. The following viewpoint is an excerpt from their book* Sound Off! American Military Women Speak Out, *in which the authors interview more than three hundred servicewomen.*

" . . . this male-dominated institution, this job that's created for men."

"I feel that our male counterparts are beginning to accept us as people they can really truly depend on and work with. It's in the first stages of its . . . I don't know what the word is. It's metamorphosis."

Its 220,000 women comprise about the same proportion of the American military—10 to 11 percent—as black people comprise in American society at large. In this traditionally male stronghold, military women confront the problems of being a minority. Without safety in numbers, often lonely or even isolated, they know that everything they do is highly visible—and therefore highly vulnerable to criticism. They are excluded by law or tradition from the military's most prestigious occupations— just as black and Oriental men were in the past. And they are the objects of antagonism from some of the male majority.

"That was one of the hardest things for me to get used to, that I was in a fishbowl. Just the minute that I would do something, someone was always around say-

ing 'I knew it. They shouldn't have women in the Marine Corps. They're more problems than they're worth.' "

"A man can fall out every time or whine on field problems [training exercises] and it's not as big a deal. It's so much more obvious when a woman does something wrong."

Women are scarce to nonexistent in some segments of the military world: in the infantry and the artillery, on fighters and bombers, and on most Navy ships. Many a woman finds herself the only woman in the unit in which she works and lives—a lonely and sometimes a desperate life, requiring radical adaptations.

"In this traditionally male stronghold, military women confront the problems of being a minority."

Their scarcity and the rapid changes of the past decades have made military women willy-nilly collectors of "firsts," for which they pay a high price in isolation and exposure to criticism. Every senior woman we talked to, enlisted or officer, had her experiences as first woman in her unit, first in her rank, first in her MOS [military occupational specialty], first to attend a war college, in the first class at a service academy. We'd guess that fully 60 percent of all the women we talked to had chalked up at least one "first.". . .

"I think we have a lot of gentlemen in the Army that work hard, and they don't want that tagged on 'em, that they're a bunch of animals, 'cause there are a lot of nice people in the Army."

"Some of them still think, 'Women didn't go out and get their asses shot off to do this. We did. Why should women be allowed in the Corps?' "

The responses of military men to military women, say our interviewees, range all the way from support and protection to assault. One extreme: a supportive and pragmatic male supervisor, extolled by an Army E-4. "This Spec-4 used to harass me. He used to make his odd little comments. He was just being perverted. Finally I told my sergeant, 'Sergeant Mack, this guy's really getting to bother me.' Sergeant Mack says, 'Hit him.' I said, 'I can't hit him. He'll kill me.' And Sergeant Mack taught me—every day, after work, he'd teach me a karate move. He says, 'He's not going to mess with you.' So next time this guy said something to me, I hit him right smack in the chest. He never ever said nothing to me again. Sergeant Mack says, 'I could tell him to stop, but you have to make him stop. You can take it to your chain of command, but they're going to put him in jail, just for being obnoxious. If you can handle it yourself, handle it.'" Bless Sergeant Mack.

And the other extreme, a young male rampant: "In basic you go to church on Sunday, boy, just to get away from your TI [training instructor], whether you believed in God or not. I met this fellow at church. We were walking around the church grounds, broad daylight, and he pushes me in the bushes. I'm not thinking about what this guy is going to do to me. I'm thinking, 'My stockings are ripped. My uniform is dirty. I'm going to get in trouble with my TI.' And he jumps on top of me. I said, '*What* are you doing?' He said, 'Isn't that what WAFs [Women in the Air Force] are for?' Ohhhh. I was livid. I slapped him. Yeah, he backed off."

A Learning Process

As a Marine staff sergeant puts it, "It's a learning process for a lot of guys. Even now there are guys at this command, staff NCOs [noncommissioned officers], male Marines, this is the first place they've ever dealt with women on a professional basis. They think we shouldn't have gotten in World War I as Marinettes, much less have our Women Marine companies and then, God forbid, become a part of the regular Marine Corps.". . .

"Women are now issued seabags in the Coast Guard. My time, we had lockers. What does it mean? Equality! The men hated that we had a locker. They had to fold everything up and put it in their seabag. Now Women get their seabags and baseball caps. The Coast Guard has finally recognized that women are not a passing fancy. The future is now."

Some servicemen allege that women are always "getting over," not doing their share of the work, because they're given special treatment, because they're not strong enough, or because they're lazy. When someone has to carry a heavy load, the supervisor always calls for a man. The supervisor lets a woman lie down because she is suffering menstrual cramps or morning sickness. Some male is always carrying the hundred-pound tool box for the woman mechanic, or helping her change the big tire or hold the heavy spare part in place for welding. She gets to ride in the front of the truck. And so on.

"This is the first place they've ever dealt with women on a professional basis."

Beyond a doubt, as most military supervisors are still male, women sometimes do get special treatment. Some women do strain and stagger under the heavy materials that they must move, and servicemen often help them—though not always. And some women do use feminine wiles to escape work or to avoid getting dirty. An Army second lieutenant struggled to understand why: "I work very hard to do what I do well. I know what's expected of me as a soldier, and that's what I'm going to do. I don't see that same feeling in most of the women, and I think part of that is because they're not pressured to do that. You know, if someone's not going to push you to your highest achievements, then you're going to sort of slack off." But, as a Navy E-7 observed, sloth is not confined to one sex: "The guys are usually always saying that the females don't want to do this; they won't want to do that. They got guys just like that. You can't say it's just females doing it.". . .

Some servicemen who enjoy competing with other males can't deal with women as competitors. "When I was at the [ROTC] detachment my freshman and sophomore years, we never had any troubles with males and females being together. It wasn't until I got to summer camp with cadets who attended military schools only for men; for some it was the first time that they had ever seen a woman in uniform. At first they were like 'Wow, she's really doing well. This is great.' After a while they felt really threatened, and they almost started not liking me, because I knew my stuff."

No Support

"I was chosen to lead a night patrol," a Marine lieutenant reminisced about her basic school. "I took this seriously. Easter weekend everybody went away. I went out and I combed my area, made sure I knew where everything was, so when they dropped us off from the helicopter I could lead everybody. They recommend that you do a terrain model. I had these little American flags, and we got bubble gum and like Juicy Fruit wrappers to indicate water, certain things for the landing zones. The next day in the classroom the instructor said, 'I want everyone to give Lieutenant Smith a round of applause. I have never seen a better-led patrol, a better terrain model in my entire career, even out in the fleet.' But the only ones that gave any applause were, of course, the Women Marines—I could not have done it without them—and one male officer. Later he said he went back to his platoon and said, 'You bunch of jerks. Are you that insecure that you cannot support a fellow Marine?'"

"Some servicemen who enjoy competing with other males can't deal with women as competitors."

Sometimes a serviceman having trouble at home vents his wrath at his wife on the nearest servicewoman. "You come in and take all the crap you shouldn't have to take. I'll take it a little bit, and then I'll just go, 'Hey, get off my case. If you've got a problem with women, go home and talk it out with your wife. I don't need to hear your crap.' If they have a problem with their wives at home, they come in and they look for the first female: 'Huh, there's another one, man. Huh.'"

Servicemen may be taken aback by servicewomen's independence. Women earning the same money as men for the same work don't respond in the expected ways, as a black Army E-4 reported. "A lot of the guys in the service, they be trying to tell you what to do. But like if you own a car, if you rent an apartment, if you tell them, 'Well, I'm here too, and I'm making my own money,' they don't like that. I guess they think they've taken over the world so they can take over you too, but it don't work like that."

"A lot of old crusty sergeants just have this straight, narrow thinking, and it's really funny. They always say, 'In my Army, I wouldn't have any women.' I tell 'em, 'Well, it's not your Army.'"

"I have found that Marines one-on-one usually are pretty nice people. But as a young enlisted Marine I also found that when you got several of them together they could be very—what should I say?—less than nice."

Two kinds of servicemen, our interviewees say, have the most trouble dealing with servicewomen. First, men nearing retirement who have worked only with men, now forced to reconstruct their image of the military *and* their images of women. "A lot of them are clumsy," a Marine corporal observed, "not used to being around women at work.

"It takes a while for them to change. Their language. Some of them change their clothes in the office, and then they find out they can't. The jokes—they don't want to say the wrong thing. What do I do with her now that she's here?"

Second, men with macho self-images, often young and unsure of themselves, brought up to believe that women are made only for men's pleasure and convenience. If an eighteen-year-old woman is sent for her first assignment to an isolated Coast Guard small-boat station, where she is the only woman or one of two among a group of servicemen like these, she's in for a testing and racking experience. They will vie for dates with her and proposition her, making it a point of honor not to take no for an answer. Her male peers and her supervisor can make her life and work a torment. Only by presenting herself "professionally" from the beginning can she survive—quite a lot to ask of an eighteen-year-old in a strange and hostile environment. . . .

Women in the Military

With 220,000 women in the military, even the old curmudgeons and the young bulls have to deal with them (though we heard stories of men who would request a transfer to another unit to avoid having to work with or for women). As a Panamanian Marine staff sergeant said, "Some of them are more macho-fied: 'Oh, a woman shouldn't be here. She should stay home.' But at the end it was like 'Well, they're here, so now we'll live with them.'"

"He says, 'Well, you want people to think you're attractive, right?' I said, 'Yeah. After five o'clock. But from nine to five I'm a sailor. Just like you're a sailor.'"

"I'm six years into the military, and these guys still see me as their little sister. I am not your little sister. I am a sergeant E-5, just like this man sitting right next to me, who I happen to outrank in time in grade, but he's in charge of me, so he thinks, because he's a man."

Sexual harassment is hard to define, servicewomen recognize, and even harder to prove. "I had one case where a female seaman wanted to book her chief," reported a lieutenant who functions as an investigating officer. "She happens to be black, and he was a Filipino, and she wanted to say that he was discriminating against her. The supervisor tells you that she is not doing the job, she doesn't show up, problems like that, which are very easy to prove. The various booking chits [records of infringements] on this seaman are all real and well founded. The seaman says 'What about So-and-so that did the same thing? You didn't book that person.' 'Well, these booking chits are the results of five other times that you've done this.' It's really hard to prove sexual harassment.". . .

Many servicewomen hear the foul language and sexual bragging that make up so much of servicemen's conversation as sexual harassment. "I've gone through the military with my own little personal crusade, I call it, just as a joke. There's a lot of cursing that goes on, a lot of foul language, dirty jokes, sexual innuendos. I make it known that I don't want to hear this. A lot of the guys feel that because of ERA [Equal Rights Amendment] and it's a work environment, I should have to listen to it. I disagree."

Men also harass women by name-calling, heavy-duty teasing, and "joking." They accuse women of being pushy, mouthy, sexually unattractive, or lesbian. Contrariwise, they allege that women get ahead by using sex. "I get highly upset," says a Marine corporal, "when you hear people talking, and they find out, 'Oh, she's an E-5 or an E-6, so where are her kneepads?'" An Army MP [military police] investigator told how "about a month ago, we had an E-8 female come in our office and when she walked out I said, 'Boy, that's something you don't see every day—a female master sergeant.' And he [a serviceman] says, 'Yeah, she's either really got her ducks in order or she's come up on her back.'"

> ## "Servicemen may be taken aback by servicewomen's independence."

"I'm getting to feel bottlenecked with what I can't do. It always comes out to the fact that I'm a female. I see no other reason why I'm not given the positions, like platoon sergeant, that I should be. I'm always the assistant platoon sergeant, even though I have more experience and more rank than the person I'm supposed to be working for."

Even more damaging are the male actions that endanger the servicewoman's career. Men ignore women, assign them meaningless tasks, refuse to teach them the skills of their MOSs [military occupation specialty], refuse to serve with them, refuse to obey their orders. When she was still a second lieutenant, an Army captain recalled, she talked to her superior about her marriage plans. "He was real snotty, and I almost detected a hint of jealousy. He basically was the cat's meow on the prowl, and here was one of his lieutenants, a female at that, getting married. Believe it or not, I didn't get selected a lot of times, most of the time, to go out and support an exercise. He would send the other platoon leader, a male. Oh, yes, I was being kept from doing my job. That was obvious."

An Army helicopter pilot told us of her amazement when an infantry company commander's hang-ups threatened her performance. Although she had formerly served in the almost entirely male artillery, this was "The only time I have ever encountered any discrimination, and I tried to put it out of my mind because it was such a shock to me. He would refuse . . . I mean he would talk to me, but he would talk to everybody else more so. He would talk to my [male] senior warrant officers even though he was really addressing me. He refused to see me as a platoon leader who could get his mission accomplished. He refused to accept that a female could be a pilot and an aviator. I just dealt with it the best I could. Talked my frustrations out a lot with the warrant officers—they were very helpful. It was just the particular individual's problem and not mine.". . .

"The only time I have ever encountered any discrimination, . . . I tried to put it out of my mind."

Men's refusal to obey a woman's orders is a particularly damaging ploy, for if supervisors cannot enforce their authority, their performance evaluations suffer. "A lot of people will not follow a female officer," observed a black E-7. "'Aw, she's just a female officer.' They turn right around and they say, 'Well, we're gonna do what we wanta do anyway.' They get away with it, because they all cover for each other, and she

never really understands what they're doing. She'll say, 'Did we get this done?' First sergeant says, 'Yeah, we got that done.' And she thinks it's done her way, when actually they didn't do it her way."

An Army captain gratefully recalls her commander's help in such a situation when she was a young second lieutenant: "The commander finally sat on one of my platoon sergeants who was being—boy, if I had him now, I would have court-martialed him, I think."

Gender Problems

Supervisors too play games. "I stayed an E-2 for fourteen months. E-3 is supposed to be automatic after six months. But I had a slight gender problem—I wasn't a guy. I hadn't done anything wrong. I had never been late to work. I won Post Soldier of the Month, got a five-day pass to go to Berlin. But that squadron leader got mad at me 'cause I was getting too many passes [rewards for outstanding performance]. I couldn't win for losing—like walking up a down escalator. Luckily one [male] E-5 stood up for me. E-5 they tried to hold up on me too. I went to a primary leadership course and got the Douglas A. MacArthur award. So when I came back, they kind of couldn't turn their heads the other way. Took 'em more than a year from when they started my paperwork—it should only take a couple of weeks. What did I do? Kept my nose clean. I'd go to my section supervisor, who treats women great, but not women in his career field. I'd go to the NCOIC [noncommissioned officer in charge], the OIC [officer in charge]. Finally I got to the promotion board. (Even though I had to borrow maternity uniforms off another lady, because mine were on order for eleven months!)". . .

Beyond obscenity, verbal assaults, and career blocks lie the direct attacks: sexual blackmail and rape. As several supervisors commented, young recruits are particularly vulnerable to sexual blackmail, overt or subtle, in that they are taught to obey the orders of their superiors. "That's hard for the young female Marine, who works for some staff NCOs who see that she's young and impressionable and naive and away from Mom and Dad," said a lieutenant. "It's easier to hit on her or to do something to her that she may not tell somebody about, touching her, saying let's go for a ride. She doesn't know any better. It's a harshness for someone to be thrown into that kind of situation. As a result, you have Marines who become very bitter, because they think the gunny [gunnery sergeant] is supposed to do this with them all the time. You have to make sure that the gunny gets prosecuted or gets handled in the correct way, and that she's pulled out of it."

If the young servicewoman does resist, the supervisor may use his powers against her in mean and petty ways. "As a young airman I had trouble with sexual harassment. I had a supervisor who told me all about his pregnant wife, he felt like he was living with a nun, why don't we go down to the . . . y'know. I flat out told him no, I wasn't interested in that type of thing. I spent the next three and a half years on midshift [at undesirable hours, instead of the normal rotation from shift to shift]."

"Young recruits are particularly vulnerable to sexual blackmail."

Even older, more experienced women must exercise ingenuity when they're confronted with demands uttered in private, where the situation comes down to his word against hers. "I had a problem where I was at odds with one particular supervisor," said an MP NCO. "The end result was, I moved to a different station, because it was that or my career would be ended by this one person. I felt sexual harassment was underneath, but I didn't feel that the people in my chain of command would have listened and been sympathetic, so I didn't bother using it. I just found a way to get out of there, and I've been very happy ever since." And a Navy chief told us about a "time when even my job was

threatened. I was between a rock and a hard spot. I didn't know whether to say something about this person, because, especially an officer, they can ruin your career. I didn't want my career ruined, but I wasn't giving in to this person either. I handled it on my own, because I didn't want their career ruined, and more importantly I didn't want them to get into trouble to where my career would be ruined."

Usually the physical assaults servicewomen told us about were reported but handled semiofficially, at as low a level as possible, by people who wished to quiet the troubled waters or swim out of them. . . .

Pressing Formal Charges

Only one victim of a physical assault who talked to us about her experience had pressed formal charges. A highly intelligent young woman, she had established a brilliant service record. The sexual assault occurred at sea. "I was asleep, and someone came into the berthing area, and I woke to certain touches, and the fact that I was asleep meant that within a certain margin of error I had no idea what was actually done to me. I booked him. It went to captain's mast [a hearing before the captain], and the captain felt that it was a serious enough charge and that there was enough evidence, so he sent it up for a court martial." She fought in vain for a transfer off the cutter. "I spent hours in a little minihell. This man, where he slept was not fifty feet from where I slept. I saw him many times. While the captain felt that the charges were serious enough to bring to court martial, he didn't feel it was serious enough to separate the two of us, i.e., put him in a locked room somewhere, in a cell.

"I will say in rape and assault cases military law is a lot more fair than civil law—civil law is hell on a woman. And I had close friends I could talk to about it. I had all the women on the ship standing behind me a hundred percent. I had men on the ship standing behind me a hundred percent. Except for this one man, they were all my brothers. I had people coming up to me and saying, 'You say the word and he'll be dog meat in an hour; I can guarantee you.' In a way I wish I'd taken them up on their offer. I don't think I'll ever find that anyplace else in the world, that sense of camaraderie, that sense of brotherhood.

"They let the man walk. I still . . . I would like to hurt him, and hurt him badly. I was obviously disappointed that he wasn't going to have a Marine with him twenty-four hours a day while he made big ones into little ones. I have seen him, and it affects me. But I'm able to control the urge to pick him up and throw him in the river at the very least." Despite the strenuous efforts of many people at her current station, who praised her in the highest terms, the effects of the assault and the way it was handled have severely limited her ability to do her job and may indeed cause her to cut short her promising career. . . .

"Only one victim of a physical assault who talked to us about her experience had pressed formal charges."

Servicewomen and servicemen work together, they socialize together, and sometimes they live in the same barracks or quarters. They have a lot in common and often enjoy each other's company. Not always. For some women the military is a disastrous experience, a place of harassment and unhappiness, which violates their ideals and principles, where they dread going to work, where no one effectively helps or understands. Many of these women leave before their terms are up. Some go mad.

Some commit suicide, or try to. Some get pregnant in order to get out. And some grimly count the days until their time is over.

But every woman faces the problem of having to earn as a privilege the place in the military that men claim—or reject—as a birthright. If, as Dr. Johnson remarked, "Every man thinks meanly of himself for not having been a soldier," the servicewoman confronts the fact that many think meanly of her for being a soldier. She must waste the energy that men can save for their jobs or their pleasures in proving herself, in smashing stereotypes and overcoming prejudice, in coping with men's questions and problems about her sexual identity and her gender roles. She must fritter away time and vigor in dealing with the question, spoken or unspoken: "Why won't you go to bed with me?" She must think about how to make men comfortable in working with her. All of these activities consume a lot of energy and a lot of time. Whatever she has left over the servicewoman can direct toward building her career.

Discrimination Makes Women Soldiers Ineffective

Michael Rustad

About the Author: *Michael Rustad is a sociologist and former research assistant for the Wellesley College Center for Research on Women in Wellesley, Massachusetts. The following viewpoint is excerpted from his study of American servicewomen living in what Rustad calls "Khaki Town," a military community in Germany.*

From the end of World War II to the early 1970s, women constituted less than 1 percent of the total strength of the U.S. enlisted forces. Beginning in 1973, each service opened noncombat jobs to women. The total number of women in the Army grew from 37,994 in 1974 to 98,459 in 1979, with much of the expansion occurring in traditionally male areas such as the military police and telecommunications. . . .

When women hold males' jobs, they find themselves subject to role strain. Paul Secord and Carl Backman defined role strain as those situations in which persons experience difficulty in meeting role expectations. Two sources of role strain are postulated. First, there is a perception on the part of males of an inherent and natural conflict between being female and participating in the military. Secondly, the presence of women in nontraditional jobs conflicts with enlisted male culture. Together, these perceptions result in stereotypes that are associated with interpersonal conflict and the failure of

Excerpted from *Women in Khaki: The American Enlisted Woman*, by Michael Rustad (Praeger Publishers, an imprint of Greenwood Publishing Group, Inc., New York, 1982), pp. 142-144, 156, 158-166, 235. Copyright © 1982 by Michael Rustad. Reprinted with permission.

women to meet their goals of adjusting to khaki-collar [nontraditional] employment. . . .

The first duty station assignment is a critical period for women to learn how to articulate successfully the soldier and female identities. The term, *Army woman* is really a contradiction in status, according to enlisted male typifications. You are either a woman or you are in the Army, according to the stereotypes of many enlisted males. . . .

Female soldiers in formerly all-male jobs are caught in a cultural transition. They are initiated into two conflicting traditions, female socialization and traditional military culture. When women began to occupy men's jobs, they threatened the jokes, language, and camaraderie of a male bastion. When they attempted to enter such spheres, males questioned their strength, emotional control, and motives.

> **"You are either a woman or you are in the Army, according to the stereotypes of many enlisted males."**

Females in khaki-collar jobs faced a double bind. If they succeeded in their jobs, doubt was cast on their femininity. If they failed, their sex role was affirmed at the expense of their work role. At the unit level, this was translated by a Khaki Town radio operator as meaning, "If I don't like a certain group of guys because they're too pushy, I am labeled as a 'dyke.' If I date a lot, I'm a whore!" The dyke and whore stereotypes were broadly representative of two actual patterns of accommodation. Females resolved the status contradiction by either carving out an identity as a hyperfemale or as a super-soldier who denied her femininity. . . .

I don't belong here. A male could do my job better.
—20-year-old teletype operator, Khaki Town

One solution to the status contradiction of being a woman in a male job within the military is to allow the soldier role to wither away. By exaggerating "femaleness," token females may find willing male role partners. When women voluntarily withdraw their claims to martial roles, male harassment can be neutralized.

Daddy's Little Girl

There are many rewards to "normalizing" relations with male enlisted culture. First, when females give up their claim to the soldier role, they are less threatening to male definitions of femininity. Secondly, since these women no longer compete for male jobs, jokes, as well as ridicule and harassment, are reduced. Those women who abandon the battle for sex integration in a retreat to femininity receive swift male rewards, including attention and assistance because the feminine role amplification involves few changes in values, attitudes, and definitions for males.

A frequent paternalistic gesture extended to women who abandon the soldier role is protection from male-oriented military duties such as field exercises and simulations. The male supervisors, the "Sergeant Daddy Warbucks" types, assign the helpless and the vulnerable to the mail room or other clerical duties when it is time for the unit to deploy to the field.

During field exercises in Khaki Town in the spring of 1978, I observed that male supervisors often failed to assign certain women to such duties as guarding the perimeter, assembling radio antennas, and changing tires on two-and-a-half ton trucks. Men assisted women and then reported to me that they were "forced" to "take up the slack" when women were assigned to field jobs. As a private first class woman put it, "The guys yell favoritism, at the same time, they are the ones who do all the favoring. They don't have to help us, but they offer. They're very quick to take over."

Paternalistic Assistance

Why do men render paternalistic assistance to females? One woman sergeant observed:

To me, men really felt outdone when a woman performs her duties better than he does. This is a very childish attitude. Men should grow up and accept the fact that some women are better able to do a specific job than some men. Women are often able to perform on the same level but aren't given the chance.

Other women argued similarly that males deliberately tried to instill doubts in women in order to allay their own fears that a woman could endure in a difficult job. A maintenance specialist made the following observation:

To me, men really can't handle women in jobs like these. They try to instill an attitude in the females that they don't know what they're doing. Once this is done, they come in and offer help. Then they say women can't do the job and we have to cover the "slack."

A radio operator added:

Men constantly think they have to look out for your welfare, to the extent that they interfere with your duties. Harassment by men and not being treated as an equal are my biggest gripes here. Men you work with are overprotective even during off-duty time. It's hard to be an equal with lots of males, because of the WAC [Women's Army Corps] reputation.

"Males deliberately tried to instill doubts in women in order to allay their own fears."

A woman team supervisor described the patterns of male paternalism in the following way:

We are treated as children by male supervisors who think they have to watch out for us. Male supervisors do not task individual women to develop their greatest potential. Men ignore suggestions to change these behaviors. Sexist attitudes of older NCOs and "timers" created divisiveness among women and limited awareness of military oppression. Women, as a result, are unwilling to discuss problems and present unified demands. Women in the military have a long way to go before they are regarded as equals rather than as novelties or servants for the services. . . .

I overheard the following incident in headquarters on an uncommonly humid day. Two women were mowing the lawn in front of headquarters on special detail:

A male colonel called and complained to the company commander. "Why do you have these women mowing the lawn in this weather?" The company commander replied that the lawn had to be mowed and these women had been assigned to the detail. Fifteen minutes later, two males from another unit appeared in the company commander's office and reported that they were sent to relieve the women.

Despite the trivial nature of this incident, it is examples like these that represent the paternalism that discourages women from performing physically demanding jobs. . . .

Creating Divisions

The social type of "Daddy's Little Girl" creates divisiveness within the nascent female enlisted culture. For women still battling to be accepted as soldiers, Daddy's Little Girl undermines female gains. When females perceive the paternalistic role expectations of Daddy Warbucks and his Dutiful Daughter, they often blame the female. The following remarks are from "isolates" who resented male paternalism. From an electronic equipment private first class:

I think that the problems of a woman in the military are often brought out by the woman. She can be treated the way she wants to. It depends on how she acts. Many women in the Army have a long way to go before they are regarded with respect.

From a woman assigned to clerical duties:

First impressions of Army women are hard to change. Some women here are the problem. A few of them can be real bitches. The behavior of a few women can affect the treatment of us all.

From a radio operator:

We have a problem here with lower class women who don't want to work. They give a bad name to those who get here and deal with their jobs. Some women are unwilling to do their MOS [military occupational specialty] and use sex to get a cushy job.

From a telecommunications specialist:

Many of us [women] work together. But from time to time an individual EW [enlisted woman] might use her role as a female to shy away from heavy, but not unreasonable work. . . .

From an electrical repairer:

Military women think they are capable for the most part. It is mostly the men who see them as delicate. Most of the women would get a hernia before asking a man for help. However, there are some women who use femininity for all it's worth. If they don't know something or can't handle something, they should tell their supervisors. I blame the supervisors because they go along with this kind of action. But when a woman goes into a Signal Corps job, she should know what to expect. If she were to go into administration, she shouldn't expect much lifting. But if you are assigned to telecommunications, you know it, God damn it, that you will have to do something requiring some physical effort.

If you have the title, you should be able to do the job. If she tries to get over, she wastes the Army's money for her schooling and she still can't do the job. And there are a lot of other people who could have done that job, but will never get the opportunity. My personal feeling is that women need to know their limitations and be intelligent enough to know when they can't do an MOS [military occupational specialty]. If you can't lift a ton of weight, you shouldn't sign up for a job which requires that. There are also a lot of women who can lift a lot and there are guys who can't lift much. If I really can't do something, I'll admit it and not play little mind games. I am not a women's libber—far from it. But I do believe that women should get equal pay and do equal effort. They should not be allowed to do any less.

"Women in the military have a long way to go before they are regarded as equals."

There is a difference between paternalism that is accepted by women and that which is rejected. Females commented on attempts by their supervisors to make them feel helpless. One female reported that while she was initially enthusiastic and confident about her ability to perform her maintenance job, males made attempts to undermine her confidence:

They made comments such as, "Hey Roy, look at the way Cathy screws in a bolt," or "Ah, you do it like a girl. Do it right."

The Dutiful Daughter role allows women honorably to remove themselves psychologically and sometimes physically from work demands. The supervisor who forms the alliance with the Daughter creates resentment from isolates who are not included. The pet is excluded from aversive work loads, while other soldiers of both sexes must perform additional duties.

The Sexpot

A second form of hyperfemininity and underachievement is the Sexpot role. Some females tried to resolve the status contradiction by emphasizing their sexuality. Certain male supervisors, whom I will call Sergeant Seductos, were always looking for sexual partners among women troopers.

By forming a relationship with her supervisor, a female could find a shield from sexual harassment. Like Daddy's Little Girl, the Sex Object was removed from work demands. This role both contributed to the divisiveness among Khaki Town women and retarded the growth of female support systems.

The following remarks are reactions of other women to the Supervisor-Sex Object set. From an electrical repairer:

Some women are screwing their senior NCOs. This is disgusting and demoralizing.

From an intercept-voice operator:

Women are sometimes treated as sex objects. I really do lack confidence in some of them. I don't know what their problem is, but they do lower themselves.

From a teletype operator:

Some women should be knocked in the head. By offering sex in return for favors, they spoil it for the rest of us who try to do our jobs.

From a radio operator assigned to clerical tasks:

First impressions of Army women are bad. A few of them do join the Army to run around. But not all of us. Most of us are here to do a job.

"The problems of a woman in the military are often brought out by the woman."

From a woman who worked as a mechanic in the motor pool:

I think there are some women here who just want to find a man.

From a vehicle mechanic:

I see most of the problems of women as self-inflicted. Many military women put themselves in the positions they complain about. I feel that women should do any job they are capable of. If they are not capable, they should be separated from the service. What I think is a real kicker is that some women don't give a shit about their Army job. They just want to get pregnant and get out.

In February of 1979, I received a letter from an enlisted woman in the Air Force that described her dismay about how an affair between a senior male officer and a junior female officer affected other women. Selected excerpts from the letter are representative of the divisive effect that such relationships can have on a work setting:

I am a woman in the United States Air Force, stationed at _____ base. It is a career I selected by choice and I have been proud to wear the Air Force Blue. Through the years of active duty, it has given me a sense of patriotism, self worth, and loyalty to my country. Until recently, I have been impressed with the professionalism of both the officer and enlisted ranks I have been exposed to, especially those of my own sex. Those women who have a job to do should do it well, with high standards and moral values.

Over the past year and a half, I have been close witness to a set of very disgusting, demoralizing, and unprofessional set of extreme circumstances.

It has taken the form of a very open and unguarded affair between _____ [a male officer] and _____ [female officer] . . . This type of activity is certainly conduct unbecoming of an officer and gives all women in the Air Force a very bad name, especially those of us who desire to make it on our own talents out of bed rather than in it with the boss . . . Weak leaders with no moral value or respect are a very poor example to younger members of the military.

A third form of hyperfemininity that women can take is the Mother role. The Mother role is often played by an older enlisted woman. Junior enlisted men bring their problems to Mom, who mollifies them. Rosabeth Moss Kanter has also observed that token females sometimes find themselves in a position in which they console groups of men in their work role. Men seem to assume that some women, especially older women, are sympathetic, good listeners, and intuitive.

In the *Fort Devons Dispatch*, there was a feature on a woman who took on the Mother role: "They called me mother—not like swearing. I was just the oldest one, the most stable—I've been a mothering person ever since I can remember." Mothers could also console junior enlisted women, as this account describes:

She had just had a baby. It was her second child. The first had died. I felt something was wrong. I just couldn't put my finger on it . . . She had no one. I made arrangements with JAG [lawyer unit] to take care of her things. Therefore, one doesn't have to have experienced the same situation to understand that feeling. She thinks that's why she's good at helping people.

The *Army Times* provides us with another twist on the mother theme. The feature story entitled, "Like Mother, Like Son," reported on the experiences of a male private and his mother who both enlisted in the Army. The Army assigned them to the same base so that they could be together:

At Fort Sill, Oklahoma, the old saying "like father, like son" will have to be changed to "like mother, like son" following Pvt. John Allen's recent graduation from basic training. Allen's mother, SP4 Jeanne Allen, joined the Army in August, 1974 and is assigned to the Training Command Field Artillery Training Center. "John's glueing them back together," [the mother-son relationship] Jeanne said. "After all these years it's hard to believe I'll still be doing it" [the mothering role].

In Khaki Town, there was a 40-year-old woman who reported that junior enlisted men frequently came to her with their problems and referred to her as "mom." However, she commented that she did not like to be treated as "mother" and preferred to maintain a more distant relationship with males. In this example, she was treated as *if* she were a motherly type. In *altercasting*, people are constrained to act in a particular way because of imputation.

Men Pushing Roles on Women

The phenomenon of altercasting may entail a key aspect of the formation of social types in Khaki Town. If women are imputed to be little girls, sex objects, or motherly types and action is directed toward them on these imputations rather than in the soldier role, women can be nudged out of conflicting roles. Women soldiers may or may not be taken in by the sexual advances and assistance given to them by their male peers and supervisors. However, the sergeant who acts in an intimate or fatherly manner defines the situation in a particular way that is difficult to block or divert, even for a woman who does prefer a more professional role. . . .

"I do believe that women should get equal pay and do equal effort."

As we have seen, there is a real question as to whether military service is really the vanguard of new sex roles or only the retrenchment of patriarchal society. Without a change in the structure of enlisted life, there will be few gains for anyone in the adjustment of women to military life.

Combat Exclusion Promotes Widespread Discrimination in Society

Robin Rogers

About the Author: *Robin Rogers, a graduate of the University of California at Santa Barbara Law School, is a California attorney.*

Reports regarding the invasion of Panama brought the increasing importance of women in the military to the public's attention and forced many Americans to examine for the first time the often unacknowledged and increasingly ambiguous rules confining military women. Much has changed in the twenty-odd years since Congress repealed the two-percent ceiling on the number of women allowed in each branch of the armed services. Women now constitute more than ten percent of the armed services and occupy vital military positions previously closed to them. Significant as these changes are, however, much within the military hierarchy remains the same. Despite the increasing importance of women in our nation's military, many military policies and procedures continue to reflect a male-enclave mentality. Facially discriminatory policies, as well as more subtle forms of discrimination, continue to obstruct women's military careers.

Congress, for the most part, views the military as a unique realm governed by standards different from those that govern the rest of American society. Consequently, Congress seems ambiva-

Robin Rogers, "A Proposal for Combatting Sexual Discrimination in the Military: Amendment of Title VII." Reprinted from *California Law Review*, vol. 78, no. 1 (January 1990), pp. 165-196, by permission. Copyright © 1990 by California Law Review, Inc.

lent toward the problem of sex discrimination in the military. Congressional policy reflects the belief that so long as the military fulfills its central task of defending the country, its values alone should determine military policies.

Congress' ambivalence towards military policy makes sense only if the effects of discrimination within the military can be cordoned off from the rest of society. Congress assumes that the larger community can achieve equity and equality while unequal treatment of the sexes continues in the military. But it is wrong—the negative effects of discriminatory military practices reverberate throughout society.

The military provides significant economic opportunities to its members. It employs more people than any single government agency or private company, and it is the "nation's largest single vocational training institution," [according to M. Binkin and S. Bach]. It offers its members a way out of poverty and provides many lower class Americans with otherwise unavailable economic opportunities. Military opportunities can be especially important to women, who as a class have historically been employed in the lower paying occupational strata. To the extent that discrimination denies women equal access to these opportunities, society as a whole feels the effects.

"The negative effects of discriminatory military practices reverberate throughout society."

The military provides its members with economic benefits that last long after they leave the military. The opportunities for education, training, and experience in the military can prepare servicemembers for future careers in the private sector. And retired military personnel receive benefits that give them "a level of financial security that few men and even fewer women would be able to achieve in the civilian sector." For example, the Veterans Administration provides benefits and services such as hospitalization and medical care, guarantees of home loans, and life insurance. In addition, the Supreme Court has validated veterans' preference statutes that give veterans an advantage when seeking government jobs. Because of the disproportionately small number of women veterans, women, as a group, enjoy fewer of these financial rewards. But the availability of greater opportunities for women in the military would lead to a larger number of female veterans, and could help women gain access to traditionally male-dominated civil service jobs.

Effect on Society

The military also affects society in significant noneconomic ways. For example, it often has a socializing effect on its members. Military service inevitably influences the values and attitudes of military personnel, and ex-servicemembers take those values and attitudes with them into the civilian sector. The cumulative impact on American society can be substantial. At a minimum, the respect and responsibility women receive within the military affects the treatment of civilian women by ex-servicemembers.

In a larger perspective, the prevalence of sex-based roles in the military propagates discrimination throughout society. As the Supreme Court has recognized, the imposition of stereotypical sex roles can harm individuals, even when the categories are apparently benign. In *Frontiero v. Richardson*, the Court rejected the concept that "[m]an is, or should be, woman's protector and defender" as an example of "'romantic paternalism' which, in practical effect, put women not on a pedestal, but in a cage." Tacit approval of discriminatory military policies gives credence to outdated notions of the proper roles for men and women, thereby limiting women's opportunities for personal achievement.

For many Americans, the concepts of citizenship and military service are integrally related. Defending one's country holds symbolic importance as a "unique political responsibility," [in the opinion of Goodman in *Women's Rights Law Reporter*]. To the extent that women are barred from sharing fully in this patriotic responsibility, they are likely to be perceived as second-class citizens.

Furthermore, women's current and potential roles in the military may shape their political ideas and choices. Gender-based military distinctions affect women's sense of commitment and responsibility toward the state. Thus, the degree to which women are involved in the military helps to determine their stake in the formulation of national security policy. As Judith Hicks Stiehm has noted, "That stake, analogous to the stake a working woman has in the economic system as opposed to the stake of a dependent wife, has the possibility of creating more informed and more intense involvement by women in matters of security, defense, war and peace." Sexual discrimination in the military burdens society as a whole. The problem deserves careful thought and analysis, rather than ambivalence. . . .

The combat exclusion affects women's military experiences in a number of ways. Most obviously, the exclusion bars women from entering certain military positions, thus closing off particular avenues of training and advancement. It reinforces stereotypical beliefs and discriminatory attitudes towards women in the military. And by showing that Congress will allow discriminatory policies in the military with little sound justification, the exclusion encourages the military to pursue other discriminatory practices.

"Internal military channels are generally hostile to sex discrimination challenges."

Most importantly, by setting forth a system in which women cannot participate in the military's central mission, the combat exclusion defines a world where women are presumed to be less valuable members of the military system.

The combat exclusion thus makes it easier for the military to justify other discriminatory policies. Starting from the premise of the combat exclusion—that men and women are not equal—a myriad of discriminatory practices may flourish.

This underlying theme of inequality reinforces and validates certain attitudes toward women in the services. These attitudes may manifest themselves in more subtle forms of discrimination than officially sanctioned policies, but the deleterious effects on women are apparent.

Direct Harms to Women

The combat exclusion precludes women from occupying not only combat specialties but certain noncombat positions as well. In some situations, the military bars women from certain positions in order to reserve rotation positions for male members serving on combat-risk missions. Also, female servicemembers cannot specialize in areas in which the number or distribution of closed positions impedes career advancement in that specialty area. Finally, women are also barred from some noncombat positions that are involved in the same conflict areas as combat units.

Beyond the job categories that it explicitly closes to women, the combat exclusion also affects women's service opportunities in a variety of other ways. In the past, it served as a justification for prohibiting women from entering the service academies. Although women can now attend the service academies, the combat exclusion continues to hamper their opportunities for training and advancement to higher paying occupations in the military. As the Supreme Court acknowledged in *Schlesinger v. Ballard*, the combat exclusion restricts women's abilities to gain the experience necessary for promotion within the military. Because military leadership training is most frequently acquired in combat-type positions, the combat exclusion places women wishing to obtain qualification for high-level positions at a disadvantage.

The combat exclusion also restricts the number of women who can enter the military in the first place. For example, the Army permits a limited number of males without high school diplomas to enlist once they have obtained a General Education Development certificate; the Army prohibits women from doing the same. In *Lewis v. United States Army*, the plaintiff, a woman who had not graduated from high school but who had obtained a General Education Development certificate and had earned some college credits, brought suit challenging the constitutionality of the Army's enlistment policy. A federal district court dismissed the claim, stating that because the combat exclusion results in fewer openings for women, the Army was justified in setting higher admissions requirements for them than for men. The court found that, because men and women are not similarly situated in the military by virtue of the combat exclusion, military enlistment standards favoring men are constitutional.

Indirect Harms

Many of the discriminatory effects of the combat exclusion are readily apparent, since they provide clear-cut examples of unequal treatment of the sexes. The combat exclusion also fosters discrimination in a less obvious manner by validating policies that differentiate the sexes, as well as attitudes that minimize women's contributions to the military. The combat exclusion reinforces discriminatory attitudes within the military, nurturing discriminatory treatment extending beyond the exclusionary rules themselves.

"The military justice system may be ill-suited to deter discrimination."

The combat exclusion sets women apart from men, reinforcing the view that women do not belong in the military. Servicewomen are perceived as being out of place in the military— needing protection from the brutality of real warfare. Male service members may resent the encroachment into the military system of these seeming incompetents, who appear to receive special treatment by being shielded from the most dangerous military work.

A more subtle effect of the combat exclusion is that it makes women's military service invisible. Although women cannot earn the distinction of taking part in the institution's "principal mission" of combat, they often share the same risks and responsibilities as those men sanctioned for front line combat duty. Classifying all women's positions as noncombat obscures the bravery of military women. The description of women engaging only in noncombat tasks eclipses the image of the women who have served in combat situations, and been taken prisoners of war.

The perception that military women contribute less than their male counterparts, a foreseeable consequence of a sanctioned exclusion, leads to tacit approval of other discriminatory policies and practices. For example, the services often bar single parents from enlisting, a policy with a disproportionate impact on women. Whereas the courts generally strike down such policies in civilian contexts, their use by the military is condoned. In addition, several recent studies have found sexual harassment, another form of discriminatory treatment, to be a particularly egregious problem in the military.

A 1988 Department of Defense Task Force Report found inequities in the facilities and services provided to male and female military personnel stationed abroad. The Report suggested that medical care provided to female servicemembers was accorded lower priority than that provided to female dependents of male servicemembers. The Task Force also reported that, as a result of the "less-than-adequate" facilities provided for service women in some locations, female members "perceive themselves, and may be perceived by others, as less than full members of the team." Like the combat exclusion, these other instances of discrimination persist without sound justification. Moreover, diverse discriminatory practices may originate with the combat exclusion. The combat exclusion, as implemented, almost guarantees that women will remain outside the central policy and planning positions. The attitudes of military personnel, in turn, conform with the fundamentally discriminatory power structure.

"The time has come for Congress to amend Title VII to extend its protection to the uniformed military."

Because the combat exclusion lies at the heart of much of the sex discrimination in the military, attaining greater equality and fairness for servicewomen requires either abolishing the exclusion altogether or finding ways to mitigate its discriminatory effects. But Congress, the judiciary, and the military seem reluctant to abandon or limit the exclusion. The legislature and the courts consistently reject petitions to eliminate the exclusion, and internal military channels are generally hostile to sex discrimination challenges.

Congressional proposals to repeal the combat exclusion may lead to its eventual abolition. At a minimum, the debate and discussion engendered by such proposals should underscore the lack of a coherent justification for the exclusion and point toward ways to lessen its impact. By bringing attention to the contributions of the growing number of women in the military such proposals may lessen the public antipathy towards the notion of abolishing the combat exclusion.

Sex Discrimination

In the short run, however, such proposals are unlikely to pass. Previous legislative attempts to abolish the combat exclusion have failed, partly because the American public has seemed committed to maintaining some sort of distinction between men and women in combat. Public opposition to women serving in combat positions remains a substantial political obstacle to repeal. Since a legislative repeal of the combat exclusion does not appear to be politically feasible at this time, other options to address sex discrimination in the military must be explored.

For a variety of reasons, legal challenges to the combat exclusion appear equally futile at the present. Any challenge to the combat exclusion on equal protection grounds would almost certainly fail, as the courts generally refrain from exercising more than a cursory review of military policy. Even when the courts undertake to review military decisions, they emphasize that judicial deference necessitates a very weak standard of review in all questions implicating military preparedness. Thus, a realistic attack on sex discrimination in the military would not seek to overturn the combat exclusion, but would instead attempt to limit the exclusion's discriminatory impact. An examination of intramilitary remedies for discrimination reveals whether the present system could be capable of effecting such a result.

"Equality within the military would give women greater involvement and responsibility both within and outside the military."

Uniformed military personnel have three options for advancing claims of discrimination: file a complaint under the Department of Defense Equal Opportunity Program, pursue a claim under Article 138 of the Uniform Code of Military Justice (UCMJ), or proceed before the Board of Correction of Military Records. These avenues are inadequate for a variety of reasons, including limited scope of reviewable claims, lack of uniform legal standards, counterproductive and ambiguous procedural guidelines, and insufficient external review.

The Department of Defense Equal Opportunity Program (DoD-EOP) allows a servicemember to bring a complaint alleging "arbitrary discrimination" based on gender. The program focuses primarily on educating servicemembers in human relations and enforcing nondiscriminatory use of military facilities and resources. It differs substantially from other federal agencies' equal opportunity programs because it is outside the jurisdiction of the Equal Employment Opportunity Commission (EEOC). As a result, the EEOC has no power to investigate or take action on charges of discrimination in the uniformed military, and the DoD-EOP does not apply the standard equal opportunity guidelines and procedural regulations.

Claiming Discrimination

Instead, the Department of Defense remedy provides that the Assistant Secretary of Defense or head of each DoD component shall "[r]eview and take action on, as appropriate, investigations . . . or discrimination complaints received by the DoD," "[t]ake appropriate disciplinary action" for arbitrary acts of discrimination, and "[e]nsure that Military Equal Opportunity and discrimination investigations are coordinated with appropriate . . . officers." No specific guidelines explain the procedure a complainant must follow, nor are any procedures set forth for adequate investigation of complaints. Complaints are handled primarily through the chain of command; thus a complainant must bring her grievance directly to her superior, the likely subject of the complaint. Appointment of an independent investigator is discretionary, and no provision sets forth procedures to be followed in such a situation.

Under the second option for advancing a claim of discrimination in the military, a servicemember may bring an Article 138 general grievance proceeding after "due application to that commanding officer is refused redress." The aggrieved party may then complain to a superior officer, who forwards the complaint to the officer exercising general court-martial jurisdiction over the complained-of officer. The officer exercising jurisdiction conducts an inquiry, takes "proper measures for redressing the wrong," and sends a statement of the complaint and any proceedings to the military department secretary. No guidelines define "proper measures," nor are accountability procedures set forth to assure that a complaint is not halted within the chain of command.

Thus, under both the DoD-EOP and UCMJ procedures, a servicewoman must pursue her complaint of discrimination through the chain of command; the regulations offer her no alternative grievance channels. The prospect of depending on the military chain of command for relief may discourage many women from bringing discrimination claims. A female servicemember pushing to bring a complaint of discrimination must often first present her claim to the offending officer—an unpleasant and discouraging task. The superior officers who next review a claim may give little credence to complaints against their colleagues brought by lower ranking servicemembers. Many servicemembers apparently believe that such claims of discrimination processed under these circumstances will go unheeded or provoke retaliatory action. Discrimination may therefore persist without complaint, under a chain-of-command system "perceived as a participant in, or thought to condone, pejorative attitudes toward military women."

Military Remedies

The only intramilitary remedy for discrimination that does not rely on the chain of command is an appeal to a Board of Corrections of Military Records (BCMR), a body composed of Defense Department civilian executives. BCMR members do not necessarily have legal training and the board lacks authority to make law or invalidate challenged regulations. Rather, the boards have authority only to "correct an error or remove an injustice" in an individual's military records. However, the regulations provide no investigation procedures or standards defining "injustice." Nor are complainants guaran-

teed a hearing before the board: a board may make determinations on applications without a hearing. Furthermore, civilian courts traditionally defer to BCMR decisions. A servicemember challenging a board's decision carries the "difficult standard of proof" that the decision was arbitrary, capricious, unlawful, or unsupported by substantial evidence.

Thus, all three of the intramilitary remedies rely on ad-hoc procedures that leave a high degree of discretion to military officials. No clear standards or procedures exist to define an adequate investigation or resolution of a claim. Moreover, complainants have difficulty knowing when they have adequately exhausted intramilitary remedies and earned the right to appeal to a civilian court.

"A servicewoman must pursue her complaint of discrimination through the chain of command."

Because complaint procedures are poorly defined, widespread discrimination may persist without coming under any substantive inquiry or review. By leaving the military to police itself, the present intramilitary remedial system may encourage members to cover up discrimination and thus avoid public criticism, rather than to investigate promptly and resolve problems of discrimination.

Furthermore, the military justice system may be ill-suited to deter discrimination since it is designed to enforce discipline, not to promote individual rights or societal norms of equity. Officers are trained in the pursuit of military effectiveness, a goal generally perceived as incompatible with individual liberties. "One who believes himself bound by and complying with this code of self-denial and subordination cannot be expected to completely sympathize with contrary values of diversity and autonomy" implicit in claims of discrimination.

In sum, the existing military remedial system cannot successfully eradicate the discriminatory practices fostered by the combat exclusion. The problem of sex discrimination in the military requires the creation of a new remedy that will eliminate much of the discrimination originating with the amorphous combat exclusion. The application of Title VII to the uniformed military would be such a remedy.

Proposal: Application of Title VII

Title VII of the Civil Rights Act of 1964 is the primary federal law used to combat employment discrimination based on race, religion, sex, or national origin. The statute addresses both "disparate treatment" of protected groups and the "disparate impact" of certain policies on such groups. Disparate treatment involves overt or intentional discrimination against an individual based upon her membership in a protected group. Disparate impact refers to facially neutral policies that disproportionately burden a protected group. Title VII allows use of a protected classification as an employment criteria only if the classification is based upon a bona fide occupational qualification (BFOQ). Similarly, an employment qualification or requirement that disproportionately excludes a protected group must be shown to be a "business necessity," rather than a mere cover for outright discrimination.

"The combat exclusion would apply only to a strictly limited number of occupations."

Almost without exception, the courts have found that Title VII, as presently formulated, does not apply to the uniformed military. Title VII's amending legislation extends coverage to "employees or applicants . . . in the military departments," but fails to define who is encompassed within the "military departments" for purposes of the statute. Significantly, the legislative history is silent on whether Congress intended to include uniformed military personnel as well as civilians in the amendment's scope. The legislature's silence strongly suggests that that Congress did not intend to apply Title VII to the uniformed military. Since the courts traditionally refuse to find a remedy for discrimination claims against the military, it is highly unlikely Congress would have remained silent had it intended to provide a Title VII remedy to uniformed personnel. Moreover, because the legislative record contains no discussion of the issue, it appears that Congress never even considered extending Title VII in this way.

The time has come for Congress to amend Title VII to extend its protection to the uniformed military. Such an amendment would institutionalize effective non-discrimination policies and procedures within the military. The new Title VII amendment could be drafted to leave intact a statutory combat exclusion, while limiting the exclusion's use as a justification for other discriminatory policies. Congress would need to establish guidelines for applying the exclusion. The services would then be required to use the guidelines when classifying military positions. This process would ensure that the combat exclusion would be applied only to the extent justified in the Congressional guidelines. Furthermore, for the first time, Congress would give the courts an express mandate to inquire into the military's reasons for combat and noncombat classifications. The courts could derive judicial standards from the statutory language, and to the extent required, from the legislative history of the amendment.

The amendment should read:

"Military departments, as provided in Sec. 2000e-16(a), shall include uniformed personnel. This section shall not preclude classification of combat as a bona fide occupational qualification, as defined in Sec. 2000e-2(e)." . . .

Making the Legislation Effective

For the legislation to be effective, the scope of a permissible BFOQ exception, and thus the scope of the combat exclusion, should remain "narrow." Accordingly, the combat exclusion would apply only to a strictly limited number of occupations, and the courts could review any combat classification to determine whether it achieves the specified purpose. Thus, the military, like other Title VII employers, would have to show why differential treatment of women is warranted.

The implementation of Title VII would grant female servicemembers a remedy for individual instances of discrimination and harassment, as well as for discriminatory military policies and procedures. The standards for the military under Title VII should be the same as those applied to all employers subject to Title VII. The legislation "precludes treatment of individuals as simply components" of a gender class. Even a statistically valid generalization about women would be an insufficient reason for disqualifying a particular woman to whom the generalization does not apply.

"Much progress in improving women's opportunities within the military can still be made."

Possibly the most significant effect of applying Title VII to the uniformed military would be its eventual impact on the attitudes of military personnel toward women. If the combat exclusion and any other gender-based restrictions were constrained to fit within legally supportable justifications, distinctions between men and women in the military would become less pervasive. Decisionmakers in the military would be required to treat men and women as equals, and could no longer assume that female members are some-how out of place in the military. An unjustified distinction between the sexes would no longer serve as the springboard for other sex-based distinctions.

With Title VII in place, the military would have consistent guidelines to follow in employment practices and grievance procedures. Although military procedures would still govern complaints at the initial stages, the system would be effectively policed by the possibility of substantive judicial review of military findings and decisions. . . .

Conclusion

The military exerts great influence on our society. To the extent that discriminatory policies are accepted and sanctioned within the military, the battle for women's equality in our society becomes even more onerous. Accepting for the present that our society remains committed to a combat exclusion for women, much progress in improving women's opportunities within the military can still be made. Expansion of Title VII protection to the uniformed military would ensure that women only be excluded from a military role based on a defensible justification.

Thus, applying Title VII would be a significant step towards instilling within the military the values and guarantees of equal treatment that are promoted in civilian society. The benefits would extend beyond the military, as women would gain new opportunities for training, education, and employment. In addition, both the military and society at large would further evolve toward full recognition of women's abilities to define their own life roles. Equality within the military would give women greater involvement and responsibility both within and outside the military, in war and in peace.

Does Discrimination Harm Women in the Military?

No: Women in the Military Are Not Harmed by Discrimination

The Armed Services Do Not Discriminate
Women Can Succeed Despite Discrimination
Black Women Can Succeed in the Military

The Armed Services Do Not Discriminate

Carol Barkalow and Andrea Raab

About the Authors: *In 1976, Carol Barkalow and 118 other women became the first females to enter West Point. After graduation, Barkalow served in West Germany from 1981 through 1983. The following viewpoint is an excerpt from Barkalow's autobiography* In the Men's House. *It begins as the author prepares to assume command of an army group at Fort Lee, Virginia. Barkalow currently works as a special assistant to the chief of staff of the U.S. Army. Andrea Raab is a free-lance writer in New York City.*

Inherent in the work of any female soldier is the call to invent, or reinvent, herself. It isn't enough to be lifted out of context, slapped into a uniform, taught a new language, and dispatched whimsically around the globe. Accompanying these generic changes is a much slower, frequently painful, and highly individualized process of self-definition. In the military, it is a challenge merely to function as best as one can within the system without losing one's sense of self. Meeting that challenge as a male within a male-oriented institution is tough enough; as a female, it can sometimes prove devastating. Women who cling to traditional ideas and images of female identity may find very few places to gain a foothold.

And yet, it is that very footlooseness that, for some, can provide the most satisfaction. Like the bob-haired, uncorseted, trouser-clad women of the 1920s who mimicked male attitudes and

dress—not because they wanted to be men, but because they wanted to be free—a woman in the military is granted a surprising freedom of movement. One is allowed—no, encouraged—to be physical. A uniform may be a rigid requirement, but in military circles it denotes respect. And perhaps more important, the female body usually is not imprisoned in pantyhose, high heels, and skirts that render one incapable of any activity more vigorous than a measured walk. One's nails don't have to be long and lacquered like bird's talons; one's hairstyle is not the center of one's existence; one's face does not need to be painted before being exposed to public view. For me, one of the greatest and most paradoxical attractions of choosing a life in the military, after accepting the yoke of missions and regulations and standards and uniforms, was living in a way that would not tie me to a fixed place, or to people, or to the obligations of domestic drudgery. If I kept body and soul together, that would be enough. The stream of my energy was channeled into work that gave me purpose and direction. Although I paid dearly for this independence with long periods of loneliness, as a professional officer with some measure of authority, I found it a relief to assume a role among men that enabled me to deal plainly and straightforwardly—a role that did not require me to project myself as a coquette, temptress, or helpless damsel in distress. Within certain professional parameters—applied equally to all soldiers—my body and image would be under my control and no one else's. Or so I believed.

> **"Inherent in the work of any female soldier is the call to invent, or reinvent, herself."**

I was introduced to the key people in the 57th Trans [57th Transportation Light-Medium Truck Company] for the first time in June 1986. The outgoing company commander had called a meeting of the platoon leaders, platoon sergeants, the first sergeant, and the supply NCO [noncommissioned officer], to make arrangements for the Change of Command Inventory. I had to account for all the property in the unit before I assumed command, which meant I literally had to count every truck, bed, sheet, dish, tent, stove, wrench, rifle, generator, and camouflage net in the company and ensure that every item listed on the hand receipts was truly present. This tedium would take approximately three weeks to complete.

A quorum gathered in what eventually would be my new office. In my company, the officers were white and the NCOs predominantly black. My first sergeant, otherwise known in military parlance as "Top," was among the first to greet me. He was an elegant man—tall, slim, and soft-spoken— with a fatherly good humor that made him extremely popular among his soldiers. Top was a Vietnam vet—one of three in the company—and, by his own account, had volunteered in 1967 to avoid the roulette wheel of the draft. . . .

Assuming Command

Staff Sergeant Kevin Randall, the supply NCO, and I spent most of our initial meeting simply leafing through the hand receipts. The supply room was right down the hall from my office, so it was easy for me to sit and chat with him, which is how we came to be friends. Privately, I referred to him as "The Quiet Man"; Sergeant Randall was a gentle, deeply religious soldier who I felt needed to be more involved with troops. So rather than having him merely in control of the Supply Room, I appointed him Headquarters Platoon Sergeant. Until then, he had worked only with property; now he'd be responsible for human beings. . . .

The Change of Command ceremony was scheduled to take place on a grassy field just east of the company area. Since a third of my company had been deployed to Yakima, Washington, in support of a fuel- and water-pipeline exercise, only eighty soldiers stood in formation for the ceremony. Six deuce-and-a-half's (two-and-a-half-ton trucks) were parked behind the unit formation to create the illusion of a crowd. One of my lieutenants was away on leave, and Top was at home nursing a migraine. At least my family was able to come.

"Sergeant Randall was a gentle, deeply religious soldier who I felt needed to be more involved with troops."

The uniform for the troops was BDUs (battle dress uniforms) with soft caps and stripped pistol belts—green web belts without the .45s, ammo pouches, and other accessories of battle that would usually adorn them. My BDUs were heavily starched, and my black leather combat boots were spit-shined.

The morning of 1 August had begun for me before daybreak, but I wasn't nervous until the stroke of nine, when the battalion commander and I commenced our slow march together into formation. As Lieutenant Colonel Edward Schuller and I approached the area, my heart started to beat fiercely. My body began to shake while I stood so rigidly at attention, and I was certain that even the meager crowd of soldiers assembled on the field could see it.

With choreographic precision, the battalion commander, the outgoing company commander, the acting first sergeant, and I maneuvered ourselves into a four-pointed diamond, then turned to face each other expectantly. In a sequence of quick, decisive thrusts, the guidon pole was passed from the acting first sergeant to the company commander to the battalion commander and, finally, to me. It crossed my hands with an authoritative slap, and the orders appointing me commander of the 57th Transportation Light-Medium Truck Company were read. At the close of this simple ritual, I was in command.

This was what I had been waiting for, it

seemed, since the day I entered West Point. Assuming command of my own company would be the true validation of my military career. . . .

Wednesday Morning Aerobics

The soldiers of Third Platoon returned to Fort Lee from Yakima on the fifteenth of October; it was gratifying, finally, to have my entire company together. Before they arrived, however, the big rumor going around Yakima had been that the new female company commander was making everybody do aerobics back home.

In fact, we did PT [physical training] three times a week in our unit—every Monday, Wednesday, and Friday morning at 0600 hours. A typical workout consisted of calisthenics for fifteen minutes on the grass in front of the company area building and then a run of anywhere from two to five miles. When that routine became a bore, I asked a friend of mine who worked at a Richmond nightclub to mix a tape of good dance music for me, and I started teaching Army aerobics in the post Fitness Center.

"The guidon pole was passed from the acting first sergeant to . . . the battalion commander and, finally, to me."

The female soldiers were pleased. Of course, none of the male soldiers wanted any part of this when they first heard about it; they were convinced that aerobics was a "sissy" exercise. But they quickly changed their minds after the first five minutes of the first day. I went easy on them in the beginning, realizing that most of them had never done anything like this.

We worked out for only thirty minutes, but I heard a lot of moaning and groaning. I had been practicing aerobics myself, so I was fine, but those guys were hurting. For three days afterward, all of them were sore. Top was walking around *real* slow. Even so, I could see a little bit of excitement in their faces, though they tried

not to show it. In any case, I never heard any of them call aerobics "sissy" again.

From that day on, we did aerobics every Wednesday morning. Often, soldiers from other units within the battalion would ask if they could join us. We once had a crowd of nearly 120 sweaty soldiers dancing at the same time.

I had a lot of fun teaching them. If one of my guys started messing around, I'd bring him up front to perform the routine with me, a tactic that usually embarrassed him enough to ward off future cutting up. It wasn't a particularly pressured PT, but everyone got a great workout. We eventually worked our way up to a solid fifty-minute routine, which I considered a personal triumph.

Disciplining Women

Mondays and Fridays, though, were still the days I reserved for the rigorous two- to five-mile runs. I would purposely turn around and run backward in front of the formation to see how many people were holding up and how many had fallen out. I have to admit that I looked specifically to see how many women had fallen out. I was very sensitive to that. Motivating people during runs, especially females, could be difficult, and I knew that some of my male NCOs were afraid to discipline the women for fear of being charged with sexual harassment. There seemed to be a rather pervasive perception among male soldiers that if you dared to cross a woman, she'd ruin you. Men were reluctant to take that chance, so they tended to go a bit easier on their female soldiers. Consequently, some of the women slacked off. But I say a soldier is a soldier, male or female, which also means that if soldiers of either sex think they can "get over," one way or another, they will. Regrettably, I had one of these ne'er-do-wells in my unit.

Before I came to the 57th, Spec-4 Louise Harper would run no more than a hundred yards before falling out. Yet no one had ever taken her to task for this. The first time she tried it with me, however, I started in on her. She complained that she couldn't breathe, couldn't stop coughing. I calmly suggested that she stop smoking.

Of course, I didn't want to do anything stupid in case the woman really did have a problem, so I sent her to the Kenner Army Community Hospital on post for a complete physical. The doctor gave her a clean bill of health, so the next time she pulled that asthma crap on me, I told her to get her ass moving. Slowly but surely, she stayed in the formations longer and longer. I think she even surprised herself.

Then, one Monday morning during a two-mile run, Spec-4 Harper quit right near the end. Well, I ran to the back of the formation and started shouting at her. She became very upset and collapsed to the ground, sobbing, which pissed me off. I was tired of her lame excuses for why she was in such terrible shape. I also wanted to prove to the other women in the company that they could be physically fit, if they tried. As Harper lay there snivelling on the ground, I yelled, "Get up and finish this run!" I really must have frightened her, because she leapt up and took off like a jackrabbit. She even caught up to the others long before they had stopped running.

I think I demonstrated to my NCOs that they didn't have to be afraid of scolding a woman for not performing up to her potential. Usually, I felt I had to be more firm than soft in these cases. At times I wasn't sure how hard I should be. I never wanted my soldiers to call me weak, so maybe I went to the other extreme to prevent that from ever happening. . . . .

Time to Think

As the months passed and our honeymoon ended, the company finally settled down to the serious business of learning to function in a new configuration. As the autumn days grew shorter, the workweeks seemed to lengthen. And when Friday afternoon arrived, I found I badly needed a place to reflect. Sometimes I would close the door to my office, sink into one of the cushioned chairs in front of my desk, and just think—or have talks with myself, which people

would occasionally overhear and wonder what the hell I was doing.

"Some of my male NCOs were afraid to discipline the women for fear of being charged with sexual harassment."

But if I really needed to talk to someone, I would wander over to the Supply Room and sit with Sergeant Randall. Sergeant Randall made me feel like a teacher—or an analyst. Now that he was in charge of forty soldiers, he'd ask me for advice on how to deal with their personalities, and, particularly, for advice on how to counsel them when they got into trouble. I didn't have all the answers, naturally, but I'd ask provocative questions and give him just enough bait to hook him into thinking like a commander and come up with solutions of his own. He was an extremely sensitive and thoughtful man, which was why I liked him so much. I'd be whirling around the company like a dervish, and Sergeant Randall would be one of the few people who could make me slow down long enough to stop and think. His decision-making process was more deliberate, which encouraged me to seek more than one solution and to recognize that situations weren't always black-and-white. West Point had pounded into my head that it was critical for an officer to make quick decisions, for one rarely had the luxury of time on the battlefield. And though this training had proved invaluable, the flaws inherent in relying exclusively on this approach were obvious. The fact was, I was a whiz at coming to snap conclusions. Now I had to study the ramifications. After all, a commander has the power to change people's lives, permanently. . . .

The ARTEP (Army Readiness Training and Evaluation Program) is one of any company's most important military exercises. It monitors and grades a unit's wartime performance from its first moment of mobilization, through four days of simulated combat, to the unit's final return to garrison.

The ARTEP is generally known among soldiers as one of those "we-have-to-pass" evaluations. All segments are graded as either "go" or "no go." If units receive a "no-go" in a particular area, they'll usually be given a chance to try again for a "go" before the evaluation is completed. War affords no second chances, of course, but peacetime offers some margin of leniency.

As far as I could determine, throughout the company's history at Fort Lee, the 57th Trans had traditionally conducted its ARTEP at Fort A.P. Hill, Virginia, located directly to the north of Fort Lee, about an hour and a half away. Most of my soldiers knew the roads at Fort A.P. Hill blindfolded. I didn't want to take them over the same boring route, so I decided to take the 57th Trans to Fort Bragg, North Carolina, home of the 82d Airborne Division. Fort Bragg was six hours away by truck, so I knew my guys would get a chance to do what they did best—drive!

"I never wanted my soldiers to call me weak, so maybe I went to the other extreme."

It wouldn't be easy, though; 90 percent of my soldiers had never been to Fort Bragg. When I introduced the idea to my junior officer staff, it was met with some resistance by one of my male lieutenants who reminded me that we had to pass this ARTEP and insisted we shouldn't take any chances. I knew it was risky going someplace new for this evaluation, but I wanted my soldiers to understand how to deploy to an area they'd never seen. Besides, I was convinced that they would rise to the occasion. I wasn't entirely rash in the way I went about it, either. The ARTEP had been scheduled for the spring of 1987, so in early March I took some of my key personnel down to Fort Bragg for a couple of days to conduct a preliminary reconnaissance of the area.

Through a fellow commander of a truck unit stationed there, I was able to arrange an opportunity for my soldiers to assume some of the company's transportation taskings, in support of a mission for the 82d Airborne. As it turned out, some of the soldiers from the 82d would be jumping into Bragg while we were on post, so it would become my soldiers' job to pick them up at the drop zone and transport them and their equipment back to their units. This, I felt, would at least give my people the feel of performing an actual mission and of being involved in real operations—not just participating in yet another exercise.

The Convoy Moves Out

Tuesday, 28 April 1987, 0800 hours. One of the biggest thrills I experienced as commander was heading out on convoy. I'd sent an advance party ahead a few hours earlier to prepare the site at Fort Bragg while the rest of us made ready for our departure from Fort Lee. The whir of the deuce-and-a-half's, the smell of the diesel fuel, and the bustling of the soldiers really had me fired up. A deuce-and-a-half makes a low growl when it starts, followed by a high-pitched squeal . . . I was almost overwhelmed. Giving my soldiers the signal to take off was a tremendous rush: The engines broke from a rumble to a roar and we pulled out of the gate, moving the entire lumbering convoy down Route 95 in a giant camouflage parade.

As commander, I was also the last member of the company to leave Fort Lee. Enroute to our destination, I would dart up and down through the convoy in my little CUCV, like a beetle skimming water in a pond, first racing to the front to make sure everything was okay, then slowing down to wait for the stragglers. Sometimes, though, I'd simply stop by the side of the road and proudly watch the entire procession go by. The teams of soldiers manning each of the huge trucks would wave or honk their horns as they drove past me, and I'd salute them, giving them a high-five in return. Sometimes I'd catch a few of them without their headgear (soldiers are always supposed to wear their camouflage-colored helmets in a military vehicle—partly for safety reasons and partly because it's "uniform"—unless they impair the soldiers' vision while driving), so I'd motion to them to put their helmets back on. I really only cared about enforcing that rule so none of them would get into trouble with someone higher up than me. I knew that in hot weather the webbed inner lining and the chinstraps on those heavy steel pots would start to itch and chafe like mad, and the longer the ride, the heavier and more uncomfortable they became.

Summer comes early in the south, and this day the sun was blazing. None of the trucks had air conditioning, and when we arrived at Bragg in midafternoon, there was no time even to cool off. We immediately had to prepare our camp area and set up a defensive perimeter. One of the first things we did was set up the mess tent, from which we'd be served two hot, cafeteria-style meals a day—breakfast and dinner—known in Army slang as "Hot-A's." We'd "eat tactical," which meant outdoors in the field, dispersed, and hunched over our individual rations like a tribe of monkeys feeding in the jungle, with at least a five-meter distance between each small group. Actually, we had to keep that distance while lining up in the mess tent, too, because if we were attacked during mealtime, the theory went, the enemy (who, in all our training scenarios, was the Soviets) couldn't take us all out at once.

"A commander has the power to change people's lives, permanently."

Lunches consisted of something called "MREs"—Meals, Ready to Eat. MREs were "boil-in-a-bag" concoctions that came in dark-brown-and-OD-green plastic bags, about a foot long and six inches wide, which we'd heat up using our electricity generators and portable burners.

Packed inside the opaque plastic we might find eight ounces of Chicken a la King, an airtight package of crackers, an ounce and a half of cheese spread, and a hermetically sealed piece of fruit cake, as well as an accessory packet containing the ubiquitous powdered coffee, cocoa, cream substitute, salt, sugar, chewing gum, matches, and toilet paper. I wished they had given us C-Rations instead; the MREs were bland and tasted like the plastic bags they came in. Being in the field always made me ravenously hungry, though, so I forced myself to swallow every flavorless bite.

Camp Preparation

Our training area became a giant campground—mostly flat, surrounded by acres of woods and sloping hills cut by trails. Now and then, when the air was still, we could hear the faint popping of simulated gunfire in the distance, a signal that other units were training nearby.

Our soldiers worked well into the night setting up the site and the equipment—pitching and camouflaging enough tents for three platoons (about 140 people) to sleep in, a maintenance tent for the vehicles, a mess tent, and a CP (Command Post) tent, from which the first sergeant and I would control all operations. Eventually, though, the fifteen female soldiers I'd brought with me drifted off to sleep inside a pair of well-insulated arctic tents, which slept six to ten each, while the male crews bedded down in GP medium tents that could comfortably accommodate up to eighteen people. I, however, spent the night curled up inside my own arctic tent—commander's privilege. But I did not sleep alone. Traditionally, during field maneuvers, the first sergeant would sleep inside the same tent as the company commander. I didn't want to behave any differently, so when my first sergeant retired, I climbed in after him. I suppose I was trying to prove a point—that a female commander and a male first sergeant could share a tent without incident. After all, we each had our own separate folding cot, and we each slept in T-shirts and fatigue pants.

Weeks before in Top's office, I had introduced the idea while discussing the administrative details of the trip. "You know, Top," I said casually, "as CO [commanding officer] and first sergeant we'll be sharing a tent at Bragg." Slightly embarrassed but not nonplussed, he'd shrugged his lanky shoulders and said, laughing, "Ma'am, I had a feeling you were going to say that."

Of course, this would not be the first time male and female soldiers would sleep together in a field tent or function as a finely tuned team to accomplish a mission without the interference of standard social conventions. . . .

"Giving my soldiers the signal to take off was a tremendous rush."

My job during this entire exercise was to coordinate and supervise the soldiers' training. So, on the second night at Bragg, my plan called for picking up and moving the entire unit to a new location. The area I'd selected was only three miles away, but for training purposes I decided we should follow a roundabout route of fifteen miles.

This driving maneuver was, in fact, a requirement of the ARTEP, but my soldiers told me that other units within the battalion had typically "simulated" the move. I told them I wanted nothing to do with simulations; we moved the unit that night. I knew it would be complicated because we hadn't been able to clear our site before dark, and after nightfall the heavily wooded roads would be much harder to negotiate. We had to take extra care not to run our trucks over any unsuspecting soldiers who might have pitched their camouflaged tents beside the vehicles. We did have one or two sprained ankles at sick call the next morning, but nothing more serious than that.

Although my soldiers were trained in defensive fighting, as a Transportation unit our primary mission was to drive—to haul ammo, equipment, soldiers, and supplies in support of combat units. But on Wednesday night we suddenly heard peals of sniper fire—they were blanks, of course. One of the truck companies at Bragg had decided to act as an aggressor and were trying to infiltrate the camp. They launched one attack and then another and another—in waves—trying to breach the 360-degree perimeter that was our twenty-four-hour line of defense. Their goal was to capture our Command Post. If they had reached that inner sanctum, we would have immediately lost the battle. We were much too clever for them, however. We'd set traps—metal trip wires strung with tin cans from the mess tent, which proved to be a primitive, but effective, alarm system. My soldiers heard the enemy stumbling noisily over the wires in the dark and alerted the rest of us, then sent for reinforcements so we were able to return their fire and head them off in time. . . .

A Job Well Done

Thursday was our last night in North Carolina. It rained, so I decided to give the troops a treat. I permitted them to leave the muddy field and go into Fort Bragg proper, where they could take showers in the post gymnasium—their first in three days. Meanwhile, both Colonel Houston and Lieutenant Colonel Schuller (the brigade and battalion commanders) had decided to pay us a visit. Fortunately, our brigade and battalion staff evaluators had been satisfied with our performance. . . . I was so relieved. My soldiers had busted their butts, and it had paid off. Thankfully, we wouldn't have to do any of our tasks over again. . . .

Looking back as a commander, I realized I had accomplished what I'd set out to do at seventeen. I'd held positions of leadership and been responsible for people's welfare. I realized, too, that the years I'd spent at West Point had been essential to that achievement. Despite its limitations, the Academy had helped to define me, and it's still the compass by which I steer.

Women Can Succeed Despite Discrimination

Anonymous

About the Author: *The author of the following viewpoint was trained as a jet engine mechanic in the United States Air Force. She worked at an Air Force base in North Dakota before being transferred to a base in Mildenhall, England.*

I am a veteran of the United States Air Force, in which I spent six years from 1974 to 1980. My job was jet engine mechanic, and I had attained the rank of staff sergeant at the time of my discharge. I entered the service in September 1974 shortly after the war in Vietnam ground to a military halt, if not a diplomatic one. . . . I went to Grand Forks, North Dakota, in January or February of '75. . . .

I checked in at the base, got settled down, got my gear, and got taken over to my shop, which worked on J57s and TF33s (engines) and KC-135 tankers and B-52 bombers. Grand Forks is Strategic Air Command (SAC), and they are part of this whole strategic triad of bombers, Polaris submarines, and missiles. It was pretty bleak, pretty bleak. They had had three other women in that shop, and all three of them had either gotten pregnant or screwed up or refused to work and were handing out tools in the tool crib or handing out technical orders in the technical order library, but none of them were working in their field. None was actually putting en-

Anonymous, "I Am a Veteran. . ." from *Arms and the Enlisted Woman*, by Judith Hicks Stiehm. Copyright © 1989 by Judith Hicks Stiehm. Reprinted by permission of Temple University Press.

gines together.

I began my on-the-job training, my apprenticeship. After six months I would be considered a mechanic and earn a level. At first I was gungho—I was ready to go. But they put me on stand maintenance, which means I worked on maintaining the stands on which engines and components were being built up. I was supposed to put safety pins in these things or oil them up. I was nowhere near a jet engine. Having just come out of school, I was disappointed. . . .

There were two parts to the shop. There was in-shop maintenance, which is where the components and the engines come in—say for an inspection—or where a brand-new engine has to be put together. The compressors, turbines, the combustion cans, the inner cases and the outer cases, and the kit or the electrical lines and hoses, and the plumbing and the extra components have to be built up. This takes maybe a week or so, to put together an engine from scratch or to tear one down. It is all shop work, and it was, to my mind, repetitive. I was much more interested in being in the other half of the shop, which was flight line or engine conditioning. This was outside—everybody worked outdoors. To do this job you had to be fairly strong.

"At first I was gungho—I was ready to go."

They had never had a woman on the flight line when I came and started making noises about it. They weren't about to have one on the flight line, either. It was a really macho group. There aren't a lot of really tough jobs in the Air Force, but bomb loaders and engine mechanics are probably two of the toughest. I was insistent, though, so they moved me from small gas engines to in-shop. We had a lot of problems in the in-shop—I mean people problems. My boss who had been on flight line was very noncommunicative. I would be standing around (by this stage I still hadn't experienced the reality of working on an engine and didn't know one part from another); he wouldn't say anything, absolutely nothing. I mean, literally, he could go all day with maybe three words. It was hard, and when I finished the study course that went with this "hands-on experience," I was really disillusioned.

"When I finished the study course . . . I was really disillusioned."

Finally there was a shake-up, and a new guy came in. Meanwhile I had asked permission to go on the flight line of my shop chief, but he kept ignoring me or smiling nicely and doing nothing. Eventually he took me into his office and said, "You can see there is nobody here, and everything I am going to tell you is strictly between us because there is nobody else here, Air Force Regulation 7-2"—his seven stripes to my two stripes. He said, "The reason I am not putting you on the flight line is (a) I am not going to have any woman on my flight line, (b) you couldn't handle the elements, the cold, heat, and whatnot, (c) if you could handle the elements you would get attacked by every male on the flight line, and (d) if you were to do better than the guys . . . well, there are twenty guys on flight line and one of you, and the mission requires that their priority come first."

Fitting In

Needless to say I was stunned. But he was right—there was no way I could report him, because there was nobody to overhear or witness it, and I had little doubt whose word was gonna be listened to. At least I knew what I was up against. A couple of weeks later, I related this to my new crew chief, and he went and bet this guy a case of beer that I would last on flight line. So in December they put me on flight line. I had no parka, and no parka pants; mind you, in winter in North Dakota it can get to 60 degrees below

zero, so it was pretty bloody cold, and they put me out there, and for a week or so I totally lacked the equipment. I lasted, and I stayed there for most of the rest of my time in service. It was rough. We had stepvans, which look like bread trucks, and those stepvans housed six people with their toolboxes and their special equipment and a driver who is usually shift chief. The procedure is that the shift chiefs go out to the flight line and drop off airmen on a particular job. Then he checks on them later. If the aircraft needs to be run to check the engine out, he does so. As I said, we worked on B-52s and KC-135s. A B-52 has eight turbo fan engines, and tankers have four regular jet engines. We took engines off the wing as "on-wing maintenance," but we never broke stuff down. We either removed or replaced components, or removed and replaced engines, or we did maintenance work while the components were on the engine. We checked oil, and we inspected them. There was a phase inspection dock that we worked in. We ran the aircraft, we trimmed it, which is sort of like tuning it up. (After you put a new engine on, it requires adjustment so it will be on line with the rest of the engines and with the parameters set for its operation.) We did essentially everything except taking the plane off the ground. It was hard work. I worked eight hours a day. For a while I worked swing shift, which I liked. That is three to eleven PM. You often get tight with people on your crew, but I had a lot of problems. I wasn't tight with these guys. I mean, most of the conversations revolved around booze, women, and cars. I like cars, but I don't drink and I couldn't talk about women. It was hard to listen when they talked about women—the way they thought about them—but it was either be a tease or be one of the guys, and I figured my options were better if I was one of the guys. So I got tough. I did it by keeping my mouth shut and biting my tongue a lot and putting up with some really insulting behavior. I don't know—sometimes I think I have done myself psychic damage and other times I feel like I have overcome it. I didn't always take it. One bitching cold day we were operating the heater so we wouldn't freeze to death while working on engines. I was standing with my parka open to the back blast area, so I could fill my parka with heat. This guy that I knew, I had worked with for a long time, a sergeant, was standing there. He came up to me and grabbed me by the crotch. It was the last thing in the world I had expected, I was humiliated, I was insulted, I mean all I could do was stutter, and the guy says, "Oh, it's my birthday; I deserve a little snatch"—like it was no big thing, like he could not see why I was upset. Sure we were friendly, sure we were working together, and of course doesn't everybody offer their physical self to be molested or harassed? Well, I mean, it is just a part of the game. I couldn't believe it. I was furious. When I could finally function, I threatened him with a wrench. . . .

A lot of stuff was beginning to pile up by then. I was getting fed up. I kept putting in for a change of orders, a change of assignment, but it was pretty hopeless. I mean, Grand Forks is one of the places that once they get you there, they are not gonna let you go because it's so damn hard to get you in the first place. I put in for a change once a week, I guess.

Orders finally came through to England. I had put in for an extended overseas tour, which I thought was for three years; it turned out to be four, but I was in ecstasy. . . .

I had just made E-4, so I was going to a new base with some rank, which always helps for women because you have to take a lot less crap the farther up the line you go. So I packed up my stuff and flew to Mildenhall, England.

The First Woman in the Shop

Mildenhall is the gateway to Europe. All flights stop there, refuel and let passengers off, and then fly on to the continent. It is a big, big airport, and it was really beautiful—all that green after North Dakota's brown and yellow! It was the most beautiful sight I have ever seen. I'm never gonna forget the view I saw from that window. Anyway, we landed. It was a World War II base, so it was kind of rustic, you know, lots of

brick and stuff, and this guy who met me—this tall, blond, nice guy—took me to the shop, and everybody in the shop was on a break and lined up out front to see the WAF mechanic. Nobody gets welcomes like that! I was not only the first woman in the shop, but one of the first women in the squadron, so it was a big deal. There I was in my class A uniform (that's something maintenance troops almost never wear, and I hadn't worn a skirt in I don't know how long). I felt like a fool. Nobody said much, everybody was just checking me out, so I talked to the shop chief. I had a lot of flight-line experience, and I would get to stay there. They were going through a big transition then to new engines, and more aircraft. I had more experience than a lot of people on the particular kind of engine we were getting, so I plunged right in. We were changing J57-43s with J57-59s. It was really busy, but it was really good. I mean I was right there, an E-4 working on flight line right from the start, and I didn't give it much thought.

"You often get tight with people on your crew, but I had a lot of problems."

The barracks situation, though, sucked. There weren't enough women for a women's barracks, so we had the third floor of the building that housed the personnel and headquarters squadrons. . . .

My roommate was a space case. It was weird. There was no community like there had been in North Dakota. Also, I had been living off the base, and it was hard for me to get used to the barracks again. I felt really alienated. The work situation was good, though; people liked me. (My shop chief personally showed me around. Later I found out that was something he only did for women and that it had caused a problem.)

It was a beautiful base; I loved it; I did a lot of traveling around.

The flight line at Mildenhall was set up differently. It was like a circuit. The taxiway went around the runway, and there were clusters of parking stands off each side of it. It wasn't just lined up wing tip to wing tip. I worked aircraft launch a lot. What happens is they fill the maintenance vans with specialists from each shop, and as the aircraft is getting ready to take off, you monitor it with the radio. If it breaks down, you zoom up to the aircraft and (sort of like Roy Rogers, I guess) put the ladder up to the cockpit to find out what the problem is, then you fix it or determine that the mission has to be scratched. It could take about fifteen minutes to do this, and it was tense. There was a lot of tension, but I liked doing it, running up there with the ground shaking from the power of the engine, and whipping off the engine cowling and looking at it with everybody depending on you and expecting you to make a brilliant decision! Saying, "Hey, it's all right, sir, you can go ahead and fly it," and having to be right. If not, everyone was out of luck! It was a real high to know that engine was or wasn't gonna make it. You've got sixty people on board; you know they are depending on you.

Sometimes I had a problem because a lot of people weren't used to women on flight line and didn't believe in me. Once I had an officer that had a problem. He said he had engine vibration. Vibration in the throttle can be a dangerous situation. So he stopped before he turned around to make his take-off roll, and there were a couple of airplanes right behind him. I hurried out. I was a sergeant. I knew what I was doing, so I went to the airplane with my toolbox, which now was about sixty pounds and hard to run with. I went to the aircraft. He was quite snobby; he showed me the throttle was shaking. I could see it was a mild case of vibration and pretty much, I still think, a case of cable slack. I checked the engine and went back to the pilot and said, "My opinion is cable slack; you can fly this airplane." He said, "What do you know about it! I want to see your supervisor. I want to see a man." So I said, "With all due respect, sir (the prerequisite formula), I don't have to take your shit." I climbed out of the aircraft and got back on the maintenance truck. The guys all went, "What's the matter, what did he say?" I said, "It's just cable slack and he said he wanted a man's opinion."

"I was not only the first woman in the shop, but one of the first women in the squadron."

It was great. My guys called over the radio (you are not supposed to be sarcastic on the radio) and said, "They have to have a man's opinion out here because the pilot isn't going to listen to a broad." The maintenance officer of the day came hurrying out, and I knew him and he respected me for my work, so he went to find the pilot. Well, the guy had shut the airplane down on the runway with other planes behind him and was getting into the crew bus. The maintenance officer stopped him and made him get back in and fly the airplane. I felt really good. It was like a victory, you know; I mean they had to listen to me, and I knew my stuff, and I didn't have to take their shit. After we got back to the shop, one of the senior NCOs [noncommissioned officers] demanded we do a vibration check anyway. I was vindicated. They did a vibration check, which takes at least a full shift, and there was nothing wrong with that engine. But that NCO didn't believe me. He was one of the crew bosses, and he should have known. He should have had faith in me. I had a lot of incidents like that where I diagnosed something and somebody overrode me and it turned out that I was right. . . .

To Be the Best

I can still remember the first time I saw a woman crew member. She was a navigator. She stepped off a plane from McGuire. We were freaked! I thought that was great, really great. And we had a couple of women maintenance officers. But as a rule I didn't see many women. I didn't work with any—no, I did work with one, and she was good. She was about nineteen and from southern California. She was one of the best. She was excellent; she had a lot of talent.

It was hard work. I mean, there is no getting away from the fact that flight line is painful work. My toolbox weighed 60 pounds. A lot of components we put on were a good 40, 50, 60 pounds, or more. The advantage I had was that I have very small hands—I'm also ambidextrous—so I could do things that a lot of people couldn't, and I could get my hands in a lot of places other people couldn't. When I couldn't do something, I had to think up a solution to the problem, a problem the guys could just use a hammer and screwdriver on. A lot of times it was frustrating, and I wasn't always successful. If you had an inch-and-a-half nut to take off of an engine mount, I would get a wrench to put on it, and then I would find an extension to put on the end of the wrench, because the longer the wrench, the easier to break the nut loose. If you are not getting anywhere, and if you fall off the stand or something, it is frustrating. And if you are the only person out there, and if you have a job to do, you're stuck with it. There is nobody around to help. It is your problem.

I had a real sense of obligation, and felt like a failure if I had to ask for help or had to have a guy come break a nut loose or something. I swallowed my pride a lot. There is a tendency to try to be Superwoman or what they used to call me—"Wonder Woman." I guess the fact is there was constant pressure to prove yourself—not just because you were a woman, but then because you were an NCO, or because you were a "flight line ramp rat." I don't know if the pressure was really there or if it was just me believing I always had to be the best.

The Turning Point

The turning point was hurting my back. I mean, I really liked my work. There was a joy about flight line work where one gets to be outside in rain and fog and the elements. You see things changing around you, the weather, the scenery. It is purifying in some strange way. Sometimes you had to be out there twelve or sixteen hours a day working on a problem that wasn't getting fixed, and it was pouring rain, and it was 11:00 PM and you couldn't see what you were doing, and you were frozen (I used to have a lot of pain in my knees), and the evenings were cold, and you spent a lot of time there, and you were in it, and it was just too bad if you got wet. There was no quitting, no crying, no saying that you want to go back to the shop.

"Sometimes I had a problem because a lot of people weren't used to women on flight line and didn't believe in me."

But I hurt my back. We had been putting up one of those CSDs, and we had been working a good six hours, and we were exhausted. It's very easy to exhaust yourself and just burn out because of the constant heavy labor. It was pouring rain, and the fuel was dissolving tarmac in the parking area where the airplane was. Because we were such a distance from the shop, a truck came around and checked on us, and they asked if we were done. We were doing the safety wire, the last few connections. I started putting stuff together and counting out tools and whatnot, and we knew that if we didn't get our shit together and get on that truck we would be stuck there another hour until the shift changed, so I just yanked up this 90-pound generator, which I normally couldn't move very far, and stuck it in the box. You had to lift it waist high and then drop it into what looks like a sawed-off 55-gallon shipping drum. I felt my back go snap, crackle, and pop, and knew that was it. I had tried for five years to be careful, but I just, I don't know, out it went, and that was it. I was in agony. I couldn't move; but the next day I came back to work, and I was running an airplane. To run an airplane, you have to set the brakes. This means you have to extend your legs and push the pedals down with your toes. You are all stretched out and lifting levers and pushing toggle switches and whatnot. I couldn't do it, I could not do it. My back went out, again. When you are carrying around 60 pounds with your back screwed up, you just physically wear yourself out after a certain point. Most of the guys I worked with were big, beefy guys, and maybe they can handle it—I don't know. I wasn't at a stage where I was willing to admit that maybe not all women can do all jobs, and although I'm strong for a woman, I'm not that big. I guess I was just sort of tired of it, and tired of physically destroying myself. My back was bad, and it would take a month for my hands to heal from a safety wire cut, or from fuel drying them out, or from a scrape or whatever. And it was impossible to get the oil out of my skin so everybody didn't know what I did for a living by looking.

"We had a couple of women maintenance officers. But as a rule I didn't see many women."

My last year in the Air Force, I went to test cell. After an engine is put together in the shop, it is sent to a test cell, where they have special equipment to see if everything is operating right. You have to hook up all these leads to test the heat, temperature, vibration, oil temperature, fuel-flow ratio, and all that stuff, then send it out to engine conditioning, and finally put it on the airplane which needs an engine. It was less work but it was inside. If you are away from the shop, you are away from some of the mickey mouse bullshit—washing floors, waxing the hangar, and all the kind of crap which I couldn't get behind. We had solved the mickey mouse to some degree in our area because it was ours and we kept it up. There weren't three shifts coming through. We worked really well together, but it was heavy work. You were pushing an 8,000-pound engine around on the stand, off the

stand, jacking it up, jacking it down—I probably got out just in time to avoid permanent injury. I did miss flight line. I guess what I missed the most was the fact that when you finished the job on an airplane (they all had their own personalities), you got to see it take off, fly, and, oh, it was beautiful. There was a sense of completion, a sense of totality, I guess. When I worked on an engine in the shop or tested something, it tested out. If it didn't, I would send it back to the shop and then test it again when it came back. It was more inanimate. I don't know if it makes sense, but it did at the time to me. . . .

I knew there was going to be an end to it with my back the way it was. I knew it wasn't going to be a career for me, so I wasn't as motivated at the test cell as I had been on the flight line. I was a staff sergeant by this time and wasn't worked up about rank anymore. I guess I didn't feel I was going to be a part of it forever. A lot of people wanted me to stay in; a lot of people wanted me to be careered, because women weren't in staff, tech, or master slots, and I had a good chance of making it to the top. But it was frustrating because parts of me weren't being challenged. I was taking night courses in a University of Maryland program, and if I brought heavy books to work, or said anything beyond shit, piss, fuck, and baby barf, it was like I was speaking another language—like I was deliberately putting myself above the guys—and it created hostility. I was also involved in a lot of local political stuff with the women's movement in Cambridge, like pro-abortion rights, and I lived off the base at this stage. I lived off the base for two or two and a half, three years in a village nearby, and I guess I was concentrating on my civilian status. . . .

Leaving the Air Force

I was feeling pretty detached from my feminine side because I wasn't around women that much, and the political contact I had was too schizophrenic. I guess I had the feeling that I had to get to a place where I could be more integrated. So I applied to some schools. I tried to stay in England, but you had to have five years residence to apply for resident alien status, so I knew I had to come back to the States. I went to the base librarian, a school friend of mine, and he showed me some books about different colleges. I had some friends in New Hampshire, and I had been there once, so I applied to go to schools in New England and got accepted to all of them except Harvard. I had thought that it would be kind of neat just to try, but I got accepted to Smith, and got a lot of mail from Smith, so I thought, well, I'll try a little women's community now. I thought it might be good for me as a balance to the total male community I was in. So in August of 1980, I got my discharge at McGuire (New Jersey) for terminal leave, went to Northampton, and started school.

"I had a real sense of obligation, and felt like a failure if I had to ask for help."

I just utterly freaked. Everybody there looked alike, blond, tan, and rich—perfect hair, perfect teeth, perfect skin, soft hands. The atmosphere was incredibly intellectual, liberal, not at all what I was used to. I talked crude; I still talk that way—a lot of slang and a lot of crude. It wasn't their way. I felt more like I was coming from a foreign country, going to a school like that, than I ever felt going to Turkey or Germany or Italy or anyplace else. It was bizarre. Now I'm getting past the adjustment phase. I feel like I'm just on leave and gonna go back to real life any minute. But people are so naive, so innocent, so righteous and judgmental about people who were in the service. And nobody knows what that means—especially for women. They can't imagine what it was like, why some of us have to go in, and why some of them don't have to. Smith has been an eye-opening experience, and sometimes I'm bitter and uptight about it, and other times I'm mellow. . . .

Women Veterans

I'm still in the process of getting adjusted, I realize that. It will be a while, because six years is a long time in an enclosed community. It's like the Air Force was most of my adult life. All I knew was the hippie years, the countercultural late sixties and early seventies, and then I was in the military. It's like all of the tremendous change taking place in the country didn't affect me. The apathy, the amnesia about Vietnam, about the whole period, is very strange to me. My parents are glad that I'm out and going to school, but we never discuss the service. I talk to my brother a lot about it because he was in for four years, and we have that in common, but I'm more involved than he is. I was in longer, and it was a different experience for a woman. Maybe this outline of what it was like is interesting. I hope so. There are a lot of women veterans and a lot of women still in service today, and not very many people seem very interested.

Black Women Can Succeed in the Military

David Dent

About the Author: *David Dent is a free-lance writer.*

The military: For many African-Americans, especially men, it has meant opportunity. Today there are more Black women in the military than their white counterparts, and Black women also have a higher reenlistment rate. . . .

Brigadier General Sherian Grace Cadoria is one of four female Army generals. As Deputy Commanding General and Director for Mobilization and Operations for the U.S. Total Army Personnel Command, she is the highest-ranking Black woman in the armed forces. Simply put, if a world war were to erupt, Cadoria would be responsible for providing replacements to the overseas commanders on the battlefields. She's got a powerful job, but Cadoria says neither the power nor the prestige came easy. In her 29-year career, she hasn't allowed the double hurdle of racism and sexism to stand in her way.

"When I started in the Army in 1961, there were jobs a Black, by unwritten code, could not do. I can never forget that the coveted position of Platoon Leader in the Women's Officers Training Detachment was denied me because a Black could not carry out all the duties the job entailed. Specifically, in Anniston, Alabama, a Black could not take the troops off the installation because of Jim Crow laws."

Cadoria entered the Army fulltime after graduating from Southern University in Baton Rouge, Louisiana. She had to do some heavy campaigning, but eventually, in 1967, Cadoria was sent to Vietnam as a protocol officer. After the war ended, she became the first Black woman picked for the prestigious Command and General Staff College, an advanced training course for majors in Fort Leavenworth, Kansas. At 50, Cadoria has never married, and she has made many other personal sacrifices for her career. While Cadoria has seen opportunities for women increase, women still face combat restrictions. "I really don't want men or women in combat, but unless all occupational specialties are opened to both males and females, our country will never be all that it can be.

I had never actually considered joining the Army, but I really wanted to do something exciting and different."

> ## "Unless all occupational specialties are opened to both males and females, our country will never be all that it can be."

Laverne Chester contacted an Army recruiter and discovered that as a college graduate she could enter a special officers-candidate school and receive a salary at the same time. After she completed the four-month program, Chester was commissioned as a second lieutenant. Today she's a captain in the military-police unit at Fort Campbell, Tennessee. One of her tours placed her at the helm of a 320-member police force. Chester's career has definitely lived up to the promise of excitement. "There are few instances where you will find a woman police chief of a small town, which is essentially what I was."

Chester, 33, and her husband, Captain Leonard Chester, are a military match. They met during her first tour of duty in Fort Knox, Kentucky. In 1989, the couple adopted a baby boy. She says they chose adoption because "it's hard to do the physical things as an officer if you are pregnant." Now she has a successful career, a supportive husband and a child. When she looks

David Dent, "Women in the Military," *Essence*, April 1990. Reprinted with permission.

back on her early days (in the insurance business), Chester says, she's "amazed at how much I've changed and grown."

Lieutenant Colonel on the Fast Track

Karen Johnson had an intense desire to go to Vietnam in 1972—not to fight, but to heal. The Jersey City, New Jersey, native was a 24-year-old nurse when she became obsessed with the numbers on the national newscasts each day—the numbers of young Americans killed in Vietnam. "I had friends who were over there and I knew that a lot of the men who got drafted were young and Black," she says.

Johnson decided that action was more effective than depressing thoughts. She was accepted into a training program for officers and was commissioned a first lieutenant. She didn't, however, go to Vietnam as U.S. troops were no longer being sent there, but her first assignment in San Antonio, Texas, was a personal battle. "I left the command one night, reached into my purse and found a note that said 'nigger we're watching you.'"

"She established a reputation and record that won her acceptance into the Air Force's . . . Institute of Technology."

However, Johnson, now 42, never let racism and sexism stop her. She just kept on climbing. From Texas she went to Thailand and then to Spain. She established a reputation and record that won her acceptance into the Air Force's highly competitive Institute of Technology. The institute provided her, along with other fast-track commissioned officers, with the opportunity to go back to the halls of academia. Johnson decided on Yale, where she got a master's degree in psychiatric nursing. In addition to paying her tuition, the Air Force paid her a full-time salary with benefits while she was a full-time student.

For all the positives, there is a down side to life in the military. The relocations every six years are obstacles to forming lasting relationships. "We don't stay in one place too long, and by the time you meet someone and think you may be ready to make a commitment to him, you get reassigned. You become a GU—Geographically Undesirable." But Johnson takes it all in stride. Although her six-year tour in Dayton is coming to an end and she doesn't know where her next assignment will take her, she maintains, "I love the change of the military."

Leader and Healer

When Clara Adams-Ender joined the Army 30 years ago, she thought she'd do her tour and then just "find a husband." But in addition to finding a husband, she learned that she had plenty of ambition and leadership ability. In 1987 her management skills were recognized by President Reagan, who appointed her Chief of the Army Nurse Corps. "I never thought I would be the chief. That wasn't really my goal. So it was kind of by divine providence that I ended up here." And in 1967 she was the first woman ever to be awarded the Army Expert Field Medical Badge, another honor she didn't expect.

Adams-Ender entered the Army's Student Nurse Program in 1959. The agreement was that the Army would pay the tuition for her remaining two years at North Carolina A & T University, and Adams-Ender would then serve as an army nurse for three years. "I just intended to do my years and get out. The orientation of women at that time was to get married and get someone to take care of you. But that didn't happen and I liked the security of the services. I liked making my own money, so I decided to stay."

Adams-Ender did manage to squeeze in marriage and has a 10-year-old stepson. She met her husband, a retired orthodontist and oral surgeon, while she was on a tour of duty in West Germany.

The 50-year-old Adams-Ender says sexism is a factor for all women in the military, even those climbing the ladders of traditionally female fields such as nursing. "Sexism is more pervasive than racism in the military." But Adams-Ender says she learned early on how to overstep sexism while growing up on a farm in North Carolina. "One of the things that helps me in a man's world is that I grew up with two brothers. I learned to play baseball and do the things boys do."

At 29, Barbara Hare-Salnave decided the only way to satisfy her deep patriotism and her zest for travel was to enlist in the Air Force. "I've always been a very patriotic person. I got it from my mother. She has always talked about God and country. She was proud to be an American," says Hare-Salnave. Because she was past the maximum age for Air Force enlistees, she chose the Navy.

"I'm really what you would call a latecomer," Hare-Salnave says. After completing basic training, she was assigned to San Diego and then to Guam. Following a year as a radio message operator, she became a Navy career counselor. Nine years later she became a Chief Petty Officer, an upgrade she says usually takes 14 years.

> **"I liked the security of the services. I liked making my own money, so I decided to stay."**

Hare-Salnave is now on the Chief of Naval Operations' Retention Team, one of the Navy's most prestigious personnel units. Based in Washington, D.C., the 42-year-old Richmond, Virginia, native travels to Navy bases worldwide to lecture to sailors on the benefits and opportunities available in the Navy. "It's so easy for me because I'm expressing to them what I've lived. I'm just a little girl from Richmond, and the Navy has given me opportunities I never thought I would have."

Power to Inform

As a child growing up in St. Thomas, U.S. Virgin Islands, Janet Mescus loved to watch the military drill teams. Soldiers stepping with strict discipline in boots that shone like glass thrilled her. "It was even more fun than dressing Barbie dolls. I've always loved marching and uniforms. It's a form of discipline that's always been attractive to me," she says. The attraction sparked Mescus's interest in the military.

Mescus also wanted to attend college, so joining the Navy Reserve Officer Training Corps (ROTC) as a freshman at the University of South Carolina was a perfect mesh. "In the Virgin Islands, the Army was very prevalent. Everyone was joining the Army, but I wanted to do something a little different, so I picked the Navy."

Upon graduation, Mescus, now 30, was commissioned a lieutenant. With her degree in media arts, she began her military career as a Navy Public Affairs Officer, responsible for providing information to the press and the public. In 1983 she was three days into her tour of duty in Puerto Rico when Grenada was invaded. "We had 25 to 30 reporters outside the main gate at most times. It was exciting. This is not a routine job. Every day when I wake up I expect something different to happen, whether it's a disaster or something positive. I will stay in the Navy as long as it's fun. When it stops being fun, I'll move on to something else. After eight and a half years, it's still fun to me."

Chapter 4:

How Have Other Nations Integrated Women into the Military?

Preface

Just as cultures vary widely throughout the world, so do their perceptions of the roles women should perform in their armed forces. Many cultures that traditionally have excluded women from male-dominated occupations—Saudi Arabia, for example—may find it inappropriate for women to serve in the military. Some cultures that place less emphasis on gender roles—Denmark, for example—do not have the same reluctance to enlist servicewomen in the nation's defense. Most nations fall somewhere in the middle ground. The United States is among the nations that continue to struggle over the question of how best to use women in the armed forces. Usually this struggle is a reflection of each nation's social struggle over the appropriate roles of men and women.

The Need for Women Soldiers

In wartime, maintaining male/female differences is less important than the nation's defense. For example, during World War II, many nations, desperate for more troops, enlisted women both for combat and combat-support positions. Soviet and Yugoslavian women fought side-by-side with men, for example, while American and Canadian women were called upon to serve in combat-support positions. In 1948, Israeli women were drafted to help fight in Israel's War for Independence. In most instances, however, when the need for women soldiers diminished after these wars, nations went back to their pre-war policies, often prohibiting women from serving in the military or in combat. Even Israel has not allowed women to serve on the front lines since 1948.

However, as career opportunities for women in many societies began expanding in the 1970s, so did opportunities for women in the military. The United States began opening up the regular military to women in the 1970s, as did European nations such as the Netherlands. For many years, most nations offered only noncombat positions to women. Recently, however, the Netherlands, Canada, Belgium, Norway, and other nations that formerly banned women from combat roles have changed their policies. The experiences of these nations will become a guide, as other nations, such as the United States, debate the role of women in their militaries.

Women's Military Participation Throughout the World			
No Participation	**Limited Participation**		**Full Participation**
Afghanistan El Salvador Iran Italy Kuwait Poland Saudi Arabia Spain	Algeria Argentina Australia Austria Brazil Britain Bulgaria Burma Chile China Colombia Cuba Czechoslovakia Ecuador Egypt Germany Finland France Greece Guatemala Honduras Hungary India Indonesia Ireland Israel Japan Jordan Libya	Malaysia Mexico Mozambique The Netherlands New Zealand Nicaragua Nigeria Pakistan Panama Peru Philippines Romania Senegal Singapore South Africa Soviet Union Sri Lanka Sudan Sweden Switzerland Taiwan Tanzania Thailand Turkey United States Vietnam Yugoslavia Zimbabwe	Belgium Canada Denmark Kenya Luxemborg Norway Portugal Somalia Venezuela Zambia

Sources: *Women and the Military System,* Eva Isaksson, ed. New York: Simon and Schuster, 1988.
Women in the Military: 1980-1990, Carolyn Becraft. Washington, DC: Women's Research and Education Institute, 1990.

Women Were Crucial in Israel's War for Independence

Shelly Saywell

About the Author: *Shelly Saywell is a television researcher and producer who lives in Toronto, Canada.*

We trained with the boys, slept in tents with them and fought with them. The unusual thing was that it was not unusual. We all did it.
—Yaffa, *Palmach soldier*

I am sure many of [the commanders] would rather have made love to me than send me out to fight. But they had no choice. It was total war.
—Shifra, *Haganah fighter*

As one historian wrote: "The Second World War was the centrepiece of the last act of the story; the generation after the war was kept busy with the epilogue." That epilogue saw the World War end and the Cold War begin, the defeat of colonialism and wars of independence in various parts of the so-called Third World. It also saw the creation of the state of Israel and the displacement of Palestinian Arabs, in an area of such strategic importance and ongoing tension that it has remained at centre stage ever since.

The horrifying revelation of the Holocaust at the end of the Second World War was the most visible catalyst for the events that followed in Palestine. Although Zionism was an ideology that had been embraced by pioneering Jews in Palestine since the late 1800s, it was the tragedy of the Holocaust, in which six million Jews lost their lives, that propelled the events that followed.

The idea of Jewish women fighting in Palestine was not new in the 1948 War of Independence. An underground army, the Haganah, had trained women in armed defence since the 1920s. Women, however, were trained for defence of their isolated settlements, not for aggressive warfare. Girls learned basic weaponry in their schools, and youth organizations taught both sexes the rudiments of fighting. By the end of the Second World War Jewish women in Palestine were members of the underground defence organization, and not unfamiliar with weaponry. . . .

"Whenever one raises the subject of women fighters, people usually refer to Israel."

Whenever one raises the subject of women fighters, people usually refer to Israel. Over the years photographs of young Israeli women in fatigues carrying Uzi machine-guns have reminded us of the legacy of women fighters that began in the first days of Jewish immigration to Palestine. Over twelve thousand women are said to have fought during the War of Independence, yet it was the last war in which Israeli women were combatant. Today women are still drafted for service in the army and trained in weaponry, but they are not allowed into battle. There have been exceptions to the rule, and there are small groups of men and women who are sent to guard isolated kibbutzim today. But officially women are not permitted to be in combat. When the underground army became official with the Declaration of Independence, a women's corps was formed. Some say the regulations banning women from combat were adopted as a result of political pressure from Orthodox groups, others that they were imposed because women soldiers had higher casualties than men in 1948. Whatever the reasons, there is little doubt that Israel, like most countries, can bear the idea of women in combat only in times of national emergency. Otherwise, it has remained traditional in its defence regulations. Now in their late fifties, the four vital women I met, whose experiences thirty-five years ago seem to them almost unbelievable, still feel that their involvement in creating a nation remains the most significant and meaningful event of their lives. Only one of them, however, would permit her full name to be used. I was told by the others that they felt they had done no more than what all young women were doing at the time and that they did not want to be singled out.

Hanna Armoni resides in Tel Aviv today, where she heads a museum of a former guerrilla organization called the Lehi, or Stern Gang, that operated against the British in Palestine. She agreed to meet me and tell me about her experiences from 1943 to 1948 because "I have a great sense of history. I feel we must talk about these things." As a member of a guerrilla group that was extremely controversial and unpopular even among most of the Jews in Palestine, Hanna says that she needed to be strong in the face of solitude. Today she exudes a strong-willed personality and a great deal of energy.

"I believed that if men could fight in battles, then so could I."

I travelled to New Jersey to meet Yaffa and Shoula, both former members of the Palmach, the fighting arm of the underground. These two women had been best friends since childhood in Haifa and after thirty-five years, by coincidence, both were living in the United States. I interviewed them together. They had not talked about those days for a long time, they said, and since they hadn't seen each other in so long there was almost the feeling of a reunion.

Shifra resides in Toronto, where she has lived for a number of years, but she grew up in Jerusalem and participated in a defence unit there during the siege of 1948, in which she fought in the trenches with the men. She is a highly energetic woman, always busy with community work and family. Although she agreed to talk to me she soon confessed that she tries never to think of the war "because I have too many unhappy memories." Her attitude towards her actions of thirty-five years ago: "I did what I had to do. If I was not there, someone else would have done it for me."

A Woman Freedom Fighter

"If you had seen me then you would never have believed I was a 'guerrilla.' I was so thin, so delicate, I didn't look as though I could hurt a fly," smiles Hanna Armoni, a former member of the Lehi or "Freedom Fighters of Israel," which operated against the British in Palestine until 1948. . . .

The Lehi advocated that the time had come to create an independent Jewish state. Like other Lehi members, Hanna believed that the British, who had ruled in Palestine since 1917, had no interest in giving it up.

During the Second World War most Palestinian Jews had joined the British to fight Hitler. The Lehi maintained that Britain was the enemy and had stabbed them in the back. In 1939, in need of Arab support against Germany, Britain had issued a White Paper that put a ceiling on Jewish immigration to Palestine. Zionists believed that it revoked promises to help the Jews create a sovereign state. There was a further moral issue: curtailing Jewish immigration to the country would leave millions of European Jews victims of Nazi Germany.

Hanna joined the Lehi after she accidentally met a couple of members. She believed that "we needed to get the British to listen to us. They had given in to Arab pressure regarding Palestine. We believed that we had to make a lot of noise too so they would listen to us. Of course, most of the population thought the Lehi was wrong until the end of the war.". . .

"There were quite a lot of women in the Lehi, which then numbered about two hundred people. I struggled for . . . feminism. I believed that a woman could do anything a man can do. I believed that if men could fight in battles, then so could I. The reaction to that was, 'Yes, all right. But you have to wait.' They said it was a matter of experience rather than sex. They said when the time came I would be chosen to help. Some men treated women as equals, some didn't. When I first joined I believed women could even do things requiring a great deal of physical strength. I said, 'I'm strong enough.' I was so determined.". . .

One of her first sabotage missions was to blow up a railway bridge near Akko to disrupt British transport of military supplies. "I had been taught to handle explosives and guns. We learned these things in a house we rented in a village.

"We planned the action carefully. One group was to blow up the bridge. My group of three people was to set off explosives farther down the tracks. As in all operations, I was scared. As we left that night I was trying not to shake. My motivation was so strong that it helped. My job was to tie the explosives on the rails. Then we hid in the bushes and waited to hear the explosion on the bridge before lighting our fuses. But just then we heard an unexpected train coming towards us, so we rushed down and untied the explosives. We didn't want to accidentally blow up a passenger train.

"Everybody was ready to die for each other and for the cause."

"When it had passed, I tied them again. As I was doing so, I noticed that one of the fuses had come out and the bomb could have exploded at any moment. Luckily nothing happened. We lived by luck, too. Finally we heard the explosion on the bridge and lit our fuses and rushed off. Later, when we learned that everything had come off just as we had planned it and that we hadn't hurt anybody, we were extremely happy."

Hanna's main job during 1944 and 1945 was

to help recruit people into the Lehi. "I had to explain to people who wanted to join exactly what we were trying to do. We didn't take any people who didn't completely understand the cause or who weren't sure they could do it." She describes those who did join: "After one minute, strangers became friends. Our common ideal was so strong. Now it seems so rhetorical, but at that time it was real and everybody was a real friend. We understood each other. Everybody was ready to die for each other and for the cause.". . .

Two Friends Join the Palmach

At the end of the Second World War, two school girlfriends from Haifa joined the Haganah's elite fighting army, the Palmach. They were in many ways a product of their generation. As Sabras, Jews born in Palestine, both were deeply committed Zionists, but they were more pacifist in their views than Hanna. They believed in expanding Jewish settlements in Palestine and still hoped that the British would eventually negotiate on the creation of a sovereign state. Like all young women who joined the Haganah youth groups, they had been taught the rudiments of weaponry and self-defence. But when the World War ended they chose to join the Palmach as full-time volunteers. Shoula and Yaffa had been friends from childhood. They shared the same upbringing and the same idealism.

Shoula: "We very much wanted to finish school, but we felt the need to fight—not only for the creation of Israel, but for the refugees who were not allowed in by the British." She explained that the Palmach's philosophy was not to attack the British, but to protect settlements and help refugees. "We did not fight for fighting's sake. Only when we were attacked."

Shoula's father had been a pioneer to Palestine early in the century, and she says that her parents were "proud of me for making that choice." Yaffa's parents were also proud. "It was not difficult for them to accept girls' doing this," she says. "You must understand that all young people believed that it was not a matter of choice, but of duty. We were educated that way—in school, after school, in the kibbutz. We were taught to do our duty because it was our duty."

The Palmach, which means "striking companies," grew out of all-Jewish units who had fought with the British during the Second World War. When the war ended they went underground (since it was illegal for them to form an army) and stationed themselves, undercover, on kibbutzim. During the war several Palmach women had served behind the lines in Europe. Hanna Senesh and Haviva Reich were parachuted into Yugoslavia to help organize escape routes for the underground. Both were subsequently caught and executed.

There were approximately twenty-one hundred soldiers in the Palmach when Shoula and Yaffa joined in 1946. Though the Haganah itself trained women only for static defence against Arab attacks, the Palmach accepted women as equal combatants. By 1947 sixteen percent of its soldiers were said to be women. It was the only organized Jewish military body, and essentially it functioned as an autonomous army, though under the Haganah umbrella. In almost all ways women were trained and expected to perform in the same capacities as men.

"During the war several Palmach women had served behind the lines in Europe."

Shoula was a fair-haired nineteen-year-old, and Yaffa, one year younger, a vivacious redhead. They were assigned to a unit that consisted of about thirty people, of which half were female. "It wasn't unusual for girls to join," says Shoula. "It was very natural for us. We trained with the boys and never considered anything like 'women's lib.'"

In addition to their training, they helped work on the kibbutz, living in tents, which would be hastily taken down whenever there was ru-

mour of British inspections. Then they would merge with the people of the settlement.

Yaffa: "Our group took a vote and decided that boys and girls could share the same tent. We either had two girls and a boy, or the reverse. We were so shy and naive that there was no problem with co-habitation," she smiles, "though that might be hard to understand today."

The days began early with long hikes, running and jogging. "They really stressed physical fitness," Yaffa continues. "We had to run three kilometres each morning in hiking shoes with knapsacks on our backs. We had to know how to run long distances in the field. We also learned judo, first aid and weaponry. We learned to shoot and throw grenades. They even taught us to fight with sticks, because it was illegal for us to possess weapons under the British Mandate.". . .

Britain and Israel

By 1947 the British wanted out of Palestine and a solution to the increasingly widespread violence between Arabs and Jews and against themselves. The Palmach, though not primarily offensive at this time, did launch attacks on British military installations at night—mainly to steal equipment. The Etzel and the Lehi continued attacks on individuals. Furthermore, the British were being pressured by Washington to allow a hundred thousand Holocaust survivors into Palestine, and pressured by the Arabs not to break the immigration ceiling. There were a hundred thousand British or Commonwealth soldiers in Palestine in 1945-46. As they came under personal attack by Jewish organizations their conduct understandably altered.

A young teenage student living in the Talpiot suburb of Jerusalem remembers that by 1946 Jerusalem had become "a city of fear. The British soldiers policed the streets drunk and wild," says Shifra. "But despite the fact that I hated them for stabbing us in the back politically, I felt sorry for the soldiers who walked around in mortal fear of being assassinated." She disagreed entirely with the tactics of the Etzel and Lehi and says, "They were ragtag, disorganized and unethical groups. They gave us bad reputations, and because of them we lost some sympathy abroad. I almost got arrested because of their actions."

A Member of the Haganah

Shifra was the only child of Orthodox parents. Her mother had died when she was very young, and she was raised by her father, a wealthy businessman who had worked with the British in the Second World War. She attended a French high school because her father wanted her to learn the French language and someday study abroad. In 1945 she joined the youth group of the Jerusalem Haganah. The blue-eyed, chestnut-haired girl had sensual good looks and though only sixteen seemed older. Because of the loss of her mother she had taken on adult responsibilities. She returned home from long school days to cook dinner for her father and helped him run the household. The end of the World War had produced in her "a personal consciousness of my own destiny and a sense of politics," she says. She had therefore joined the youth group without telling her father.

"My father would not have approved," she explains. "So my girlfriend's mother covered up for me by saying I was staying at their house on weekends and holidays." As an Orthodox Jew her father was a pacifist and believed in traditional roles for women. "He would have liked not to see wars, and would ask, 'Why my little girl?' but by 1945 things were seething and boiling in Palestine and I wanted to be part of it."

Great Britain now turned to the United Nations for help in finding a solution to the conflict between Arabs and Jews that would ensue once the British had left. All Palestinians knew that there was little hope of avoiding war. As one Jewish leader said, "If the UN votes for a partition, the Arabs will not accept it. If they vote against a partition, we will not accept it." Both sides geared up for war.

In early 1946, at nineteen years of age, Hanna Armoni married one of the Lehi boys who had recruited her in 1943. They had fallen in love in part because of the shared idealism that made all members very close. They asked the organization for permission to marry, not because they needed to but out of respect. Though they were told not to expect any special treatment such as the opportunity to go on joint missions, she says, "We did seem to get them quite often."

Hanna didn't know she was pregnant when the Lehi planned their next action, an attack on the train repair factories near Haifa. Over forty members took part. Hanna was assigned with a man to mine one section of roads leading to the factories, to act as a road block. Other groups blocked the other roads, and the rest were to sneak into the huge buildings and blow them up.

"In almost all ways women were trained and expected to perform in the same capacities as men."

Hanna and her colleague took lamps to light up the warning signs they placed before the mined section of the road in the pitch black night. It was an extremely dangerous area because there were British military bases and police stations nearby. The group sent in to blow up the buildings had twenty minutes to complete their mission. Hanna's husband was among them.

When the explosion was set off the groups began their hasty retreat, but two members did not turn up at the prearranged spot. The others went back into the huge complex to look for them. When they finally found them they rushed to leave the area, but it had been forty-five minutes since they had begun the action and the British troops in the area had already cleared one road of its mines. The Lehi group was ambushed as it retreated. Eleven Lehi members were killed and twenty-three captured; only a few managed to escape. "My husband was among the nineteen boys who were captured and all were sentenced to death," says Hanna. "Four girls were also caught and sentenced to life imprisonment.". . .

After the birth of her daughter, Hanna returned to live with her parents in Tel Aviv. Six weeks later the Etzel and Lehi broke into the Akko Prison to get their people out. During the escape British soldiers shot and killed Hanna's husband, who was in a get-away car.

"I had often thought about the possibilities of him or myself dying," she reflects. "But it was a great shock. He was only twenty-two, but I believe that in his short life he accomplished more than most people could in a hundred years. It took years to understand, to get over the sorrow, but now it has its proper place.

"Age was an important factor. I think that if such a thing happened today, God forbid, I would be much more frightened, much less strong. But then I had strength. I told myself there would be better times, when we would no longer need war and could live in peace.

"Still, I had my baby and my battle to fight. I refused to stop. I went to Haifa and one of the member's wives took care of my baby. I kept very busy. I was made responsible for education of the youth groups."

"I never allowed myself to think in terms of where I got the courage."

Despite the united resistance agreed upon by the Haganah, Etzel and Lehi immediately after the end of the World War, the tactics utilized by the Etzel and Lehi, predominantly acts of urban terrorists, were condemned by Jewish leader David Ben-Gurion. On 22 July 1946 the Etzel's assault group blew up Jerusalem's King David Hotel, the British military headquarters. Eighty-eight people were killed, including Arabs and Jews. The Haganah immediately denied involvement in the action. The united resistance had come to an end.

Shoula and Yaffa remember the split. Shoula: "They did not have the same philosophy as us. The Palmach believed in building the state slowly by settling the land and protecting the settlements from attack. The Urgun and Lehi thought the way we worked was too peaceful." Yaffa: "We acknowledged their devotion and bravery but took those things for granted, as everybody was ready to give all he or she had. We did not agree with the tactics they used. We felt they were irresponsible and hurt our cause.". . .

Working on a Kibbutz

Yaffa worked at a kibbutz near Jerusalem, functioning as "a secretary without papers, meaning I did everything no one else had time to do." She adds, "Everybody else had a specific thing to do. One would be in charge of arms, which were hidden in deep holes in the ground. Another was a driver. Another was the officer. I feel funny saying officer," she smiles, "because he didn't wear a uniform or anything. He didn't look special. He was a friend in every way. We didn't have special dining rooms or anything. We all ate together. I was in charge of communications. I was the only woman there, but we had people to cook for us, so I didn't have to do stereotypical female jobs. In the headquarters I shared a room with one other guy, but nothing went on between us. If I wanted to get dressed or undressed, I would just say 'curfew' and he would turn his head. Curfew meant the other one had to hide under the sheets or turn around. I felt secure with him in the room even when I was undressed. I never worried about it. A lot of people can't understand that. I lived for six months that way and nothing ever happened, because we weren't in love. There was no reason for us to get into any other relationship than the true friendship we felt for each other.". . .

Fighting in Jerusalem continued day and night. Shifra remained in her old stone home in Talpiot. Her father helped get food and water supplies to the beleaguered forces but eventually left the suburb and stayed in the city.

Talpiot was on the road from Bethlehem and

was surrounded by Arab villages. It had become a military zone. Shifra was given a gun. The tumultuous and quickly paced events have merged and become confused in her memory. She says, "It is all fused. I guess I've blocked some of it out. I remember walking around with a gun all the time." Her unit was given orders to capture the rich Arab neighbourhood of Baka, a first step towards opening the road into the city. "When we got this order everyone was extremely afraid," she remembers. "We had to go through the Arab neighbourhood in units of three people. We planned the attack for night, as we always did. We were to go in and take the area, house by house. None of us thought we would leave there alive.

"We walked in and it was incredible! The coffee was still hot and the beds had been slept in, the closets were full of food and clothes. The entire population had fled. We just walked in and took it.

"Some of the houses had already been looted—by our own people. There are many things that we are not proud of."

Also merged in her memory are the endless nights spent in trenches. "The Arabs attacked by night, so we had our guard shifts. We would just lie there waiting for a sound. We sat there and didn't know if they were coming or not. We didn't hesitate if we heard anything. We began shooting. I killed people.

"Only the Jews used women as fighters."

"I never allowed myself to think in terms of where I got the courage. We had an attitude: it was live and let live, but the Arabs weren't going to let us live, so we had to fend for ourselves. It meant I had to fight. We took care, tried to be careful, but we didn't think in terms of courage. We just did it. Maybe there were times I became hysterical and someone had to slap me out of it. I don't remember. But I never saw the people I

killed. I never shot point-blank except at target practice.". . .

Jewish and Arab Women

Shifra's unit fought in Operation Nahshon, an attack to reopen the road into Jerusalem from the north. But as the Haganah fighters fought to reclaim mile after mile of the road that led in from the heights, the IZL (Fighters of the Irgun) attacked a nearby Arab village of Deir Yassin, killing two hundred men, women and children. Shifra witnessed the results of the massacre only hours later. "When I saw what our side had done I felt sick to my stomach. I felt apologetic. But I shouldn't have because this was the Irgun—Menachem Begin's doing—not ours. He was smearing our war with shame." The tragedies and atrocities of the unofficial war did not spare innocent civilians. Guerrilla fighting obstructed order and front lines. Civilians huddled in the basements of both mosques and synagogues.

But in this "total war" for each block of each city, each acre of every settlement, only the Jews used women as fighters. There may have been exceptional cases in which Arab women picked up guns, but for the most part Arab women would not fight until later conflicts. It was something they learned from the Jews. Arab reaction to enemy women fighters was reportedly demoralization. More than affronting their chauvinism, the presence of Jewish women in battle clearly indicated to the Arabs that this was a war in which the Jews were prepared to use every possible force.

Though even the Palmach tried to keep their women fighters relegated to the jobs of arming convoys and defending settlements—to protect them from the most severe combat—the women fought alongside the men and suffered injury, maiming and death. Most frightening were reports of what happened to women soldiers captured by the enemy. "Our commanders did feel protective," says Shifra. "I am sure many of them would rather have made love to me than send me out to fight. But they had no choice. It was total war."

A founder of the Palmach, Yigal Allon, later wrote about the importance of women in the fight:

The presence of women in combat units blurred and decreased the harshness of military life; it lent substance to the Palmach concept of an armed force free of militarism; and it precluded the brutalization of young men thrown into an all-male society for months on end. The mobilization of daughters, sisters, sweethearts, and often wives turned the Palmach into a true People's Army.

Shoula agrees: "When a woman was in the group the men behaved much more nicely and politely. They seemed happy to have us. I don't think we affected them in any kind of negative way. Sometimes, I thought, women were even stronger emotionally in bad situations. In war some men are strong and some are not. It really boils down to education. If you are educated and trained to do your duty, you do it, whether you are a man or a woman. Women don't like killing, perhaps—but neither do a lot of men. We felt terrible when anyone was killed or maimed, and did not take it any more badly if it were a girl rather than a boy. We were in it together.". . .

Peace Missions

Just before the final withdrawal of the British from Palestine Ben-Gurion sent a personal envoy on a peace mission to Amman to discuss with King Abdullah of Transjordan means of avoiding full-scale war. His envoy was a woman who would be famous to the world in years to come. Disguised as an Arab, Golda Meir made safe passage to the top-secret meeting. But the talks broke down when she was told that the Arab nations would call off a full-scale attack only if the Palestinian Jews would relinquish claims to a sovereign state. Mrs. Meir, who would lead her country to war in years to follow, relayed this final ultimatum to Ben-Gurion. A few weeks later, only two hours before the official end of the British Mandate on 14 May 1948, Ben-Gurion read Israel's Declaration of Independence to an emotional audience in Tel Aviv. Hanna Armoni, then residing there with her family, remembers that the first Egyptian air attack on the city came that same night.

The next day the new state of Israel was simultaneously invaded by armies from Lebanon, Syria, Egypt and Transjordan. In total the invading armies were said to number about twenty-three thousand men. The Arab armies had tanks, superior firepower and air support. The Haganah, which overnight had become Israel's official army (the Zahal) had no tanks and no air force.

"Political as well as practical arguments favoured taking women out of direct combat."

Fierce fighting continued in Jerusalem, where Zahal fighters attacked and attempted to seize the Old City as soon as the British were gone. In the month-long fighting that ensued the Jewish quarter of the Old City was almost completely levelled, and the Jewish fighters eventually surrendered to officers of the Arab Legion. In other sections of the city water and food shortages had become critical. On 11 June a truce was negotiated by the United Nations, and fighting throughout the country temporarily stopped. Shifra was given five days' leave and went to stay with a friend near the beach in Tel Aviv. She says, "I just stayed on the sand, staring at the water for the whole five days. I was burnt to a crisp, but I didn't care. I hadn't seen water for so long. I kept staring at it, and it helped me a lot. It helped me get back to myself."

Both sides used the month-long cease-fire to regroup and resupply. The Israeli army now numbered nearly sixty thousand soldiers, of whom twelve thousand were women, and was in the process of becoming a conventional army. As its numbers grew the policies regarding women changed. Because it was now the official army, run by the government, political as well as practical arguments favoured taking women out of direct combat and putting them in their own units. As a large body of the electorate, Orthodox Jews pressured the leaders to stop women from fighting. They and others argued that it was immoral to billet men and women together; some statistics indicated that mixed-combat units had higher casualties; no other civilized country accepted women into combat roles in the armed forces. Because the Israeli army no longer needed "every able-bodied man or woman," and because pressure was extreme, the army enforced the change. Where possible women were assigned new roles, out of combat.

Shifra was sent to an officers' training course in Tel Aviv. "They taught us to forget everything we had been previously taught and learn things all over again," she muses. "It meant a new kind of discipline, and even uniforms. I actually preferred it. I liked the change because I am a very organized person. I got a rank and became a sergeant major in charge of a nurses' unit." But was there no resentment, after having been a fighter? "No. Women continued to do vital jobs that allowed the men to go forth and fight. These jobs had to be done by someone, and I don't think they were any less valuable to the war effort. There was a fear of what might be done to a woman caught by the Arabs. And anyway, we girls weren't fighting to prove anything. I have no hang-ups about my femininity. I fought when there was no choice, but when I was no longer needed in that role I was happy to move on to something else. Besides," she smiles, "I had my uniform tailor-made and looked good in it."

"Both sexes were expected to fight—to do their duty."

For Yaffa and Shoula the change had no personal effect. Though the Palmach was no longer sending new women recruits to mixed fighting units, they did not reassign those who were there. Shoula remained in the Negev where fighting was intense and continued in the same capacity. Yaffa remained a communications operator in a fighting unit, and her commander's adjutant. When asked if they nonetheless resented the policy change and its implications, they both seemed surprised. Sexism was hardly an issue while the fighting lasted, they said. Yigal Allon wrote about some of the reactions:

> The girls stormed at any proposed discrimination, arguing that it ran counter to the spirit of the new society being built in Palestine to restrict women to domestic chores, particularly since they had proven their competence as marksmen and sappers. In the end, the wiser counsel prevailed. The girls were still trained for combat, but placed in units of their own, so that they would not compete physically with men. Whenever possible, they were trained for defensive warfare only.

Yaffa says, "They stopped letting girls go in action units where they had to run a lot. Physically girls couldn't run as well—and if they couldn't run fast enough they could endanger the whole unit, so they were put in other units. But they still fought."

Shoula: "Yes, I remember they made decisions on these things. They found it very hard for women. But mainly I think it was because of political pressure." . . .

Doing One's Duty

Shifra married her English officer and managed to take the final exams that she needed to graduate from high school. They moved to a new settlement, "with very few amenities," where she gave birth to the first Jewish baby who had been born there in two thousand years.

"We women of Israel fought because we had to. We fought because we had no choice. It wasn't a feminist thing. It was our duty.

Now women are not allowed combat roles, but Shoula thinks current wars would be too difficult for women. "But my daughter, like my son, does her duty, and if there was ever total war again, I'm sure that she and all the girls would fight."

Yugoslavian Women Fought Effectively in World War II

Barbara Jancar

About the Author: *Barbara Jancar is a political science professor at the State University of New York in Brockport. A former fellow in the East European Program at the Smithsonian Institute's Wilson Center, Jancar has written numerous articles and books on women in Eastern Europe.*

The military role of women in Yugoslavia's National Liberation Struggle (NOB) is only one way of studying the participation of Yugoslav women in those decisive years which determined that country's postwar political shape. The official figure for women's total participation in the partisan cause is 2 million, or about 12 per cent of the prewar population. Of these, 100,000 were soldiers in the partisan guerrilla forces, of whom 25,000 died and 40,000 were wounded. Some 2,000 women achieved officer's rank. Some 282,000 of the women participants on the side of the partisans are estimated to have died or been killed in the concentration camps. A dedicated but indeterminate number were engaged in terrorist and guerrilla activities in the territories occupied by the enemy. The balance of the women were employed in logistic and supply operations in the rear in what were termed the liberated areas.

Given the more massive participation of women in other aspects of Yugoslavia's revolution, why should we single out the women soldier? Above all else, the *partizanka* was the dual

Adapted from *Women and Revolution in Yugoslavia, 1941-1945* by Barbara Jancar. Reprinted with the author's permission.

symbol of women's fighting contribution to the revolution and of her stake in the emerging socialist Yugoslavia which promised women an equal place with men. The Second World War in Yugoslavia was not one war but three. It was a war against the invader. It was a war between the country's feuding nationalities to achieve equal status in her political system. And it was a political war between the Communist-led partisans desiring to overturn the old order and create a socialist Yugoslavia along Soviet lines, and those who wanted varying degrees of a restoration of the *status quo ante*. Women were caught up in all of these wars.

> ## "Some 282,000 of the women participants . . . are estimated to have died or been killed in the concentration camps."

The typical woman of prewar Yugoslavia was a mother in a peasant household, illiterate, and whether Christian or Moslem, subordinate to the patriarchal rule of her husband. In the mountainous regions of Macedonia, Montenegro and Bosnia, peasant women had long held a reputation as fierce fighters for their homes and families against the invading Turk. This tradition came to life again in the Second World War, symbolized by the *partizanka*. In the industrializing cities, women were at the bottom of the labour ladder, the worst paid, the last hired, and the first to go when a crisis came. It was not surprising therefore that they should have been active in the strikes and wage protests which characterized the interwar labour movement in Yugoslavia. The urban woman's most urgent demand was the right to vote, and the civil rights movement attracted the largest number of adherents. As constitutional government was washed away in the rising tide of dictatorship, the movement appeared to grow in strength. Its culmination was a massive demonstration for the right to vote in all of Yugoslavia's major cities in

1939. To no avail. The realities of fascism, German occupation and civil war cut short the dreams. The *partizanka* came to stand for women fighting not only for national liberation from the invader but for their own rights and freedom.

Who were the women who joined the partisan army? Official wisdom and analysis of available data indicate that the huge majority of them were under 25 and probably as much as 70 per cent under 20. The partisans admitted women volunteers between the ages of 18 and 45, and accepted 17 year olds if they requested. In Croatia, these young fighters were known as *djeca borci* (child warriors). Because of their youth, many women soldiers were still in school or holding first factory jobs. According to Danisa Milosavljevic, commander of the 1st Battalion of the 2nd Proletarian Brigade during the final operation in Serbia, the majority of the young women who served under her had never seen military service before. In the older age groups, the partisan women came from a variety of occupations. Some were Serbian Orthodox nuns. Others were workers and teachers from the cities, but again the large majority were peasants. Most needed by the partisans were doctors and nurses. Because nurses in the interwar period had come from the nuns, young recruits had to be trained in medical work. For this reason, the partisan army treated women doctors with respect, and the few who joined, like Sasa Bozovic, developed legendary reputations.

Women in a World War

The women came from all over Yugoslavia. Probably, the greatest number were Serbian, although there are no data to support this assertion. Very few Moslem women joined the partisans. But one would not want to insist on the preponderance of any one nationality. Young girls came from all nationalities and regions where the war was fought. The majority of these young women came from villages under occupation, or that had been a target of war. The chair of the Yugoslav women's organization, Sasa Javorina, drew a distinction between these women who joined 'by instinct' and the more ideologically oriented women who volunteered in the first partisan units. Those mainly came from the large cities and towns, where they had come in contact with progressive ideas through literary circles and school clubs.

"The bravery of the woman soldier was legendary."

Motives for joining the partisan forces were diverse. In the forefront, doubtless, were personal reasons. A parent, brother, or fiancé had been massacred or sent to a concentration camp. In the hill country, where most of the battles were fought, the war entered women's lives directly, and personal tragedy forced them from the sidelines into action. Often whole families joined the partisans together.

Personal experience was not the only reason for joining. For many, the partisan life in the woods seemed infinitely preferable and safer than remaining in the exposed villages or cities, where enemy reprisals were sudden and unpredictable. Another factor was the camaraderie of the partisan experience. The single most precious memory for the former women partisans interviewed by the author in December-January 1985 was the common experience and danger of the war. They shared hunger and cold, and the exhilarating realization that one was tough and could bear infinite hardships. Such experiences forged permanent bonds between soldiers in the same unit. Women also joined because of the adventure and excitement the partisans offered. In some of the more remote villages, young women danced to radios for the first time in their lives. When the partisans were in town, the evenings were filled with music, dance and impromptu and professional theatre. The war brought not only danger but a new life-style to the village. Young girls wanted to be a part of that.

Because of their simple origins, many young women recruits had only the most confused idea of Tito or the Communist Party. One young courier thought the Party was a lovely woman from the Soviet Union who was stronger and more intelligent than the woman commissar of her unit. In some villages, women were discouraged from joining the partisans. They were told that the Communists recruited young women for immoral purposes and that the women soldiers led dissolute lives or were raped for the partisans' pleasure.

Probably only a minority of the young women joined the partisans for consciously held political or ideological reasons. Most of these had either been active in the prewar anti-fascist or women's movements, or their childhood experience had led them to become convinced nationalists. The most politically aware were the first recruits from the cities. For the majority, political education began in the partisan forces. While most ended the war with respect for the Party and a special loyalty to Tito, most entered it because of personal tragedy, the need to survive and the overriding desire to defend home and family.

"Women never deserted the units and were among the most heroic."

Initially, the Party leadership was not sure it wanted women soldiers. But the evident eagerness of women to serve changed its mind. Women were the first to volunteer when partisan detachments were organized. Thirty girls from the Bosnian village of Dvar were among the first to sign up in 1941, and the first woman national hero was from Dvar. Women actively participated in the abortive Montenegrin uprising of July 1941. Women were in the original partisan detachments of Macedonia, Slovenia and Serbia, and were also among the first to lose their lives.

When a woman joined the partisans, she assumed definite obligations. At induction she swore the partisan oath, pledging to destroy old habits of thought, commit herself to the 'working masses' and be full of love for her comrades-in-arms. Once inducted, the woman soldier was assigned generally to a unit in the territorial forces, which operated close to her home village. If she had more experience, she might be assigned to a unit in the proletarian divisions which were authorized to fight all over Yugoslavia and were subject to the orders of the partisan command. In both kinds of groups, there was strict discipline and a sense of commitment to an ideal which was larger than self. Many women embraced this new life eagerly. The 100,000 Yugoslav women who became soldiers rank numerically among the largest contingents of women ever to go into battle under military command at any time in history.

Distribution and Functions

As noted above, women were exceptionally eager to sign up. Vladimir Dedijer, one of Tito's closest associates during the war, recalls that women wanted to join so badly that they were shaking lest they be rejected. When the first women's battalion was formed in Lika, a village of Serbian peasant immigrants in southern Croatia, 700 women volunteered. Only 110 could be taken. A major disappointment was to be assigned a job that was not 'soldiering.' National Hero Albina Hocevar-Mali from Slovenia burst into tears when she was assigned her first duty as nurse. The doctor turned to her and said coldly, 'How can you cry? You, a SKOJka [a member of the Communist Youth League].' Communists must do as they are told cheerfully and willingly.

The first all women's partisan *ceta* (band or unit) was formed in Lika on 25 August 1942. In September of that year a second women's unit was formed in Turjanski, and a third and fourth a month later. These uniquely female units were later phased out by absorption into other *cete*. As a rule, a *ceta* of 300 would have five or six women. The *partizanke* were distributed in these mixed units throughout the territorial and operational commands.

An analysis of the relative strength of women to men in the units of the I Corps of the National Liberation Army (NLA) in Croatia provides some idea of their functions. The largest percentage of women appear to be at staff headquarters in this corps, and the next largest percentage in the artillery. The smallest percentage of women are not in the specialized units but in the regular territorial units. In none of the units does the proportion of women reach even 10 per cent. Data on the distribution of women in Dalmatian units analysed earlier by the author show without exception a concentration of women in the medical assistance jobs, although the largest number of women served as soldiers (42 per cent). Specialized soldiers and service personnel were far fewer as were political officers.

While women did not form a very large part of the overall fatalities in the I Corps, the share of women who lost their lives relative to the total number of women in the corps was almost 20 per cent. The share of men who died compared to the total was 24 per cent. The corps would appear to be representative, perhaps even a little low in female fatalities, since the total number of women partisans who died as compared to the total number enlisted was 25,000, or 25 per cent. In the VI Corps of the NLA Croatia, where 183 women had lost their lives as of 1944, we find that the common perception that nurses and staff personnel shared danger equally is illusory. The data suggest that it was far riskier to be a partisan soldier than a medic. The inexperienced peasant woman under 25 did not survive much beyond her baptism of fire. . . .

The Bravery of Women

The bravery of the woman soldier was legendary. National Hero Milka Kufrin became a symbol of partisan resistance for her courage in sabotaging the Zagreb-Karlovec railroad line and 'cleaning' the area of enemy units. Javorina proudly asserted that women never deserted the units and were among the most heroic. Milovan Djilas, who later broke with Tito over postwar policy, insisted that women were braver than men. Danisa Milosavljevic, one of the few women partisan officers, stressed women's stamina in the war and estimates that the soldiers in her command had walked over 4,000 miles of roadless terrain by 1945.

"The partisan male knew he could not openly oppose the position of the woman fighter."

Such courage is even better appreciated when it is placed within the context of the difficult conditions in which the soldiers lived. As stated earlier, most of the first women partisans came from the cities, where they had been workers, students or teachers. The peasant women were recruited later as the war developed in the mountains of Montenegro, Bosnia and Serbia. The professional women, in particular, were not used to physical work nor the rough primitive surroundings. Exposure to the harsh wartime conditions made it impossible for many of them to bear children after the war. According to Sasa Bozovic, numerous women, even the younger ones ceased to menstruate or had difficulties with their periods, a condition which was not uncommon elsewhere in wartime Europe, where proper food was scarce and living conditions deteriorated.

Women partisans lived the same life as the men, slept in the same quarters, ate the same food, and wore the same clothes. A partisan strict moral code governed daily living. Sexual relations were severely discouraged among the common soldiers. Love, said Javorina, showed itself in carrying a rifle for one's beloved or in giving an apple. Bozovic, however, recalled that youth would have its way, and that young people frequently succeeded in avoiding the strict eyes of the partisan command, even though they knew that swift punishment would follow if discovered. Women found the time to be women. The posed photographs in the published documents are full of handsome young women with smiling faces dressed in partisan uniform with surprisingly chic hairstyles under a partisan cap perhaps set a tiny bit askew to give a jaunty effect. Although the partisan code frowned on such frivolities, it seems only human nature that after the battle or before the camera, the girls would want to pretty themselves up, especially if there were evening activities scheduled. But no young *partizanka* could openly admit she was interested in such things. . . .

The documents and interviews provide no evidence of special military training for women. The standard formula was a one month's short course for all soldiers before being sent to the front. Frequent references are made to one-month 'political military courses' where both men and women received training. The partisans also offered courses in encoding and decoding, and artillery courses, but none of them was specifically directed towards women. The basic training courses were rudimentary at best, and in view of the urgency of the situation, could not last as long as they should have. The high mortality rate of young women suggests that women might have benefited from additional training. . . .

How can we fairly assess the role of women as fighters and the impact of this role upon the consciousness-raising process? The data and interviews indicate women sought the role of fighter as indicative of higher status, commitment and adventure. When they were admitted into the partisan units, they proved excellent, dedicated fighters. For the women active in the prewar Communist underground, admission was nine-tenths of the battle. The prewar programme both of the non-Communist Women's Movement and the Communist Party demanded that women be permitted to acquire male roles. The male role *par excellence* was that of the warrior. Thus the old generation of urban-born women Communists accepted woman's fighting role as proof of the programme achieved.

"The role of soldier was a personal breakthrough in which [women] successfully played a man's part in a man's world."

For the younger generation of peasant women, the wartime warrior role represented both a continuation of a valued patriarchal tradition and an uprooting from this tradition in the communist leadership's insistence on the equality myth translated into specific norms of conduct. This insistence expanded their sense of personal worth, giving them a *perception* of equality never before experienced. For both generations, the role of soldier was a personal breakthrough in which they successfully played a man's part in a man's world. . . .

Through their participation in the partisan forces, Yugoslav women proved to the world that women could fight as soldiers in a modern war as well or better than men.

Canada Successfully Allows Women to Serve in Combat Positions

Mary Suh

About the Author: *Mary Suh is a writer for* Ms., *a monthly women's magazine.*

Isabelle Gauthier just wanted a chance to drive a jeep. "I've got my license and all that," she explained. "I was able to drive, you know, just like everybody else." In 1981, she had fulfilled all the major requirements to be in the Regiment de Hull, a reserve armored division of the Canadian Armed Forces (CAF). During three months of training, she held her own in target practice, strength tests, and drills. But after the initial training ended, the men were tooling around in jeeps, and she was behind a desk, shifting papers.

Gauthier could never be in the driver's seat, because rules preventing women from engaging in military combat put operating jeeps, tanks, and rifles off limits. Worse, after only seven months, she got fired. Not for incompetence or insubordination, but because the regiment had its 10 percent allotment of women.

Gauthier fought back by suing the forces in 1981, and in 1989 she finally won. The Canadian Human Rights Tribunal, which hears cases of discrimination against federal employees, ruled that all combat positions must be opened to women, and no restrictions may be placed on their numbers. So for the first time, qualified

Mary Suh, "Canadian Women at Arms," *Ms.*, June 1989. Reprinted with permission, *Ms.* magazine, © 1989.

women can be fighter pilots, tank commandos, and naval officers—serving everywhere except in submarines where privacy needs preclude mixed gender crews.

Canada (and recently Sweden) joins three NATO [North Atlantic Treaty Organization] countries that employ women in combat jobs, but Belgium, the Netherlands, and Norway only draft men and their female forces are very small. Israel and the United States employ about 10 percent women, but have laws or policies excluding women from combat.

The CAF, which will not appeal the ruling, has inched toward a greater role for women, who serve in all ranks, including one brigadier general. In 1987, it launched CREW (Combat Related Employment of Women) trials, a five-year empirical study of mixed gender combat groups in the army and navy.

"Women should serve their country wherever men serve."

"We thought we might be able to demonstrate [to the tribunal] that putting women into combat situations was going beyond the experience we had to date," said Commander Judith Harper, director of the CREW trials. "We argued to let us continue the trials. We were in the spirit of the law, but we wanted to have an evaluation."

During the two-year existence of the tests, 41 women made it to combat positions in the army and navy. Greater success can be found in the skies: in 1987, the air force—without benefit of CREW—opened all combat jobs to women, and it has the largest number of women, including 45 pilots and 25 navigators.

The progress is real—albeit slow—but nothing would have happened without two decades of outside pressure. In 1970, the Royal Commission on the Status of Women noted that the military employed women in a small number of positions, such as nursing and personnel, and recommended opening up more opportunities, particularly in skilled trades like electronics and engineering. Three years after that report was issued, over two thirds of military occupations were opened to both sexes. But combat jobs were still off limits, and in other fields, like the armored units, a quota was established to ensure a certain percentage of men, as high as 90 percent.

Then the 1978 enactment of the Canadian Human Rights Act (CHRA) forced the complete reassessment of military policy. The act stipulated that there should be no discrimination against women, except under bona fide occupational requirement. "We never had a law, as you have in the United States, that prohibits women from going into combat," said Harper. "It was just a policy." And with the CHRA, the armed forces had to demonstrate why it was *not* possible for women to go into combat. "The prejudgment of the law was that women should serve their country wherever men serve," said Harper.

The tribunal ruling forces the military to continue the trials, but as the first stage of full integration of women into all units of the army and navy. And the Human Rights Commission will monitor the forces' compliance.

In the trials so far, women have been unable to meet the stamina standards required by the infantry. Of the 60 who started, only one has passed (four are still in training). But under CHRA, all physical standards must match job requirements, so the military may be forced to revamp its training and recruitment program.

Changing Macho Attitudes

A far bigger problem may be changing macho attitudes. "Nobody would come up and say that they didn't want women because they were women," said Anne Trotier, attorney for Gauthier. "But there was a lot of reluctance."

But the military isn't expecting armies of women to flood recruiting centers either. "There are not many women who want to get into this kind of employment," said Harper. "You can take an ordinary man and make a soldier of him, but you have to have an extraordinary woman to be a soldier."

"Oh, we heard that for so long," said retired Lieutenant Colonel Shirley Robinson. "The whole idea is that women would never want to be in the infantry. But let's face it; there's not that many men who want to go into the infantry either."

"Women went into combat roles during World War II."

Feminist groups are divided about the ruling. "We had an ambivalent reaction to it," said Lynn Kaye, president of National Action Committee on the Status of Women. "We take a strong pro-peace position, and we are very concerned about the militarization of our economy."

But the Association for Women's Equity in the Canadian Forces was ecstatic. Like other feminist military experts, they argue that the ruling is a clear-cut victory for Canadian women. About 60 percent of the country's mothers work outside the home, and their opportunities for training in marketable skills will vastly improve.

"Women went into combat roles during World War II," said Linda Grant De Pauw, director of the Minerva Center, a U.S. group that watches women in the military. "But now that war is only hypothetical, being described 'in combat' gets you status and career advantages."

One person not looking for combat duties is Isabelle Gauthier, who is still sitting behind a military desk in Ottawa. In 1981, she was younger and wanted different things. "Right now I'm very satisfied with my job," she said.

South Africa Uses Servicewomen to Promote Its Racist Ideology

Elaine Unterhalter

About the Author: *Elaine Unterhalter is a senior research officer in the sociology department at the University of Essex in Great Britain.*

White society in apartheid South Africa is characterised by marked racism and sexism. Nonetheless, despite the legal and economic barriers to women's equality and a highly developed ideology of the inferiority of women, white women have served in the military since 1971. This study examines some of the ambiguities that have resulted from the recruitment of white women for white South Africa in general and the South African Defence Force (SADF) in particular.

My argument is that the ideological need to unify whites around the military policy of the regime in support of minority white rule has been of paramount importance in recruiting white women. The increasing military mobilisation of white society against the black majority and the growing problem the SADF faced in staffing its permanent force, led to white women beginning to perform some important back-up roles for the military. But when the economic climate changed, and recession and unemployment meant that more white men took jobs with the military, the pressures to recruit white women purely for their labour were reduced. To date, the actual role of white women in the

Adapted from "Women Soldiers and White Unity in Apartheid South Africa" by Elaine Unterhalter, in *Images of Women in Peace and War: Cross-Cultural and Historical Perspectives*, edited by Sharon Macdonald, Pat Holden, and Shirley Ardener. Reprinted with permission of the author and the University of Wisconsin Press, © 1987, Elaine Unterhalter.

SADF in no way matches the grandiose claims made for their participation. Their mobilisation seems most important in terms of their white race. However, the actual presence of white women members of the SADF itself poses questions about their gender identity, and a whole barrage of popular ideological representations have been forged to maintain a 'feminine identity' for women doing somewhat similar jobs to men in a society in which sexism is deeply entrenched. . . .

"The actual role of white women . . . in no way matches the grandiose claims made for their participation."

White women served in the South African armed forces in the Second World War; there were 25,000 women recruited into the permanent force and 65,000 women in temporary positions, but they were all demobilised at the end of the war. In 1963 the Transvaal Congress of the NP [Nationalist Party] voted for military training to be made available for white women and this form of political pressure culminated in 1971 when, largely through the initiative of the Minister of Defence P. W. Botha, the Civil Defence Army Women's College, a military training college, was opened at George in the Cape, Botha's own constituency, to train white women for the civil defence structure of the commandos and the citizens' force. The significance of the location of the College appears to be primarily as an act of local patronage. At the opening ceremony of the George College, P. W. Botha described this recruitment of white women as:

> an act of faith in the women of South Africa and a manifestation of faith that the civilian population was preparing, in an organised way, a national 'wall' against military threats as well as emergencies and national disasters. (*Sunday Times*, 12 April 1971)

Linking the recruitment of white women to

acts of faith appears almost an elevation to religious heights; at the same time white women are identified as representing *all* South African women and, indeed, the civilian population as a whole, while South Africa itself is presented as a country facing imminent military attack.

Threats to White Rule

Both this speech and this initial mobilisation pose several problems of interpretation. In 1971 the external military threats to white rule in South Africa in the immediate future seemed negligible. Portugal, militarily supported by NATO [North Atlantic Treaty Orgnization], appeared firmly in control of her southern African colonies despite many years of guerrilla war; Ian Smith and his Rhodesian Front also appeared well able to withstand the efforts of the liberation armies to end white domination in Zimbabwe; the newly independent countries of Botswana, Lesotho and Swaziland were economically dependent on South Africa with no armed forces of any note. In 1973 a prominent military journal in South Africa, assessing this situation, concluded:

> South Africa faces no real threat from its immediate neighbours. None of these are likely to launch an attack against South Africa or even countenance harbouring an 'Army of Liberation' within their borders.

Within South Africa too it appeared that the massive repression imposed during the 1960s, combined with an economic boom, had crushed the popular militancy and mass mobilisation of the liberation movement that had been so evident during the 1950s. Thus, at the time of the initial military mobilisation of white women, it appears there was no internal or external threat to the South African regime, and it is difficult to identify the 'military threats' against which the women in civil defence were meant to erect their physical 'wall'. I believe this mobilisation can be understood only if the recruitment of white women is seen not so much as a search to provide the SADF with new recruits because of labour shortages or pressing military need, but

as a move to foster and reinforce white political unity portrayed (as P. W. Botha put it) as 'an act of faith in the women of South Africa'. . . .

From 1974 white women began to be recruited into the permanent force as well as the citizen force and commandos, and an increasing number of job categories within the SADF opened to women. This expansion of women's deployment took place against changing strategic conceptions of the SADF, but, as I will show, the need for women's labour remained overshadowed by the greater desire to use the recruitment of white women to foster and preserve a sense of white political unity.

"The recruitment of white women is . . . a move to foster and reinforce white political unity."

In 1974 leaflets giving details of the career opportunities the permanent force offered white women were delivered to every house in the white residential areas of South Africa. The leaflets were aimed at women aged between eighteen and thirty with a minimum of Standard 8 education (minimum school leaving qualification). An army career was portrayed as providing:

> belongingness, thoughtfulness, recognition, security, fairness and opportunity. (*Cape Times*, 25 November 1974)

At the same time considerable publicity was given to the first commissions for women in the Air Force and the Navy since the Second World War, and the promotion of a small number of women in the Army. In 1974 the SADF as a whole boasted two women colonels, one commandant, five majors, ten captains, eight lieutenants, and thirteen second lieutenants (*South African Digest*, 12 April 1974).

In 1976 P. W. Botha announced that women would be trained for a range of new jobs in the permanent force. Women would also be recruited into the commandos and trained in the use of weapons (*Rand Daily Mail,* 17 December 1976). At the end of 1976 there were 300 women in the permanent force and seventeen job categories open to them. Botha's changes involved opening eleven new job categories to women in the permanent force while eighteen administrative stores and clerical posts became available to women in the commandos. The Civil Defence College at George was renamed the Army Women's College and it was enlarged to take 500 recruits a year (*Cape Times,* 17 December 1976). These changes appear to be the first serious attempts to use white women's labour in the SADF, even though on a very small scale.

The trend of slight increases in recruitment and small expansions in the job categories open to women continued in subsequent years. This was the period of huge growth in the size of the SADF and continued discussion about a white skilled labour shortage. In 1978 the courses on offer at George College were expanded. In an attempt to attract more women to military service a new twelve-month course was introduced which involved seventeen weeks' basic training at George and seventeen weeks' work at a military base near the women's homes. All women volunteering for the Citizen's Force or entering the permanent force were sent to George on nine weeks' basic training (*Star,* 24 May 1978; *SA Digest,* 10 February 1978). For the first time, white women were encouraged to volunteer for national service in the South African Medical Corps, which provided facilities for 500 women a year to be trained as medical orderlies.

Recruiting White Women

This drive to recruit white women volunteers into the SADF did have results. In 1973 women made up only 0.6 per cent of the permanent force; in 1977 this had increased to 5.9 per cent and in 1978 7 per cent. By 1981 women made up 12.5 per cent of the permanent force (*Star,* 12 July 1979; *Cape Times,* 16 February 1982). In the mid-1980s there are 3500 white women in the permanent force (some 9 per cent of the to-

tal), with 10,000 women serving with the commandos out of a total of 26,000 volunteers, in a commando force totalling 200,000. If one includes 500 women in training at George College the total number of women in the SADF is 14,000. In *Brutal Force: The Apartheid War Machine,* G.Cawthra calculates the total armed strength of the SADF as 639,000 in 1985, which makes women recruits 2.19 per cent of the total. While women are numerically significant in the commandos, their numbers in the permanent force appear to have declined; their overall small numerical representation in the SADF is a function of the large numbers of national servicemen who make up the great bulk of SADF recruits.

"Attitudes to women soldiers in South Africa as a whole are complex and sometimes patronising."

The expansion of women's deployment took place in the decade which saw the SADF mount attacks on the neighbouring states of Botswana, Lesotho, Mozambique, Angola and Swaziland in search of African National Congress (ANC) members and supporters, as well as in efforts to destabilise the governments of the front-line states and militarily undermine them. At the same time the SADF built up and maintained a huge force in Namibia to fight the South West Africa Peoples Organisation (SWAPO), the national liberation movement. Increasingly within South Africa the SADF takes on the role, formerly played by the police, of breaking up demonstrations, carrying out house-to-house searches in black townships, manning roadblocks around townships, surrounding and searching black schools, forcing students into classes and attacking and killing black South Africans on the streets. With white minority rule in South Africa and Namibia increasingly under threat Botha's 'total strategy' is being put into effect, but what is striking is (commandos aside) the small role that white women play in the

SADF, despite the rhetoric of 'total onslaught'. With the recession of the 1980s the number of women in the permanent force has declined, and attempts to recruit women have become low key. The exclusion of white women in plans for the expansion of national service bears this out.

Expansion of the Military

In 1982 a White Paper laid out the expanded needs of the SADF in funds and manpower. Before the publication of the paper there had been much speculation that it would contain recommendations for compulsory national service for white women. But this did not prove to be the case. Instead the White Paper called for an increased period of national service for white men, and an elimination of the loopholes through which immigrants were able to escape national service. In introducing the White Paper in Parliament, the Minister of Defence said it was in the 'national' interest that white men should no longer be utilised as the SADF's only manpower source:

> the SADF will be more and more dependent on other sources of manpower, such as white females and members of other population groups, and to involve these people in a meaningful manner their utilisation is already being based on programmed manpower development plans which extend to 1990. (*Rand Daily Mail*, 3 April 1982)

He went on to spell out his perspective on the mobilisation of white women through national service:

> As regards white females, efforts in the short term will be directed at expanding the permanent force. It is envisaged in the medium term to increase the intake of female recruits for voluntary national service. A large scale increase in the number of female recruits cannot however take place until the permanent force has been expanded to such an extent that the larger numbers can be accommodated. (*Cape Times*, 3 April 1982)

Thus, although it appears that there is some labour shortage in the SADF which some increase of white women in the permanent force will help to alleviate, there is no pressing need to extend national service to women. The minister's speech seems to suggest that national service for women might even undermine their usefulness, as there has not been adequate preparation for such an increase in conscripts.

It has been claimed that the importance of white women in the SADF is to relieve men from administrative tasks. According to the *Cape Times* defence correspondent women are important in the SADF because in their roles as:

> air traffic controllers, nursing aides, radar operators and pilots of light aircraft, [they] release a lot of men from administrative work for fighting. (*Cape Times*, 16 April 1982)

In recent years considerable numbers of women have taken over administrative posts within the SADF. The personal assistant to the present head of the army is a woman. But I consider it still needs to be proved that white women provide labour for the SADF that cannot be found from any other group. At the time of rapid military expansion, which coincided with fears about a white skilled labour shortage, relatively large numbers of women were recruited, but as the labour shortage has become less pressing, with unemployed white men joining the permanent force, white women have not been conscripted as white men have been. Yet white women volunteers continue to be recruited and deployed even though they are not, at present, a crucial source of labour.

"Women are more important... because they are white than because of the labour they perform."

I believe that the fact that women's presence in the SADF has been maintained at a fairly low level (the commandos aside), and that plans for national service for women have not been given high priority, indicates that in the mid-1980s as in the early 1970s political and ideological motives supersede labour requirements in the recruitment of women.

The period of the recruitment of white women in the SADF is both the period of the rapid growth in armed forces and military spending and of the reformulation of military strategy in South Africa. But it is noteworthy that the recruitment of women into the permanent force preceded both the *débâcle* of the defeat of the South African invasion of Angola in 1975-6 and the Soweto uprising of 1976-7, both of which are cited as the chief reasons for the formulation of the 'total strategy' designed to mobilise all whites in defence of the regime. It seems to me that the fact that white women were being recruited into the permanent force indicates the thinking that contributed to the 'total strategy'. The recruitment of white women was based on ideas about white political unity which preceded it and which informed the publication of the 'total strategy'. The expansion of women's deployment should be seen primarily in terms of 'total strategy' and only secondarily in terms of filling labour requirements.

"Women members of the SADF are virtually invisible in the higher ranks."

The ideological dimensions of the expansion of women's deployment seem particularly important here. The 1974 recruiting leaflet portrays life in the SADF as a cross between a chummy boarding school and a girl guide troupe. Botha's 1971 speech exalts the nature of women's recruitment, seeing it as an act of 'faith'. In neither of these portrayals is there any hint that the defence force is involved in *war* or that, in consequence, the reality of the work might be a lot less cosy and exalted than it was portrayed. There is one projection of the SADF for women—where 'feminine' values are stressed; and there is another depiction for men —such as that which appears in the SADF's magazine and newspaper which stresses grit, grime, sporting prowess, cunning and malevolent enemies, military hardware, alongside semi-naked and apparently available young women.

Attitudes to women soldiers in South Africa as a whole are complex and sometimes patronising. The SADF's gender images are a double-sided image of the female, both the 'thoughtful, belonging' fellow-worker and the passive sexual object. It seems to me that if the presence of white women in the SADF was of critical strategic significance, these stereotyped images—absorbed untransformed from white society as a whole—would have been reformulated. It is the very mirror they hold up to certain images of white women in white society that underlines my belief that women are more important in the SADF because they are white than because of the labour they perform. . . .

Women's Roles in the Military

Despite the argument set out here so far giving reasons for the recruitment of women, it would be misleading to suggest that the role of white women in the SADF was merely symbolic and decorative. The job categories open to women in the services have expanded since the early 1970s and the SADF does offer white women certain unique experience in work. In 1974 the Air Force began training women as radar operators, fighter aircraft controllers, and telecommunication officers, in addition to the tasks they had performed before as clerks and typists; they also formed a squadron of women pilots to fly communication flights and undertake the evacuation of casualties (*SA Digest*, 12 April 1974 and 4 July 1974; *Star*, 14 February 1976). From 1976 the army employed women both in administrative and clerical posts, and in such tasks as doghandling, topographical work and draughtsmanship. The commandos, where the biggest deployment of women takes place, employ women as adjutants, radio operators, pay clerks, store managers, personnel officers, and a range of other administrative roles (*Star*, 24 June 1978). But even these new job categories for women perpetuate a distinction between male servicemen in active, decision-making roles and women in back-up services. Women members of the permanent force are barred from active service and similar restrictions apply to women in the commandos.

Invisible Women

Women members of the SADF are virtually invisible in the higher ranks. By 1979 there were only two women brigadiers, five colonels, and 581 women holding rank, although the total number of women serving in the permanent force numbered around 1000. The most senior women officers have responsibility for welfare services, the training of women recruits and personnel management (*Star*, 12 July 1979; *Cape Times*, 30 November 1980). The areas of strategic planning and overall defence policy, to say nothing of active service, are closed to white women officers.

Although women in the services earn the same basic pay as men in the same job categories, it is difficult for them to qualify for all the benefits for which men are eligible. Until 1981 women serving with the permanent force had no access to housing subsidies, and the prohibition on women going on active service prevents them claiming the 'danger money' bonuses with which men supplement their pay. Although child-care is generally not a problem for white South African women because most white families employ a black servant, the low priority given by the SADF to the needs of the children of working mothers in the permanent force is illustrated by the tale of the nursery at Voortrekkerhoogte near Pretoria where large detachments of the permanent force are stationed. In 1976 the Women's Federation at Voortrekkerhoogte founded a nursery school, but the only accommodation they were provided with was a prefabricated hut opposite the detention barracks. There were sixty children enrolled, and a long waiting list. It took nine years before more suitable accommodation and adequate staff could be provided by the army command (*Paratus*, December 1985).

Despite these inequalities the SADF projects itself as an exemplar for the rest of the society. Major-General Neil Webster, at the time a member of the President's Council and an influential policymaker in the SADF, stated:

> If a conservative organisation like the army can accept the equality of women, why should the rest of the civil service and the private sector not do the same? Discrimination based on sex is morally wrong and economically indefensible. If more organisations could genuinely accept women as equals—instead of just paying lipservice to this ideal—a lot of the country's staff shortages would be alleviated. (*Sunday Times*, 22 November 1981)

Major-General Webster's portrayal of the army as an ideal version of the society masks the way in which the SADF continues to perpetuate discrimination against its own white members (to say nothing of its role in maintaining in power a regime which has created and perpetuated thousands of political, legal and economic constraints making for the oppression and inequality of all black women and men).

"White women are no more equal in the SADF than blacks are."

The reason why the SADF is portrayed as an equal-opportunity employer, and the creator of 'spiritual and material welfare', seems to lie in the new role it has taken on as the guiding hand navigating apartheid policies away from their hidebound past, condemned by the world, to a new dynamic future in which, it is believed, the rulers of South Africa will be able to sit down in comfort with other conservative world leaders. There have been attempts to portray the SADF as the epitome of the new South African society, where blacks serve side by side with whites and petty apartheid has disappeared. It is as part of this image-building by the SADF that statements about the equality of women within the armed services must be seen. White women are no more equal in the SADF than blacks are, but they, and the society of which they are a part, must believe they are in order to accept the SADF as a go-ahead institution and the engine of a new dynamic form of apartheid. This role for the SADF was made explicit in the farewell message of General C. L. Viljoen, who retired as head of the SADF at the height of the state of emergency in 1985 as troops patrolled the townships, assaulting and killing:

> We in the Defence Force serve South Africa to the benefit of all its people. If we continue to do our task as well as we have in the past we will gain enough time and maintain the peace long enough for peaceful solutions to be found to our problems. If we fail all the inhabitants of this country will face chaos, poverty, famine and civil strife. We must accept that this is a worthwhile task, protecting all our people against the disaster that is revolution. (*Paratus*, November 1985)

Although the SADF career structure makes it plain that women will be confined to administrative jobs and support roles, the training given to women at the George College stresses toughness and endurance. There is an emphasis on combat situations which is out of key with the fact that the women are unlikely to encounter these within their actual working lives.

Basic Training

The training at the George College for women going into the permanent and citizen forces involves nine weeks of basic training in the use of firearms, parade ground drill, military discipline and fieldcraft, including map-reading and long-distance marches in rugged country (*Star*, 24 May 1978). Subsequently women in the permanent force get training similar to male recruits, but with more emphasis on clerical tasks and somewhat less emphasis on physical activity (*Paratus*, December 1982). Young women doing the one-year training course, not necessarily for a career in the SADF, have the same basic instruction with special courses in telecommunications and administration and lectures on current events, the army and revolutionary war, and much stress on crafts and music (*Paratus*, Octo-ber 1985).

It appears puzzling that women who are going to be office-bound are given so much costly, traditional, basic military training, and that women who know their work will never involve active service elect to undertake a training that is so very 'macho' in tone, and in the face of which they have to work so hard to maintain their 'femininity'. But this contradiction dissolves if women's participation in the SADF is seen to be as much about maintaining an ideology as it is about fulfilling labour requirements. The training of women seems to stress the inculcation of *esprit de corps*. The feeling of 'belongingness', which the SADF promised its recruits, can well be cultivated under the stress of route marches or in parade ground drill. Training women in the use of firearms underlines the political role they will play in maintaining white supremacy, even though they will never use these skills. If women are being recruited more because they are white than because they are women, it is important that their training gives them a sense of their race being under threat and of their contribution to white unity. Hence, the heavy emphasis on tasks the women will never perform except in imagination by identifying with white men fighting in defence of the regime.

Minnie Dreyer, an award-winning student at the George College in 1980, said of her training:

> It has really been worthwhile because you get to know yourself. A woman should know how to shoot, to do first-aid and to be prepared for whatever may happen in life. It's not necessarily preparation for war. (*Cape Times*, 14 April 1980)

"Women in the military have helped to maintain white identity in South Africa."

Despite the disclaimer, according to Minnie Dreyer, all the skills the training had inculcated are skills associated with maintaining a society under threat. This seems to be the essence of the ideas the women acquire at the George College and which may be much more important than any work-experience as clerks, typists or personnel officers. In the words of the College song their training brings the young women together:

In endeavour heart and mind
To protect our citizens
We shall be strong and conquer.
(Own Trans. from *Paratus*, November 1985)

At the passing-out parade in 1978 Désiree De Swardt, who joined the Air Force as a member of the Permanent Force, gave her reasons for taking this course:

I could do something for the country, study through the Air Force, be treated as a lady, and get almost the same salary as a man. (*Rand Daily Mail*, 21 April 1978)

I suggest that the country for which she wanted to do something is the territory of white power. The rigorous training which the SADF recruits undergo ensures that the women will define their country in these terms, and forge links of fellowship with other recruits in a way that a typing course or ordinary nursing training could not. . . .

The sanctified and esteemed role the SADF confers on women soldiers within white South African society, by word if not in deed, does not reflect all views of women soldiers, which in certain circles or at particular times range from the patronising to the openly hostile or dismissive.

The press, for example, has a condescending tone when referring to white women in the services. They are often depicted by diminutives, for example 'Botha's Babes' (a reference to P.W. Botha who introduced women's recruitment when Minister of Defence), 'trooplets' and '*sol-doedies*' (an Afrikaans diminutive of the word for soldier). In other characterisations they are identified with rather useless, specifically feminine accessories, for example as the 'powder-puff squadron' and the 'petticoat privates'. In all of this the press mirrors the marked sexism of white South African society as a whole, which has been virtually untouched by the moves toward sexual equality which have been an important element in the post-war history of so many countries. . . .

Conclusion

I have shown how the use of women in the SADF was born not so much out of the need for women's labour as the need for women's identification with white supremacy in a context where the majority of the population is black. The expansion and modernisation of the SADF has led to some use of skilled women workers, but their role in the services has been portrayed not for what it is, a continuation of white women's subordination to white men in terms of pay and job opportunities, but as an advertisement for the modernity of the SADF and as an instrument to create white political unity. Women in the military have helped to maintain white identity in South Africa. Their training, which stresses white unity and aspires to the 'feminine', attempts to preserve certain 'traditional' white values. In my judgement, recruitment into the armed services on these terms is no liberation for white women, it is merely an advance into backwardness.

The Netherlands Failed to Fully Integrate Women into the Military

Annemiek Bolscher and Ine Megens

About the Authors: *Annemiek Bolscher is a researcher at the University of Nijmegen in the Netherlands. Ine Megens is with the Scientific Office of the Pacifist Socialist Party in Amsterdam.*

During the Second World War the foundation was laid for the military auxiliary women's corps. In 1943 the auxiliary women's corps, the Vrouwen Hulp Korps (VHK) was founded from Great Britain. This corps aided evacuees, assisted with food distribution and took part in the organizing of the transportation of children. The strength of the force amounted to about 200 women. After the war the VHK remained. In particular, it became a reservoir of administrative personnel.

In 1944 the women's section of the navy (Marva) was established. In view of the so-called 'liberation' of the Dutch Indies, it was thought that too few men would be available for the navy. Accordingly, women were recruited with the slogan 'Free a man for the fleet'. In 1948 the strength of the Marva was about 700 women. Within the navy they were employed in the administrative section, as cooks, tailors and drivers.

Although women had entered the army during the Second World War, it was not until 1951 that a political decision was made that the participation of women in the army had to become

Adapted from "The Netherlands" by Annemiek Bolscher and Ine Megens, in *Women and the Military Service*, Eca Isaksson, ed., pp. 359-369. Copyright © 1988, St. Martin's Press, New York. Reprinted with permission.

permanent. From 1955 the Dutch army had three female corps: the Marva (women's section of the marines), the Milva (the military women's section) and the Luva (women's section of the air force). Although the corps had military status, separate legal rules were applied to them with respect to the training and career. The reasons for discharge were different too: marriage and pregnancy involved dismissal. The possibilities of women in the military were limited. Most women were employed in the administrative, social or nursing sections. A few were drivers. Women constituted only 1 per cent of the total amount of military personnel. The work of women was considered to be temporary and supporting. In advertisements to recruit women for the corps it was said, 'the only weapons of the female soldier, her accuracy and charm—weapons we should call "disarming"' and 'here women are not trained in readiness to fight but to fulfil a useful function'.

The position of military women in this period was essentially different from that of men. Most of the jobs remained closed to women. The jobs they fulfilled were of a traditional female character. The unequal position of women is an accepted fact in this period, about which nobody seems to care. At the end of the 1970s, however, the policy changed.

"The participation of women in the army had to become permanent."

In 1978 the Netherlands decided to dissolve the women's corps, to give women access to all jobs in the military and so integrate them completely. It was intended that in future all functions, including combat functions, would be open to women. As professional soldiers, men and women could take part on an equal base in the Dutch military. With this decision the Netherlands has a unique position in the world. Military conscription for women, however, was not opportune. The integration policy has been under development now since 1978; in these eight years a lot of experiments have been held; a dozen or more reports have been written and several enquiries have been held. A definite policy concerning women and the military still has to be approved by the Parliament.

"Officially, women have the same rights and duties as men."

From 1 January 1979 new legal rules for women came into force. Women who now joined the army were given the same contracts as men and went through the same training. The women's corps were slowly dissolved and completely abolished in 1982. From that date on there were no longer separate functions for men and women: officially, women have the same right and duties as men. Still, in the early 1980s one could not speak of any real equality. First of all, there were several 'practical' problems to be solved, like the adaptation of barack and ship accommodation and the apposition of physical requirements. These were still totally attuned to men. Often it was not possible for women to satisfy these requirements. After a few years of experimenting it appeared that more was needed to bring about actual integration than just formal admittance. The interest of women in the army seemed to diminish more than to increase. In the beginning of 1983 there were about 1,450 women employed within the army; a small 3 per cent of the total numbers of professional personnel. Because of this small number of women, the risk of an isolated position was very high. The physical requirements remained a problem and so did the acceptance of women by their male colleagues. The decision to integrate women was mainly a political decision, one which many men and women in the military itself were not very pleased with. Many prejudices against women and doubts concerning the integration policy were expressed. . . .

A formal policy of equal rights and duties does not mean that in practice all women had equal chances. In 1979 the integration of women in the military forces was started cautiously. One can speak of a formal admittance to all jobs. In practice this meant that many training schools still had their doors closed to women. Hardly any effort was made to interest more women in a job in the army. A sex-neutral recruitment policy was followed, to that effect that the usual 'M/F' was added to advertisements. The attempts to facilitate access to the army for women were rather different for each of the military forces. The navy decided on a large experiment with women in jobs on ships. The land forces distinguished all jobs according to their physical demands, within functional groups. The integration policy did not lead to a great increase in the number of women in the military forces. . . .

Integration Without Reserve

We would like to stress two points which are important for understanding the background and range of the integration policy. First of all, there is the issue of combat functions, and second, we want to restore something about the discussion of military service in the Netherlands.

Most Western NATO [North Atlantic Treaty Organization] countries where the integration policy took shape in the 1970s made some kind of reservation. But not the Netherlands. From the beginning there were no formal limitations: no combat jobs were closed to women. With this policy the Dutch army seems to affirm its image as an institution open to social influences—an army in which the 'new leadership' and 'socialization of the army' made a great impression. Elsewhere I have hypothesized that because of this, the Dutch army may have been used by NATO as a test case for the integration of women in the army. After careful examination of the internal information of several ministries however, we have now come to the conclusion that the decision to open combat function to women was probably not the intended result of a formal decision ten years earlier.

The Netherlands made no reservation regarding the army when they signed the Treaty of New York (1953) in which the political rights of women are guaranteed. Article 3 of the Treaty reads as follows: 'Women are entitled to hold public office on an equal footing with men and occupy all public positions which are instituted in accordance with the national law, without any distinction.'

The Netherlands did not sign the treaty until 1971. At that time the civil servants at the Ministry of Defence stated that making a reservation for the army was attracting attention in an unwanted way. Some thought that the treaty still offered opportunities for a 'reasonable discrimination', such as the exclusion of women from fighting man to man. The treaty, it was said, 'couldn't be meant to correct the job of God'.

"Many training schools still had their doors closed to women."

It took some time, but in 1979, eight years later, the complete integration of women in the Dutch army was formally launched. Whether the ideas about 'reasonable discrimination' had changed by that time is an open question. The fact that there was no legal possibility to limit the jobs of women in the army had to be taken into account. A lack of manpower, or the more technical way of fighting, reasons which in other countries contributed to the growing part of women in the military, did not have a decisive influence on Dutch policy makers. In the back of their minds they may have thought of the declining birth rates, but in the Netherlands that will not be an acute problem until the 1990s, probably even later. Moreover, manpower problems are more of a problem with conscripts than with the professionals. Introducing compulsory service for women is the only way to increase the number of women in the army on a larger scale. Using women as a reserve army because of manpower problems would probably meet with difficulties in society. In the Netherlands only 35 per cent of the women between 15 and 65 are active on the labour market, which is far less than in other countries in Western Europe. The issue of military service for women has not been debated in public, but it gave rise to a new discussion between policy makers.

In a situation where there is compulsory service only for men, women will always keep a special position. Because they can only take part as professionals, they are always in a minority position and have to prove themselves as leaders of male soldiers. . . .

Military conscription for women is out of the question for all policy makers. In pursuance of the Treaty of New York of 1979 concerning the banishment of all discrimination of women, this policy was explicitly formulated. Perhaps they learnt wisdom after the experiences with the first Treaty of New York, or they just wanted to be sure and so made a reservation regarding military service. Women will not be obliged to follow military service because they have less opportunities in society, the official argument goes. Military service usually means a break in a career and hampers men in their development. For women this would mean an extra problem because of their backward position.

The Dutch government also saw some more practical problems: introducing military service for women would enlarge the amount of potential candidates. Making an objective selection which distributes the weight justly and equally will become much harder. The load of work, the financial consequences and the expected mass of exemptions from military service for women all lead to the conclusion that military service for women is not desirable. One of the reasons for freedom from military service probably would be pregnancy. Military service might then become an undesirable pressure to become pregnant—a very curious argument.

Integration Policy

For years now the integration policy has been under debate. In these years a load of papers and reports have been produced by the military and policy makers at the Defence Ministry. There has also been rather wide media coverage of the issue. The first woman helicopter pilot or the first woman on board a minesweeper is always good for a picture in the newspapers. Women are still considered curiosities. Some newspapers also gave attention to rumours and scandals concerning women on board. An action committee of concerned wives of (male) marine personnel against the presence of women on board received much attention.

A questionnaire about the integration policy in 1982 showed that 52 per cent of the Dutch people were of the opinion that women should be able to fulfil combat functions.

"The idea that women can enter combat jobs is a myth."

In the beginning of the 1980s a few small anti-militaristic women's groups were formed which took up the issue of women in the army, sexual harassment and pornography. They got a lot of publicity, and the issue of sexual violence is under investigation now. More and more information is becoming public and incidental cases are brought to the military courts. No women were involved in these cases, which of course does not mean that women are not troubled by sexual harassment. The actions of anti-militaristic groups seemed to have been successful in highlighting these problems. To stimulate a political debate on the integration policy as such, has failed.

Therefore we need to discuss not only the actual measures but also the nature of the military.

We are of the opinion that we cannot speak of any real integration of women in the military forces. There are still a lot of problems to be solved. The defence administration describes the factors which obstruct the integrations as follows:

1. The lack of interest shown by women in a military career.

2. The high ratio of women that don't pass the examinations and selections.

3. The isolated position of women.

4. The lack of acceptance of women as colleagues by male soldiers.

Nowhere are the problems with the integration connected with the specific task and the resulting characteristics of the armed forces. The army resembles a mainly male-oriented society. This expresses itself, for example, in requirements for job performances, communications structures and in a general cultural environment. Women are expected to adapt and to adjust to this *status quo*. It was never intended to change the traditional organization in this respect. On the contrary, the integration of women must not be on the cost of the operational readiness and war-fighting capability of the armed forces; it is 'only' a personnel problem. But even from the point of view of efficiency and management, we see that few attempts or adjustments are made to optimize the new situation. The best reason we can think of for this is the fact that the integration was introduced mainly for political motives and was more or less forced on the military.

Chronology

A Chronology of Women's Participation in the U.S. Military Since World War I.

World War I 1917-1918

About thirteen thousand women serve in the United States Navy and Marine Corps. Most occupy clerical roles, but some work as translators, recruiters, and in other traditionally male positions. Women are not allowed to enlist in the army. An additional twenty-one thousand women serve in the Army and Navy Nurse Corps, units separate from the regular army and navy. Members of the Army and Navy Nurse Corps do not have military rank. After the war, the navy and Marine Corps are prohibited from recruiting women.

World War II 1941-1945

Half a year after the Japanese attack Pearl Harbor, Congress establishes the Women's Army Auxiliary Corps (WAAC). The WAAC is organized as an auxiliary branch of the army with a separate command structure. It does not grant its members military benefits or rank. Two months later, Congress creates the Navy Women's Reserve and the Marine Corps Women's Reserve. Women in these reserve units, known as WAVES (Women Accepted for Voluntary Emergency Service), are given full military status. In 1943, the WAAC becomes the Women's Army Corps (WAC). To encourage women to join, the WAC gives its members full military status. About 350,000 military women serve during the war. Most are in clerical and health care positions, though some hold nontraditional jobs. The army excludes women from combat and from being supervised by men. The navy prohibits women, except nurses, from serving in foreign countries. Enemy fire kills more than two hundred women. In the Philippines,

seventy-seven military nurses are held as prisoners of war (POWs) by the Japanese for thirty-seven months.

1948

Congress passes the Women's Armed Services Integration Act, giving women permanent status in the armed forces. The act limits the number of military women to 2 percent of enlisted personnel and prohibits women from attaining the rank of general or admiral. Other restrictions are placed on the number of female officers permitted. A provision of the act, later known as the Combat Exclusion Law, bars navy and air force women from occupying combat roles. The army later develops its own regulations prohibiting women from holding combat positions.

The Women in the Air Force (WAF) is established as the women's branch of the air force.

Korean War 1950-1953

The number of women serving in the armed forces reaches 49,000 in 1952. Women nurses serve in the combat zone. WAC and WAF women also serve at bases in the Far East.

Vietnam War 1965-1973

Between five thousand and six thousand women nurses and about fifteen hundred other military women serve in Vietnam. Nonmedical servicewomen are officially excluded from combat areas. Nine military women die in Vietnam.

1967

Congress eases restrictions on the promotion of servicewomen and removes the 2 percent limit on female enlisted personnel.

1970

The air force allows women into the Reserve Officers' Training Corps (ROTC), a leading source of officers for the military. The Army Nurse

Corps' Anna Mae Hayes and the WAC's Elizabeth P. Hoisington become the first women generals in American history.

1972   Women still comprise less than 2 percent of military personnel. The army and navy open the ROTC to women.

1973   The Department of Defense announces that it will no longer draft civilians into the military during peacetime. Instead, the armed forces will be comprised entirely of volunteers. This change forces the military to compete with civilian employers to attract qualified personnel. Eventually, the scarcity of male applicants for military service puts pressure on the armed forces to accept more women.

1976   Women enter the army, navy, and air force service academies for the first time. These academies provide the military with their most highly trained commissioned officers. Forty percent of enlisted women hold traditionally male jobs.

1978   The Women's Army Corps is dissolved. Military women are no longer organized separately from men, but they are still prohibited from serving in combat positions.

1980   The U.S. military includes 151,000 women, who make up 8.8 percent of enlisted personnel.

1983   U.S. Marines and Army Rangers invade the island of Grenada to rescue U.S. citizens and overthrow the Marxist regime. About 170 army women provide support in the invasion as military police, helicopter crew chiefs, and communications and maintenance personnel.

1986   In retaliation for the Libyan bombing of a West Berlin disco, U.S. planes bomb Tripoli and Benghazi, Libya. Women copilot noncombat airplanes in support of the U.S. attack.

1989   The United States invades Panama to oust dictator Manuel Noriega. Military women participate in the invasion of Panama in noncombat positions as military police and in supply, communications, and transport operations. Circumstances force two women, however, to command troops in combat when they encounter enemy soldiers.

Persian Gulf War 1991   The armed forces of the United States and other nations expel the Iraqi military from Kuwait, which Iraq had invaded six months earlier. The U.S. military deploys 35,355 women troops, who serve in almost every role except combat, from which they continue to be barred. Eleven army women die. Two servicewomen, Rhonda Cornum and Melissa Rathbun-Nealy, become Iraqi prisoners of war. Rathbun-Nealy is the first woman POW in the regular army.

Approximately 379,000 women comprise 11 percent of active-duty personnel and 13 percent of the reserves. The House of Representatives passes a bill repealing the restrictions on women flying combat aircraft.

Bibliography

Books

Carol Barkalow with Andrea Raab — *In the Men's House: An Inside Account of Life in the Army by One of West Point's First Female Graduates.* New York: Poseidon, 1990.

M.C. Devilbiss — *Women and Military Service: A History, Analysis, and Overview of Key Issues.* Maxwell Air Force Base, AL: Air University Press, 1990.

Jean Bethke Elshtain — *Women and War.* New York: Basic Books, 1987.

Jean Bethke Elshtain and Sheila Tobias — *Women, Militarism, and War: Essays in History, Politics, and Social Theory.* Savage, MD: Rowman & Littlefield, 1990.

Cynthia Enloe — *Does Khaki Become You? The Militarisation of Women's Lives.* Boston: South End Press, 1983.

Jeanne Holm — *Women in the Military: An Unfinished Revolution.* Novato, CA: Presidio Press, 1982.

Eva Isaksson, ed. — *Women and the Military System.* New York: Simon & Schuster, 1988.

Joint Center for Political Studies — *Who Defends America? Race, Sex, and Class in the Armed Forces.* Washington, DC: Joint Center for Political Studies. 1989.

Nancy Loring — *Female Soldiers—Combatants or Noncombatants? Historical and Contemporary Perspectives.* Westport, CT: Greenwood Press, 1982.

Sharon Macdonald, Pat Holden, and Shirley Ardener, eds. — *Images of Women in Peace and War.* London: MacMillan Education, 1987.

Brian Mitchell — *Weak Link: The Feminization of the American Military.* Washington, DC: Regnery Gateway, 1989.

Helen Rogan — *Mixed Company: Women in the Modern Army.* New York: G.P. Putnam's Sons, 1981.

Michael Rustad — *Women in Khaki: The American Enlisted Woman.* New York: Praeger, 1982.

Shelly Saywell — *Women in War.* New York: Viking Press, 1985.

Dorothy and Carl J. Schneider — *Sound Off! American Military Women Speak Out.* New York: E.P. Dutton, 1988.

Mady Wechsler Segal — "Personnel." In *American Defense Annual, 1990-1991,* edited by Joseph Kruzel. Lexington, MA: Lexington Books, 1990.

Mady Wechsler Segal — "The Military and the Family as Greedy Institutions." In *The Military: More Than Just a Job?,* edited by Charles C. Moskos and Frank R. Wood. Washington, DC: Pergamon-Brassey's, 1988.

Judith Hicks Stiehm — *Arms and the Enlisted Woman.* Philadelphia: Temple University Press, 1989.

Periodicals

Shelley Anderson — "A Soldier's Story," *Fellowship,* March 1991. Available from the Fellowship of Reconciliation, 523 N. Broadway, Nyack, NY 10960.

Clare Ansberry and Carol Hymowitz — "Gulf War Takes a Toll on Soldiers' Children," *The Wall Street Journal,* January 29, 1991.

Stephen Chapman — "Easing Obligations Would Limit Opportunity," *Conservative Chronicle,* February 27, 1991. Available from PO Box 11297, Des Moines, IA 50340-1297.

Stephen Chapman — "Military Women and the Meaning of Equality," *Conservative Chronicle,* February 20, 1991.

Don Feder — "Women in Combat Is a Feminist Fantasy," *Conservative Chronicle*, April 25, 1990.

Alice Fleming — "Women: Their Changing Military Role," *The American Legion Magazine*, March 1990.

Glamour — "Letters from the Gulf," June 1991.

Glamour — "We Are *All* Woman Warriors," June 1991.

Ellen Goodman — "Military Orphans Bill: Balancing Loyalty to Country and Family," *Liberal Opinion Week*, February 18, 1991. Availabe from 108 E. Fifth St., Vinton, IA 20003.

Anne Gowen — "Soldiers, Gender, and 'Warmones,'" *Insight*, March 4, 1991. Available from PO Box 91022, Washington, DC 20090-1022.

Barbara Grizzuti Harrison — "Should Women Have the Right to Fight?" *Mademoiselle*, June 1990.

Carol Kleiman — "Hell No, She Won't Go!" *Ms.*, January/February 1991.

William Murchison — "Women in the Middle East Lines," *Conservative Chronicle*, October 10, 1990.

Jon Nordheimer — "Women's Role in Combat: The War Resumes," *The New York Times*, May 26, 1991.

Clarence Page — "Soul Searching About Women in War," *Liberal Opinion Week*, February 18, 1991. Available from 108 E. Fifth St., Vinton, IA 20003.

People — "A Mother's Duty," September 10, 1990.

Jeannie Ralston — "Women's Work," *Life*, May 1991.

William Raspberry — "Sending Mothers to War Is Wrong," *Liberal Opinion Week*, March 4, 1991.

Charlie Reese — "Women Have No Place in Combat," *Conservative Chronicle*, January 21, 1990.

Phyllis Schlafly — "Sending Mothers to the Gulf War!" *The Phyllis Schlafly Report*, March 1991. Available from the Eagle Forum, PO Box 618, Alton, IA 62002.

Phyllis Schlafly — "The Lesson of Women in Combat in Panama," *Conservative Chronicle*, February 7, 1990.

Anne Summers — "Pat Schroeder: Fighting for Military Moms," *Ms.*, May/June 1991.

Women's Research and Education Institute — *Women in the Military: 1980–1990.* June 1990. Available from 1770 18th St. NW, Suite 400, Washington, DC 20009.

Women's Research and Education Institute — *Women in the U.S. Armed Services: The War in the Persian Gulf.* 1991.

Molly Yard — "Should Military Women Serve in Combat?" *American Legion Magazine*, May 1990.

Frank Zepezauer — "Military Moms and the Battle of the Family," *The Human Life Review*, Spring 1990. Available from Room 840, 150 E. 35th St., New York, NY 10016.

Organizations to Contact

The editors have compiled the following list of organizations that are concerned with the issues debated in this book. All of them have publications or information available for interested readers. The descriptions are derived from materials provided by the organizations. This list was compiled upon the date of publication. Names and phone numbers of organizations are subject to change.

American Defense Institute
1055 N. Fairfax St., 2nd Fl.
Alexandria, VA 22314
(703) 519-7000

The institute is a nonprofit educational organization that supports a strong national defense. The institute believes that women serving in combat would weaken America's defense. It publishes the quarterly newsletter *American Defense Initiative* as well as occasional articles.

Center for Defense Information (CDI)
1500 Massachusetts Ave. NW
Washington, DC 20005
(202) 862-0700

CDI analyzes military spending, policies, and weapons systems. The center believes that military servicewomen should be allowed to serve in any positions they are capable of, as long as the nation's defense is not compromised. The center publishes *The Defense Monitor* ten times a year and sponsors the television program "America's Defense Monitor."

National Organization of Women (NOW)
1000 16th St. NW, Suite 700
Washington, DC 20036
(202) 331-0066

NOW is one of the largest women's organizations in the nation. It supports equal rights for women, including equality for military servicewomen. NOW believes that women serving in combat would strengthen the nation. The organization publishes the bimonthly *NOW Times.*

United States Defense Committee
3238 Wynford Dr.
Fairfax, VA 22031
(703) 280-4226

The committee supports a strong national defense and believes women in the military weaken the nation's defense. It lobbies Congress on defense issues. Publications of the committee include the bimonthly *Defense Watch* as well as defense briefs.

U.S. Department of Defense
Public Correspondence Division, Defense Information Services
Assistant Secretary of Defense, The Pentagon
Washington, DC 20301-1400
(703) 545-6700

The Department of Defense provides the military forces needed to deter war and protect the security of the U.S. With the Congress, the Department of Defense determines the role of women in the U.S. military. Write for a list of publications.

Women's International League for Peace and Freedom (WILPF)
1213 Race St.
Philadelphia, PA 19107
(215) 563-7110

WILPF is an international network of women activists who oppose militarism. While it supports equal rights for women, it believes that neither women nor men should participate in the military. WILPF publishes the bimonthly magazine *Peace and Freedom* and the book *The Women's Budget.*

Women's Research and Education Institute (WREI)
1700 18th St. NW, Suite 400
Washington, DC 20009
(202) 328-7070

WREI is an independent, national public policy research organization that studies women's issues. It manages an ongoing project on women in the military. The institute publishes frequent reports and analyses concerning women's issues, including *Women in the Military: 1980-1990* and *Women in the Armed Services: The War in the Persian Gulf,* and the book *The American Women.*

Index